Sports Lingo

BOOKS BY HARVEY FROMMER

Sports Lingo   (1979)
The Martial Arts: Judo and Karate   (1978)
A Sailing Primer (with Ron Weinmann)   (1978)
A Baseball Century: The First Hundred Years of the National League   (1976)

SPORTS LINGO

A Dictionary of
the Language of Sports

HARVEY FROMMER

ATHENEUM 1979 New York

Library of Congress Cataloging in Publication Data

Frommer, Harvey.
Sports lingo.
1. Sports—Dictionaries. I. Title.
GV567.F76 1979   796'.03   78-12130
ISBN 0-689-10939-3

Published simultaneously in Canada by McClelland and Stewart Ltd.
Composition by Connecticut Printers, Inc., Hartford, Connecticut
Printed and bound by Halliday Lithograph Corporation, Hanover and
Plympton, Massachusetts
Designed by Kathleen Carey
First Edition

TO MY SON, FREDDY,

who gave me the idea by
asking all those questions.
Now he knows the answers.

ACKNOWLEDGMENTS

Marvin Brown of Atheneum is owed many tips of the cap for his sensitive coaching and highly beneficial strategy sessions.

My wife, Myrna, my "designated hitter," is publicly thanked for her invaluable aid in researching, writing, typing, editing, and encouraging.

Deluxe pinch hitters: Granny (Gertrude Katz), Jennifer, Ian—and my very able copy editor, Dan Flanagan—thank you, too.

CONTENTS

Sports Lingo

WARM-UP TIME

Do you know the differences among the following: penalty (football), penalty kick (soccer), penalty killer (hockey), penalty shot (basketball), penalty box (hockey), penalty goal (soccer), penalty-kick mark (soccer), penalty shot (hockey), penalty timekeeper (hockey)?

How well can you explain the differences among these terms from basketball: free throw, bonus free-throw, free-throw area, free-throw circle, free-throw lane, free-throw line, free-wheeling offense?

How well do you know the sports meanings and the sports they belong to of each of the following: own goal, goal area, goal-area line, goal-line stand, goal average, goal crease, goalie, goal judge, goalkeeper, goal kick, goal-less, goal light, goal mouth, goal post, goaltender, goaltending?

Can you identify the sports and the meanings of the following colorful terms: gold, yellow card, red card, black flag, checkered flag, red flag, body in white, greens fee, gold or red handkerchief, red-dog, blue line, red line, black belt, blueprint, yellow light?

After reading this book, you'll know the meaning of these terms and many more, for *Sports Lingo* is aimed at all those who want to better understand and more fully participate in the world of sports.

Sports lingo is a language that has died and a language that is waiting to be born—a language that grows each year, changes and attempts to adjust to the ever-expanding world of athletics which it describes. It is technical yet colorful, simple yet tremendously involved—a language for those inside of sports and at the same time an important part of the general cultural vocabulary.

Individual sports have a language personality all their own. A lot of fencing lingo is spoken in the accents of Italian and French. The racquet sports are relatives and there is a good deal of inbreeding of language among them. Football has a military aura surrounding its language, while soccer—or what the rest of the world generally refers to as football—is characterized by an international flavor and many British expressions. Bowling's language contains a quaint and colorful application of this sport's reliance on words taken from the general cultural vocabulary—Cincinnati, Christmas tree, and mother-in-law, for example. Skateboarding, with its origins in surfing (in fact, the sport is called sidewalk surfing), is filled with expressions borrowed from surfing. And if there were a championship trophy awarded for the richest and most varied of sports lingo, baseball would win it easily. More than 100 years old, played over a very long season in all sections of the United States, baseball's language is aimed at explaining and describing the nuances of our national game.

It is fascinating to survey the sports lingo that lives and dies depending on developments in sports. The *set shot* (a stationary, two-handed shot at the basket) in basketball was replaced as the game changed with the *jump shot*. The *three-point shot* (awarding three points for a basket made from 26 or more feet out) and the *30-second rule* (mandating that an offensive team shoot within 30 seconds), and the *red, white, and blue basketball* all vanished with the end of the American Basketball Association.

The *spitter,* or *spitball,* was supposed to die as a term as a result of a rule in major league baseball that outlawed this type of pitch. The *designated hitter* was born as a result of an American League baseball rules change. The *shoot-out* and the *tie breaker* were new additions to the language of sports as a result of new rules in the North American Soccer League. *Super Bowl* and *Soccer Bowl* are relatively new terms used to describe the championship games of the National Football League and the North American Soccer League. National Football League officials didn't even like the name for their chanpionship game, which was coined by a sportswriter. The public did, and the rest is sports lingo history.

Some expressions live out their time because of the popularity of the figures who use them. Mel Allen's "How about that?" and Red Barber's "In the catbird seat"—phrases that marveled at a baseball player's accomplishments—departed the sports lingo scene when Mr. Allen and Mr. Barber left their play-by-play announcing roles.

Within the clubhouses and in their private conversations with each other, athletes use another level of language. This sports speech, this special language, provides another view of sports. Some of these terms are also included in this book. *Bringing it* is baseball slang to describe a pitcher who is throwing the ball hard, or *putting some mustard on it* in pitching to his *cousin* (a player he does well against). A player who hits the ball hard and with straight force is one who manufactures a *frozen rope*. A basketball player who *shoots in your face* is one who attempts to show up another player who is guarding him. A loose and relaxed basketball player *shakes and bakes*. One who *picks someone's pockets* is able to steal the basketball from another player. Such terms and expressions are no longer as "inside" as they once were. Each time a sportscaster or sportswriter hears them, there's a good chance that they become public, part of the culture, and part of sports lingo.

Some sports terms belong to all sports. A *player-manager* is a team member who both plays and manages. A *player-coach* performs the same role no matter the sport. All sports have *home teams* (the ones that play at their home site) and *visiting teams* (the ones that travel to play at the home team's location). The *bleachers* (those seats beyond the outfield in baseball) are generally the same in all sports, although the Los Angeles Dodgers give their bleacher seats a touch of class by referring to them as *pavilion seats*. *To be up* (ahead) or *down* (behind) or *to rally* (come from behind) or to be *in the lead* (to be winning) or *to trail* (to be losing) or *to falter* (to fall behind) or *to clinch* (to assure victory)—these are all general words that apply to all sports.

Sometimes the same word or phrase varies greatly in meaning from sport to sport. *Dribbling* in soccer takes place with the feet, while in basketball it is performed with the hands. *Fan* in football is a pass pattern. In baseball, to *fan* means to strike out. *Down* in baseball means out, whereas in football it signifies one of a series of four attempts to gain ten yards. To *center* a ball in football is to have the center hike the ball back to the quarterback. In hockey, a meaning of the word *center* is to get the puck back to the center of the rink.

To *trap* a baseball is to gain control of it after it has bounced. To *trap* a soccer ball is to gain control of it by cushioning it with any part of the body except for the arms or hands. To *trap* in football is to block off a defensive lineman in order to allow an offensive ballcarrier to have ease of movement. To *trap* in basketball is the act of two players tightly guarding the player with the ball in an attempt to take the ball away. The *pocket* as used in baseball and lacrosse refers to the part of the glove or the head of the stick most useful for gaining control of the ball. *Pocket* in football is a field location a few yards behind the line of scrimmage that a quarterback stays in for protection in his passing attempts.

Sports lingo is not only a way to understand and appreciate the language of athletics, it is also a plus to many in everyday speech and writing. It is a tool to describe positive and negative feelings, special situations, awkward moments. It is even a wonderful crossword puzzle aid.

To strike out (baseball) is not to do well. To *hit a home run* (baseball) or *score* (all sports) is to succeed. To hit a *homer with the bases loaded* (baseball) is to succeed mightily. To be *out in left field* (baseball) is to be nowhere, while to be *caught off base* (baseball) is to be surprised. To score a *hole in one* (golf) is to have a triumph akin to winning the *Super Bowl* (football). To *come on strong down the home stretch* (swimming, track, etc.) is to finish fast and successfully, while to *break quickly* (track and field) or *get a jump on the pitcher* (baseball) is to have an edge on the opposition.

To *quarterback* (football) is to lead, to be a *backup quarterback* (football) is to wait to lead, to be a *Monday Morning Quarterback* (football) is to second guess. To *pinch hit* (baseball) is to take someone's place, while to *hit a foul ball* (baseball) is to make a mistake. To *throw a curve ball* (baseball) is to attempt to trick someone, while to be *thrown a curve ball* (baseball) is have someone attempt to trick you. To get a *rain check* (baseball) is to have an opportunity to do something again. To *get to first base* (baseball) and to *kick off* (football) is to begin . . . the examples go on into *sudden death, overtime, extra innings* . . .

. . . *kissoff* (archery), *ace* (racquet sports), *dunk* (basketball), *mod* (auto racing), *hairy* (auto racing), *bomb* (football), *mag wheels* (auto racing), *raunchy* (auto racing), *zap* (motorcycling), *bull's-eye* (archery), *hot hand* (basketball), *K.O.* (boxing), *take a dive* (boxing), *split* (bowling), *belly whopper* (diving), *caddy* (golf), *duffer* (golf), *in the soup* (surfing), *wiped out* (surfing), *hacker* (tennis), *pug* (boxing), *on guard* and *parry* (fencing), *dead heat* (track and field), *gun lap* (track), *half-nelson* (wrestling).

There is even a sports lingo of letters that forms a language and symbolism all its own. Here's a sampling:

A	assist (baseball)
BA	batting average (baseball)
BB	base on balls (baseball)
BK	balk (baseball)
C	catcher (baseball)
CC	cubic centimeters (auto racing)
D	defense (basketball)
DH	designated hitter (baseball)

D.O.H.C.	double overhead camshaft (auto racing)
E	error (baseball); end (football)
FG	field goal (basketball)
G	goaltender (hockey)
H	the shape of the goalposts (football)
I	a type of formation (football)
JV	junior varsity
K	strike out (baseball)
L	loss (baseball pitcher)
M	a formation (soccer)
MX	moto-cross (motorcycling)
N	novice slope (skiing)
O	(combined with X to diagram football plays)
P	pitcher (baseball)
PH	pinch hitter (baseball)
R	run (baseball)
RBI	run batted in (baseball)
S	sacrifice (baseball)
SB	stolen base (baseball)
SF	sacrifice fly (baseball)
T	technical foul (basketball); formation (football); time-out
U	utility player (baseball)
V	victory (all sports)
W	formation (soccer); win (baseball)
WFO	wide-open throttle (motorcycling)
WP	wild pitch (baseball)
X	combined with O to diagram football plays
Y	another shape of football goalposts
Z	zig-zag pattern (football)

The world of televised sports has its own language—slo-mo, instant replay, hand-held camera, overhead blimp, mini-cam instant isolate, spotters, graphics, miked officials, freeze, radar gun, split screen, promo, half-time shows . . . but that's the subject matter for another book.

This book is for parents interested in helping their children better understand sports vocabulary; it is for participants who wish to better comprehend the language of sports; it is for fans who wish to follow just a little more intelligently the words and phrases used by sportscasters and sportswriters.

Sports lingo is now part of the culture—a term that seeks to describe the language, vocabulary, slang, expressions, and definitions of the world of sports.

H. F.

ARCHERY

ANCHOR The spot on the archer's face or neck where the string hand rests at the time of release.

ARMGUARD Piece of leather wrapped around the forearm to protect it from string slap.

ARROW A thin shaft shot from a bow.

ARROWHEAD The point or head of the arrow (see PILE).

ARROW PLATE Vertical section of the bow against which the arrow rests before release.

ARROW REST A projection on the side of the bow which supports the arrow.

BACK The side of the bow that faces the target.

BACKED BOW A layer of material bonded to the back of a bow for reinforcement.

BARRELED ARROW An arrow that is tapered at each end and thicker in the middle.

BELLY The side of the bow that faces the archer.

BLUNT An arrow that has a flat tip.

BOLT A short arrow that is shot from a crossbow.

BOW An instrument that is used to shoot arrows. A bow consists of a flexible strip that is tapered at either end and connected to an arc.

BOW ARM The supporting arm for a bow.

BOW HAND The hand that grasps the bow.

BOWSIGHT An aiming device fastened to a bow.

BOWSTRING A string used to propel an arrow.

BOWYER One who makes or deals with bows.

BRACE The act of stringing a bow.

BRACER An arm guard.

BROADHEAD A triangular-shaped flat and sharp arrowhead used in hunting.

BULL'S-EYE The centermost ring in a target.

BUTT A backstop behind a target.

CAST The speed at which a bow can shoot; the privilege of shooting first in a competition.

CHESTED ARROW An arrow that is thickest near the nock.

CLOUT TARGET A target that is twelve times the standard four-foot target. A clout target is laid flat on the ground and used for distance shooting of up to 180 yards.

COCK FEATHER A feather that is set at a 90-degree angle to a string and is of a different color than the other feathers to facilitate locating the nock.

CREEP The edging forward of an arrow during the aiming process.

CREST Colored identifying bands that are located on the shaft of an arrow.

DOUBLE ROUND A round that is shot two times in succession, with the scores of both added together.

DRAW The act of pulling back the bowstring.

DRAWING HAND The hand that pulls back the bowstring.

DRAWING WEIGHT The specific power needed for pulling the bow all the way back.

DRIFT An arrow's movement sideways because of crosswinds.

END In target competition, the number of arrows shot and scored as a group.

EYE A loop at the bowstring's end.

FACE The front of a target.

FIELD ARCHERY Competitive events held in forestlike areas to approximate hunting conditions.

FIELD ARROW An arrow used in field archery.

FIELD POINT A tapered arrowhead.

FIELD ROUND A round in field archery.

FIELD ROVING COURSE A course set in forestlike areas to approximate bow-hunting conditions.

FINGER STALL Protective coverings for the draw fingers.

FINGER TAB Protective leather coverings for the string fingers.

FISTMELE The distance from the belly of a bow to the string.

FLETCH The act of putting feathers on an arrow.

FLETCHER An arrowsmith.

FLETCHING The vanes or feathers attached to an arrow.

FLICK A change in direction of an arrow in flight.

FLIGHT ARROW An arrow designed for distance shooting.

FLIGHT SHOOTING Distance shooting.

FLIRT A flickering of an arrow just after it is shot from the bow.

FLU-FLU An arrow with a broad point, designed for bird hunting.

FOOT BOW A bow that is placed against the feet and drawn with both hands.

FOOTED ARROW An arrow with strong material inserted behind the pile for greater strength.

FREESTYLE Competition that allows various kinds of bows, aiming devices, and types of shooting.

GOLD A bull's-eye in a target.

GRIP The bow handle.

HEAD The point of the arrow.

HEN FEATHERS Two out of three feathers of a three-feather bow that are colored alike.

HOLD The pause at full draw.

HUNTER'S ROUND A field-archery round on a roving course.

HUNTING BOW A bow used for hunting game.

IN The second unit in a field-archery round.

KICK Jolt when a bow is let go.

KISSER A button or knot located on the bowstring, against which the lips are pressed to fix draw and arrow elevation.

KISSOFF An arrow that bounces off one already in the target and lodges in a lesser scoring area or misses the target altogether.

LET DOWN The loss of bow weight.

LIMB Bow ends.

LONGBOW A long, straight bow, such as those used in medieval England.

LOOSE The act of releasing the drawstring and shooting the arrow.

MATT The straw or grass coil on which the target is placed.

NOCK The grooves on an arrow or on limb tips into which the bowstring fits.

NOCKING POINT The place on the bowstring where the arrow nock fits.

OUT The first unit shot in a round of field archery.

OVERBOWED A bow that requires greater strength to draw than the archer has.

OVERDRAW The act of drawing an arrow back too much.

PETTICOAT The white rim of a target, which is scoreless.

PILE The metal tip of the arrow.

PIN HOLE A point in the center of a target that aids aiming.

POINT Pile.

POINT BLANK The distance from the target at which the point-of-aim and the gold coincide.

POINT-OF-AIM The object an archer sights on to get proper elevation.

POPINJAY SHOOTING A shooting competition in which blunt arrows are shot at artificial birds; scoring values are attached to high overhead perches.

POWER FORM A stance used for target shooting that is aimed at increasing body-muscle tension. In the power form, the feet are turned out more toward the target than ordinarily, and the upper body is twisted to some degree away from the target while the archer aims.

QUIVER A carrying device to hold arrows that is usually a long leather bag worn over the shoulder.

RANGE FINDER An aid in estimating the distance to a target or in determining the point-of-aim.

RECURVED BOW A bow whose tips are formed with a reverse bend.

REFLEX BOW A bow with limbs that curve away from the archer when unstrung and held in shooting position.

RELEASE To loose an arrow by releasing the bowstring.

RISER Additional stripping glued to the bow handle's belly side for depth or reinforcement.

ROUND A specific number of arrows shot at given distances; in field shooting, a two-unit or 28-target course.

ROVER An individual who engages in the old method of field archery by shooting progressively at casual, or random, targets.

SELF A bow or arrow made from a single kind of material; an arrow with no footing; a bow created from only one type of wood.

SERVING Additional wrapping around the bowstring to prevent chafing and make for longer wear.

SHAFT An arrow's cylindrical body from the nock to the pile.

SHAFTMENT The part of the shaft at which feathers are attached.

SPINE Arrow-shaft stiffness, firmness, elasticity; the arrow's ability after being released from the bow to resume its original shape.

STACKED BOW A narrow-limbed bow whose limbs are not as thick as they are wide.

STAKE A shooting position in field archery.

STRING To get set for shooting the arrow by bending the bow (see BRACE).

STRING ARM The string-pulling arm.

STRING DAMPENER A device that helps cut down the twanging sound made when an arrow is released. It is composed of rubber or plastic and is fitted on the bowstring to cushion vibrations (STRING SILENCER).

STRING HAND The bowstring-pulling hand.

TAB Leather covering for the fingers that pull the bowstring.

TACKLE Archery equipment.

TARGET A circular outline positioned on a backing of straw and having concentric rings representing scoring areas of different values. The bull's-eye in the center has the highest scoring value.

TARGET ARCHERY Competitive events where archers shoot at a target from specific distances.

TARGET ARROW The target-shooting arrow composed of a fairly small fletching, an equal-diameter shaft, and a pile that is pointed.

TARGET POINT A cone-shaped pile that is pointed.

TARGET ROUND A target-shooting round.

TILLER To find a bow's curvature at all bends and to adjust unequal bending.

TOXOPHILITE A word derived from the Greek *toxon* ("bow") and *philos* ("loving") and meaning an archer or someone who is a fan of archery.

UNDERBOWED An archer with a bow that is too weak for his strength.

UNDERDRAW To draw back just shy of full draw, diminishing shot power.

UNIT Half of a full field course; a fourteen-target loop.

UNSTRING To take the bowstring off the nock(s) of a bow.

VANE Fletching; generally refers to plastic types.

WALK-UP Progressively placed shooting stakes.

WAND A long, narrow target stuck into the ground.

WAND SHOOTING Competitive events where 36 arrows are shot at a wand.

WEIGHT The force necessary to pull a bow all the way back (BOW WEIGHT).

WHIP The act of putting a serving (wrapping) around a bowstring.

BADMINTON

ACE A winning point.

BACKHAND Stroke hit by right-handed players on the left side of the body or by left-handed players on the right side of the body.

BACKSWING Movement of the racquet backward in anticipation of the forward swing.

BASE A spot on the middle line, a bit closer to the net than the baseline, where players in singles games should attempt to return to after most shots.

BIRD A cone-shaped missile with rounded cork at one end and 14–16 feathers at the other end (SHUTTLE; SHUTTLE-COCK).

CLEAR A lofting stroke that projects the bird to the back of the opponent's court (LOB).

CROSSCOURT A stroke that gets the bird to go diagonally across court.

DRIVE A flat, fast stroking of the bird.

DROP SHOT The bird barely clears the net and descends almost vertically as a result of this stroke, which may be hit underhanded or overhanded.

FAULT(S) Foul(s) that cost the server the serve.

FLICK Rapid wrist-movement shot, performed with little motion in the player's arm, that gets the bird high in the air and to the rear of the opponent's court.

FOLLOW-THROUGH After racquet contact with the bird, the smooth continuance of the stroke in the direction of the bird.

FORECOURT Front court.

FOREHAND Right-handed players' natural stroking of the bird from a position to the right of the body, or a stroke hit on the left side of the body by left-handed players.

FRONT SERVICE LINE The forward boundary of the service courts; a line parallel to and 6½ feet from the net on each side of the court (SHORT SERVICE LINE).

GAME In singles, 15 points for men and 11 for women; 15 points in the different types of doubles play.

HALF COURT The serving court for one player, which is diagonally opposite the receiving court of his opponent.

HIGH SERVE A serve delivered high and deep into the half court of the receiver (LOB SERVE).

KILL A hard and quick shot that is virtually impossible to return (PUT-AWAY).

LET A point that is played over; an expression that indicates that because play has been interfered with, a point must be played over.

LOOSE SHOT A poorly hit, weak shot.

LOVE A scoring term that indicates zero.

LOVE-ALL No score.

LOW SERVE A serve that is softly hit and just skims over the net (SHORT SERVE).

MATCH A three-game set; the first player to win two games wins the match.

MIXED DOUBLES A pairing of a man and woman as partners against another man and woman.

NET SHOT A shot played from close to the net; a type of drop shot.

OVERHEAD A stroke hit from a level above a player's head.

PLACEMENT Stroking the bird to a part of the court where the opponent will have difficulty in returning the shot.

POSITION During a rally, the point occupied by a player on the court at a particular time.

RALLY Exchanges of the bird over the net between players or teams prior to the finishing of a point.

RECEIVER The player designated to receive a serve.

REPLY The stroking back of an opponent's shot (RETURN).

ROUND-THE-HEAD A stroke executed from the area of the left shoulder, utilizing the forehand grip, that results in an overhead shot smashed with some degree of force.

SERVE To put the bird into play at the start of a rally.

SERVER The player who serves.

SERVICE COURTS The half-courts designated as areas where players must serve to.

SETUP An easy chance at a winning shot.

SLING The act of not hitting the shuttle cleanly but carrying it on the racket, which is a fault (THROW).

SMASH A powerful downward stroke hit with much speed.

STROKE The hitting of the bird with the racquet.

BASEBALL

ADVANCE The moving ahead of a base runner to the next base as a result of a hit, error, sacrifice, balk, etc.

AHEAD To be winning; a pitcher can be ahead in the count if he has more strikes on the batter than balls.

ALLEY The space between the center fielder and right fielder or between the center fielder and left fielder.

APPEAL PLAY An appeal play occurs when a defensive player claims a runner did not touch a base and urges the umpire to call the player out. The defensive player must tag the runner or the base to get the appeal considered.

AROUND THE HORN A phrase describing a ball thrown from third base to second base to first base, generally in a double-play situation.

ASSIST A player's throw to another player on his team that results in a putout.

AT BAT An official time up at the plate as a hitter.

AWAY A pitch out of the reach of a batter. A side retired in its half of an inning.

BACKSTOP Another name for the position of catcher.

BAIL OUT The movement of a batter away from a pitched ball as a result of fear of being hit by the pitch.

BALK Illegal movement by a pitcher that, when executed with runner(s) on base, allows the runner(s) to advance one base; with the bases empty, a ball is added to the count of the batter.

BALL HAWK A speedy and sure-handed outfielder.

BALTIMORE CHOP A hard-smashed ball in or just beyond the home plate area that bounces high in the air and gives the runner a good chance to beat the fielder's throw to first base.

BANJO HITTER A "punch and judy" or weak batter.

BASE The white canvas bags, set 90 feet apart in professional baseball, and designated as 1st base, 2nd base, and 3rd base. (See HOME PLATE, which is technically a base); (SACK; BAG).

BASE HIT Any fair hit that results in a player reaching a base safely; generally refers to a single (BINGLE).

BASE ON BALLS The yielding of a fourth pitch outside the strike zone to a batter, which allows him to move to first base (WALK; PASS; FREE TICKET).

BASES LOADED A situation where there are runners on 1st, 2nd, and 3rd base.

BASKET CATCH A catch of a ball by an outfielder with glove at waist level, palm side up; made famous by Willy Mays.

BAT AROUND A situation where each batter in the lineup receives a chance to hit in the same inning.

BAT BOY/GIRL A youngster who takes care of bats and other baseball equipment.

BATTER The player who is up at bat, hitting (BATSMAN).

BATTER'S BOX A rectangle on either side of home plate in which the batter must stand in order to hit.

BATTER'S WHEELHOUSE That part of the plate where the batter hits most effectively from.

BATTERY The pitcher and catcher.

BATTERY MATE The catcher is the pitcher's battery mate; the pitcher is the catcher's battery mate.

BATTING AVERAGE A means of indicating the effectiveness of a hitter; to compute the average, the number of hits is divided by the number of official times at bat.

BATTING ORDER The sequence in which hitters on a team come to bat in a game.

BEAN To strike a batter in the head with a pitched ball.

BEANBALL A pitched ball aimed generally at the head of a batter.

BEHIND To be at a disadvantage; describes a team that is losing, a batter that has a count with more strikes than balls, etc.

BELT The hitting of a ball with much force by a batter.

BENCH JOCKEY A loud-mouthed player who teases the opposition from his position on the bench in the dugout.

BLANK To shut out; to hold the opposition scoreless (WHITE-WASH).

BLAST A very powerfully hit ball that travels for distance.

BLOCK THE PLATE The act of a catcher straddling the baseline between home plate and an oncoming base runner in an attempt to be in a good position to tag out the runner.

BLOOPER A softly hit ball that generally has some backspin and which barely drops in beyond the infield. A lobbed pitch.

BOBBLE A fielder's fumbling of a ball.

BOOT A fielder's mishandling of a ground ball.

BOTTOM The second half of an inning; the time reserved for the home team to bat.

BREAKING PITCH A pitch that does not come in straight to a batter, but moves about, such as a curve or a slider.

BRUSHBACK PITCH As opposed to a beanball, a pitch not thrown *at* the batter, but thrown close enough to him to make him move back from a too choice position in the batter's box.

BULLET A hard-thrown fastball. A powerfully hit ball.

BULLPEN An area, generally in the left or right field vicinity, where relief pitchers are allowed to warm up during a game in case they are needed to come in and pitch (PEN).

BUNT To tap, but not swing, at a ball to get it to roll just a bit onto the playing field. Bunters can try to make it to first safely in order to get a bunt hit, or they may place the ball in such a way as to sacrifice or give themselves up while moving a teammate up to another base.

BUSH LEAGUES The low minor leagues or not well-known leagues.

CACTUS LEAGUE Spring training schedule of major league teams in the Southwest.

CALL Announcement of an umpire, or the keeping track of balls and strikes.

CALLED STRIKE A strike that a batter does not swing at but which is announced as a strike by the umpire.

CAN OF CORN A lazy, high fly ball (RAINMAKER).

CATCHER The player positioned behind home plate who catches the ball thrown by the pitcher.

CHANCE A fielder's opportunity to catch a ball.

CHASE To cause a pitcher to leave a game because a team scores quite a few runs off him. An umpire forcing a player, coach, or manager to leave the game because of what the umpire deems to be misconduct.

CHEST PROTECTOR A stuffed pad worn over the chest by catchers and umpires to ward off damage from thrown or batted balls.

CHINESE HOME RUN A home run that barely clears the outfield wall.

CHOKE UP To grip the bat nearer to the middle than down at the handle in order to get better bat-control. To panic in stress situations.

CHOP To smash the ball down onto the ground.

CLEAN-UP HITTER The fourth man in the batting order.

COACH'S BOXES Rectangular boxes eight feet outside first base and third base in which the coaches of the team at bat stand, giving signals and advice to the batters and base runners.

COMEBACKER A ground ball batted back toward the pitcher.

COMPLETE GAME A game that a pitcher starts and finishes.

CORNER The inside and the outside portions of home plate.

COUNT The number of balls and strikes on a batter during his turn at bat.

COUSIN A player whom another player has luck performing against.

CROSSFIRE A sidearm pitch that angles across the plate.

CROWDING THE PLATE A situation where a player moves up close to the plate, either to increase his chances of walking or his ability to hit an outside pitch.

CUP OF COFFEE A very brief time as a player in the major leagues.

CURVEBALL A pitch that breaks and curves as it crosses the plate.

CUT A batter's swing.

CUT DOWN A fielder's throw that results in a base runner being put out in the act of trying to reach the next base.

CUT OFF A throw, usually from an outfielder to a catcher, that is stopped by an infielder on its way to the catcher or infielder.

CYCLE A batter achieving a single, double, triple, and home run in the same game (HITS FOR THE CYCLE).

DEAD BALL A ball that does not carry far. A ball that is out of play either because play has been temporarily suspended or because the ball is outside the boundaries of play.

DELAYED STEAL A stolen base executed after the pitcher has thrown the ball to the catcher and not while the pitch is underway, as in a traditional stolen base.

DESIGNATED HITTER A rule in the American League that allows a team to designate a batter to hit for the pitcher; the designated hitter doesn't play in the field and the pitcher never comes to bat.

DIAMOND The baseball infield, whose four bases resemble the points of a diamond in the shape they outline.

DIE A situation where a runner is left on base at the end of an inning because his batting teammates cannot score him. A situation where a baseball drops abruptly in its flight.

DIG IN The act of a batter getting firmer footing in the batter's box by using the spikes on his shoes to loosen the ground. Metaphorically, a situation where a batter bears down in his concentration against a pitcher.

DOUBLE A hit that allows a player to run from the batter's box to second base (TWO-BASE HIT; TWO-BAGGER).

DOUBLEHEADER Two games played on the same day, usually right after each other and usually for a single admission price for the fan.

DOUBLE PLAY The retiring of two players for two outs on the same play.

DOUBLE STEAL A situation where two base runners each steal a base on the same play.

DOWN Losing or out ("one man down in the top of the ninth"), or trailing in the score ("down by three runs").

DRAG BUNT A ball purposely hit slowly by a batter facing away from the pitcher to give himself a head start in his run to first base in pursuit of a hit.

DRIVE A batted ball hit for distance.

DRIVE IN To bat a run in, to cause a run to score.

DUGOUT An area on each side of home plate where players stay while their team is at bat. There is a visitor's dugout and a home-team dugout.

DUSTER A pitch thrown high and inside to a batter and intended to make him "hit the dust" or jump out of the way to avoid being hit by the pitch.

EARNED RUN A run scored without the aid of an error or passed ball.

EARNED-RUN AVERAGE (ERA) The average number of earned runs scored against a pitcher for every nine innings he pitches; the average is obtained by dividing the total number of earned runs by the number of innings pitched and multiplying this figure by nine. A low ERA is preferred.

ERROR A misplay of a ball by a fielder.

EVEN THE COUNT A situation where a batter or pitcher is able to get the count even—that is, a like number of balls and strikes.

EXTRA-BASE HIT Any hit other than a single.

EXTRA INNING Any inning beyond the regulation nine.

FAIR BALL A ball that is in play.

FAIR TERRITORY The area between the foul lines that makes up the playing field's fair-ball territory.

FAN To strike out (WHIFF).

FASTBALL A pitch thrown with power and speed.

FAT PART OF THE BAT The area of the bat, near the trademark, that contains the most contact or striking surface.

FAT PITCH A pitch that is easy for a batter to hit.

FENCE BUSTER A long-ball hitter.

FIELD The handling of a batted ball by a defensive player.

FIELDER A defensive player other than the catcher or pitcher.

FIELDER'S CHOICE A situation where a fielder, after gaining possession of a batted ball, can elect either to throw out the batter who is running to first base or to attempt to throw out another base runner. A batter who reaches base because the fielder elected to go after the base runner is credited with reaching base on a fielder's choice. A time at bat is charged to the batter.

FIELDING AVERAGE The percentage of chances fielded successfully versus errors committed, which reveals a player's defensive skills, at least from a statistical point of view.

FIND THE HANDLE The ability on the part of a fielder to control a ball hit to him; an inability to "find the handle" results many times in the commission of an error.

FIREBALLER A fastball-throwing pitcher (HARD CHUCKER; FLAME THROWER).

FIREMAN A relief pitcher.

FIRST Refers to first base.

FIRST BASEMAN A player whose position is first base (FIRST SACKER).

FLY A batted ball hit high in the air (FLY BALL).

FORCE-OUT The retiring of a runner on a force play.

FORCE PLAY A condition where a runner must leave his base and move to the next base because of a ground ball the batter has hit. The runner's failure to reach the next base before it is touched by a defensive player in possession of the ball creates a force-out.

FORKBALL A pitch thrown by a pitcher who grips the ball with his index and middle fingers spread apart; this pitch dips downward as it crosses the plate.

FOUL BALL A ball hit into foul territory.

FOUL LINES The boundary lines of fair territory that extend on a right angle from the back corner of home plate past the outside edges of first and third base and on into the outfield.

FOUL OFF To hit a pitched ball foul.

FOUL OUT To foul off a pitch and have it caught by a defensive player before it touches the ground, for an out.

FOUL POLES Vertical extensions of the foul lines whose lower portions are generally painted on the outfield walls, above which extends the actual pole.

FOUL TERRITORY The opposite of fair territory.

FOUL TIP A ball swung at and tipped back by the batter and then caught by the catcher.

FOUR-BAGGER A home run (CIRCUIT CLOUT).

FULL COUNT Three balls and two strikes on a batter.

FUMBLE To bobble a ground ball.

FUNGO A batting practice procedure in which a player throws up a ball and hits it with his bat as it drops down to strike-zone level.

FUNGO BAT A specially designed bat with a long handle and a thin shape, used to practice hitting fungoes.

FUNGO CIRCLES Circular areas near to the baselines on either side of home plate, from which fungoes are hit.

GIVE ONESELF UP A sacrificing effort by a batter who hits the ball behind a runner on base in order to advance the runner, even though such an effort usually causes the batter to be thrown out.

GIVE UP Mental lapse or courage breakdown on the part of a player, allowing his opponent to gain an advantage.

GLOVE MAN A fine fielder.

GO FOR THE FENCES To consciously swing for a home run.

GOOD WOOD To make contact with the ball with the fat part of the bat, thus hitting the ball well.

GOPHER BALL A pitch that "goes for" a home run—not a very well-thrown pitch from the pitcher's point of view.

GO WITH THE PITCH To hit the ball where it is pitched and not to attempt to overpower it.

GRANDSLAMMER A bases-loaded home run.

GRAPEFRUIT LEAGUE The spring-training schedule of the major-league teams in Florida.

GRASS CUTTER A powerfully-hit ground ball that skips along the ground and "cuts the grass."

GROOVE To throw a pitch over the fat, middle part of the plate. To be in a good, flowing playing condition, such as a batting groove.

GROUNDER A ball that is hit along the ground.

GROUNDOUT To be retired at first base on a grounder to an infielder.

GROUND OUT To hit into a groundout.

GROUND RULE A special rule governing the course of play that is put into effect because of the particular features of a ball park.

GROUND-RULE DOUBLE The awarding of two bases (a double) to a batter who hits a ball into a special ground-rule situation—the batted ball, for example, bouncing into the stands.

GUESS HITTER A batter who swings at a pitch that he guesses will be a strike, a ball, low, high, etc.

GUN DOWN To throw out a player with a strong throw, generally referring to an outfielder's or catcher's throw.

HANDCUFFED A condition occurring when an infielder has trouble controlling a powerfully hit ball.

HANG To throw a pitch that does not break (HANGING CURVE).

HANGER A pitch that does not break.

HEAVY BALL A pitch that a batter has trouble hitting for distance.

HIGH PITCH A pitch that is above the batter's strike zone.

HIT AND RUN A play in which the batter swings at the ball and the runner on base breaks for the next base.

HIT THE DIRT A situation in which a batter drops to the ground to avoid being hit by a pitched ball or where a base runner jumps back to the base to avoid being picked off by the pitcher.

HOLD ON BASE A condition in which a pitcher, by keeping an eye on the runner and sometimes throwing the ball to the defender stationed at that base, attempts to keep the runner from taking too big a lead or stealing a base.

HOLE The space between two infielders.

HOLLER GUY A player that has a lot of enthusiasm and screams out encouragement for his teammates.

HOME A short way of saying home plate.

HOME PLATE A slab of white rubber with five sides that the pitcher throws to; it is also the final base touched by a runner to score a run.

HOME RUN A hit that leaves the ball park in fair territory; it is worth one run, or more if there are men on base. The batter is allowed to trot around the bases uncontested (FOUR BAGGER: CIRCUIT CLOUT) (see INSIDE-THE-PARK HOME RUN).

HOME STAND A stretch of games played by a team at home.

HOOK SLIDE An action where a runner slides into the side of a base, hooking it with a bent, back-stretched leg as he passes the base.

HORSE COLLAR Describes a situation when a player gets no hits in a game.

HOT CORNER Third base; the term originated because of the number of hard-smashed balls that arrive there.

HOT STOVE LEAGUE Designation for winter-time baseball doings and gossip.

HURL To pitch (CHUCK).

HURLER A pitcher (CHUCKER).

INFIELDER The positions of first baseman, second baseman, third baseman, and shortstop.

INFIELD FLY A situation that occurs when, with less than two men out and with either all three bases occupied or first and second bases occupied, a hitter pops the ball up to the infield; the hitter is automatically declared out and the runners may advance at their own risk.

INFIELD HIT A hit achieved by hitting a ball that does not leave the infield.

INFIELD OUT The retiring of a batter on a ball hit in the infield.

INNING A period of play that consists of three outs for each team. A regulation game consists of nine innings.

INSIDE-THE-PARK HOME RUN A home run that takes place when the ball is hit and is in play and the batter is able to reach home plate before being tagged out.

INTENTIONAL WALK A situation in which a pitcher deliberately throws four balls to a batter in a strategic attempt to prevent the batter from hitting.

INTERFERENCE Getting in the way of a runner, a fielder, or hitter and making it difficult for that player to perform unhindered action.

JAM THE HITTER To pitch a ball close to a hitter so as not to give him anything good to hit and to keep him off balance.

JUG-HANDLE CURVE A wide-breaking curveball.

JUNK PITCHER A hurler who throws slow and deceptively-breaking pitches, or "junk."

K The scorecard symbol for a strikeout.

KEYSTONE Second base.

KEYSTONE COMBINATION The second baseman and the shortstop.

KNOCK OUT OF THE BOX To score runs against a pitcher in such a way that he is removed from the game.

KNUCKLEBALL An unusual pitch that flutters as it comes to the batter (FLUTTERBALL; KNUCKLER).

KNUCKLE CURVE A combination knuckleball and curveball.

LAY DOWN A BUNT The act of bunting the ball.

LEAD The amount of steps a base runner takes off a base. A short lead takes place when the runner is close to the base. A long lead describes a proportionately longer distance off the base.

LEADOFF BATTER (MAN) The first hitter in the team's line-up or in an inning.

LEAD OFF To bat first in an inning or in the team's lineup.

LEAVE MEN ON BASE A situation at the end of an inning when a team has been retired and one or more base runners have been left on base, unable to score (STRAND BASE RUNNER[S]).

LEFT FIELD Viewed from home plate, the left side of the outfield.

LEG HIT A base hit awarded to a runner who beats out a ground ball to the infield by using his speed.

LETUP PITCH A pitch from which something is taken off, generally speed, so that it comes in to the batter with less velocity than he expects (CHANGE-UP).

LINE OUT To hit a line drive that is caught for an out.

LINER A ball hit straight and solidly (LINE DRIVE).

LINE SCORE A printed summary account, inning by inning, of a game.

LIVE BALL A ball that, because of its alleged composition, will travel a long way when hit—as opposed to a dead ball (RABBIT BALL).

LOAD THE BALL The illegal placement by a pitcher of saliva or some other foreign substance on the ball, to gain an edge by causing the ball to move about unpredictably.

LOAD THE BASES An offensive team's placing of runners on each base (BASES FULL).

LONG-BALL HITTER A batter who hits the ball for distance.

LONG RELIEVER (LONG MAN) A relief pitcher counted on to pitch approximately three innings or more.

LOOK FOR To come to bat expecting a certain pitch. (The term also covers many situations involving expectation, such as "looking for a player" to supply home-run power.)

LOOK THE RUNNER BACK A situation in which a pitcher attempts to control a base runner by staring at him, implying a throw; the pitcher's gaze alone will most times convince a runner to stay close to the base.

LOOPER A batted ball that drops in flight.

LOSING PITCHER The pitcher who is officially charged with a loss.

LOW PITCH A pitch that comes in below the strike zone.

MOUND A raised surface in the center of the diamond on which the pitcher stands and throws to the batter.

MOUNDSMAN Another name for a pitcher.

MUFF To misplay a ground ball or a fly ball.

NAIL The act of throwing out a runner.

NIGHTCAP The second game of a doubleheader.

NINE A baseball team (STARTING NINE).

NO-HITTER A game in which a pitcher (or pitchers) on one team does not allow any hits to the opposition.

OFFICIAL GAME A game that goes 4½ innings with home team ahead or five innings with visitors leading.

OFFICIAL SCORER The person who records the score and statistics of a game and rules on whether a hit or an error, etc., should be charged to a player in a particular situation.

OFF-SPEED PITCH A pitch that is slower than others a pitcher usually throws, so that the difference in velocity affects the timing of a hitter.

ON DECK A term describing a player stationed in the batter's on-deck circle in front of the dugout, preparing to be the next batter to come up and hit.

ONE-BAGGER (ONE-BASE HIT) A single.

OPPOSITE FIELD The part of the field opposite the batter's box a hitter occupies. Thus, right field is the opposite field for a hitter who bats right, and left field is the opposite field for a hitter who bats from the left side of the plate.

OUT To be retired by the defense.

OUTFIELD The playing area beyond the infield where outfielders are stationed.

OUTFIELDER The positions of left fielder, right fielder, and center fielder (PICKETMAN).

OUTHIT To get more hits than another player or team.

OUTPITCH To pitch better than an opponent.

OUTSLUG Usually, to defeat another team by displaying more extra-base power.

OVERMANAGE To bother and hamper a team with excess strategy and suggestions—generally the suggestions and strategy come from the manager.

OVERSLIDE To slide into a base and then past it.

PALMBALL An off-speed pitch, not often used, for which a pitcher grips the ball between the thumb and the palm.

PASSED BALL An error charged to a catcher for a pitch he is unable to control; usually, the runner on base is able to advance to the next base because of the error.

PEG A forceful throw (catcher to second baseman, for example) aimed at retiring a base runner.

PENNANT A pennant-shaped banner that symbolizes the winning of a league championship (FLAG).

PENNANT RACE The battle for the pennant among contending teams.

PEPPER GAME Pregame warm-up action where a player chops the ball on the ground to teammates who field the ball and flip it back to him.

PERCENTAGE PLAYER OR MANAGER One who goes by past form or logical odds and acts on the basis of these considerations.

PERFECT GAME A no-hitter in which all 27 opposing batters in a nine-inning game, for example, are not allowed to get on base.

PICKOFF The retiring of a base runner through a throw to the player covering the base, who tags the runner before he can get back to the base.

PICKOFF PLAY A set play aimed at picking off a base runner.

PILOT Another name for a baseball manager. To manage a team.

PINCH HIT To come up to the plate to hit for another batter.

PINCH HITTER The player who comes up to the plate to hit for another batter.

PINCH RUN To function as a substitute runner for another player. The substitute takes the other player's place at the base that the player had occupied.

PINCH RUNNER A generally faster runner who comes into a game to take the place of a man on base and to run for him.

PINE TAR Cloth saturated with tar that is rubbed on a batter's hands or bat for better grip.

PITCH To throw the ball to the batter from the pitcher's mound.

PITCH AROUND A BATTER To consciously refuse to give a batter a good pitch to hit, out of respect for the ability of the batter. A base on balls is sometimes given so as not to allow the batter to see pitches that he might be able to hit.

PITCHER The player who is positioned on the pitcher's mound who throws the ball to the plate (HURLER; MOUNDSMAN; CHUCKER; TWIRLER).

PITCHER-OF-RECORD A pitcher officially liable to be charged with a win or loss even though he has been removed from a game. This condition prevails until or unless the score is tied and a new pitcher-of-record is established.

PITCHER'S DUEL A tough, low-scoring game, highlighted by effective pitching on both sides (SQUEAKER).

PITCHER'S MOUND Located on a line between home plate and second base, this raised surface is the area a pitcher operates off.

PITCHING CHART A record; a complete statistical accounting of a pitching performance in a game, usually kept by the pitcher who is scheduled to start the next day.

PITCHOUT The pitcher's intentional throwing of the ball a bit wide of the plate. This maneuver is aimed at giving the catcher an edge in throwing out a base runner he suspects will be attempting to steal.

PIVOT A second baseman's turning maneuver as he touches the base with one foot and whirls about to throw to first base to complete a double-play attempt.

PLATE UMPIRE The home-plate umpire.

PLATOON To alternate players at one position.

PLAYOFFS Postseason competition to determine league entry into World Series.

POLE THE BALL To hit the ball with power.

POP FLY, POP IT UP, POP-UP, POP All signify a short fly ball.

POP-FOUL To hit a short, foul fly ball.

POP OUT To be retired on a short fly ball.

POPPING THE BALL The act of a pitcher throwing the ball so hard at the catcher that it can be heard "popping" into the catcher's mitt.

POTENTIAL TYING RUN A base runner or a hitter who, if he eventually scores, will tie the game up. Thus, each time a team losing by one run gets a man on base or to the plate, that player is the potential tying run.

POWER ALLEY An area in the outfield that a particular player can hit to with power; the areas between center field and right field, and center field and left field where many home runs are hit.

POWER THE BALL The ability to hit or throw the ball with force.

PROTECT THE PLATE The defensive behavior of a batter swinging at pitches that he thinks may be called strikes.

PROTECT THE RUNNER The act of a hitter swinging at any pitch in a hit-and-run or steal situation to attempt to hamper a catcher's throw aimed at putting out the runner.

PULL HITTER One who pulls the ball.

PULL THE BALL The act of a hitter swinging in such a way that the ball will be hit to the same side of the field from which he bats: a right-handed pull hitter thus hits the ball to the right side; a left handed pull hitter hits to the left side. This situation is the reverse of hitting to the opposite field.

PUTOUT The actual act of retiring a player; the first baseman who catches the ball thrown by a shortstop to retire the runner streaking down the first-base line gets credit for a putout, for example.

RABBIT BALL A lively baseball; one that can be hit for distance.

RAIN CHECK That portion of the ticket that permits a fan to attend another game in place of one that has been rained out.

RAIN DATE The alternate date for a game that was rained out.

RAIN DELAY The interruption of a game because of rain; the game may be continued if the rain lets up.

RAINOUT A game that is called because of rain (WASHOUT).

RBI Abbreviation for a run batted in (RIBBY).

REACH BACK Describes a pitcher who summons additional energy or skill to throw an effective pitch to a batter.

REACH BASE (REACH) To manage to get on base; usually refers to first base.

RELIEF PITCHER A pitcher who comes in to take the place of another pitcher on his team who is not hurling effectively or who has gotten injured or tired (RELIEF; RELIEVER).

RETIRE THE SIDE IN ORDER The act of a pitcher facing only three batters, none of whom does he allow to get to first base.

RHUBARB A passionate difference of opinion that produces an extended argument on the playing field.

RIDE THE BENCH A phrase that describes a substitute who sits on the bench in the dugout.

RIFLE THE BALL To throw the ball with force and speed.

RIGHT-CENTER FIELD The area between right field and center field.

RIGHT FIELD Looking from home plate, the part of the outfield on the right side.

ROLLER A rolling ground ball.

ROPE A ball hit to the outfield on a line.

ROSIN BAG A pouch with powdered rosin used by pitchers to keep their throwing hands dry.

ROUNDHOUSE CURVE A pitch that breaks wide and slow.

ROUND THE BASES To trot around the bases, touching each one, after hitting a home run.

ROUND TRIPPER A home run (CIRCUIT CLOUT; FOUR BAGGER).

RUBBER The white rubber slab positioned on the pitcher's mound, the front edge of which is 60 feet, six inches from home plate. The pitcher cannot throw to home unless his foot is in contact with this object, or else a balk is called (SLAB; PITCHER'S RUBBER).

RUBBER-ARMED PITCHER A pitcher, usually a relief pitcher, who is capable of pitching often and long and whose arm does not reflect the stress and strain of hard work.

RUN A score of one run is made each time a player crosses home plate (TALLY; MARKER; SCORE).

RUN AND HIT A situation where a player on base runs and then the batter at the plate hits.

RUNDOWN A situation where a player is trapped between two bases and is chased back and forth by the defenders as he attempts to wind up safely on one of the bases.

SACK Base (BAG).

SACRIFICE A bunted ball that advances a teammate, or a ball hit to the outfield that enables a runner to tag up and score. The player committing the sacrifice does not reach base, but he also does not get a time at bat charged against his batting average (SACRIFICE BUNT; SACRIFICE HIT; SACRIFICE FLY).

SAFETY Base hit, bingle.

SAVE Credit given to relief pitcher for insuring team's victory.

SCATTER THE HITS The yielding of a good number of hits by a pitcher that are spaced over several innings to hamper opposition scoring.

SCORE The amount of runs each team achieves or is achieving at a given moment in a game. To drive in a run. To cross the plate and tally a run.

SCOREBOARD A highly visible board, generally beyond the outfield, that gives information about the score, the batting orders, the pitchers, other games in progress, or scheduled coming events.

SCORECARD A program purchased at ballpark by fans, who use it to keep score of the game in progress.

SCORING POSITION Location on the bases (generally second or third) from which a player can score on a hit or a fly ball.

SCRATCH FOR RUNS To have difficulty in scoring.

SCRATCH HIT A questionable hit that barely enables a runner to reach base safely.

SCREEN A wire barrier covering the area in the stands behind home plate to prevent fans from being hit by foul balls.

SCREWBALL A seemingly straight pitch which unexpectedly swerves to the right (when thrown by a right-handed pitcher) or to the left (when thrown by a left-handed pitcher) (SCROOGIE).

SECOND BASE The base midway between first base and third base and lined up with home plate (SECOND).

SECOND BASEMAN A fielder positioned, as a rule, to the right of second base. This player is a key man in double plays and in covering the area around his position and between first and second base.

SET DOWN IN ORDER To retire a side in order with no hits, no walks, no errors, and no runs.

SET POSITION A pitcher's stance assumed after a stretch—the ball is held in front of the body, with one foot positioned on the rubber.

SEVENTH-INNING STRETCH A baseball custom that enables fans to stand and to stretch a few moments before the half of the seventh inning that the team they are rooting for comes to bat.

SHADE The act of defensive players moving slightly toward the side of a position they expect a batter to hit to.

SHAKE OFF A SIGN A situation where a pitcher will not accept a sign for a pitch given by a catcher and will indicate this by head or glove movement.

SHELL A PITCHER To get quite a few hits and runs off a pitcher, generally in a brief period of time.

SHIFT To move players from traditional defensive positions to other locations to compensate for a hitter's pattern.

SHOESTRING CATCH The grabbing of a fly ball by an outfielder just as it is about to hit the ground.

SHORTEN UP THE INFIELD A defensive move in which infielders move in closer to the plate.

SHORT-HOP To grab a batted ball by charging in at it and seizing it before it bounces high.

SHORT RELIEVER A relief pitcher who pitches for a brief time (SHORT RELIEF; SPOT RELIEVER; SHORT MAN).

SHORTSTOP A player positioned between third base and second base, closer to second, who has double-play responsibilities as a main part of his job.

SHOT A hard-hit ball.

SHOTGUN ARM A powerful throwing arm.

SHUTOUT A game in which a pitcher holds the opposition scoreless.

SIDEARMER A pitcher who throws the ball to the plate from a sidearm position, as opposed to overhanded.

SINGLE A one-base hit.

SINGLE IN A RUN To score a runner by hitting a single.

SINKER A pitch that drops as it nears the plate.

SINKING LINER A line drive that drops as it gathers distance.

SKIMMER A batted ball that rapidly glides across the ground.

SKIPPER Another name for a manager—the person who directs a baseball team (PILOT).

SKIP ROPE A quick, jumping movement by a batter to get out of the way of a pitched ball that is coming too close to him.

SKULL To bean or hit a batter in the head with a pitched ball.

SKY OUT To hit the ball high in the air and have it caught (RAIN-MAKER).

SLAB The pitcher's rubber.

SLASH THE BALL To hit the ball sharply to the outfield.

SLICE THE BALL To hit the ball so that, for example, it veers left when batted by a left-handed hitter, or vice-versa.

SLIDE The action of a base runner hitting the ground and coming into a base head- or feet-first. A belly slide is a variation in which a player flops on his belly with hands outstretched toward the base.

SLIDER A hard-breaking pitch with less overall motion than a curve ball.

SLIP PITCH A dropping pitch that comes toward the plate with off-speed velocity.

SLUGGER A player who gets long extra-base hits.

SLUGGING AVERAGE The ratio of total bases achieved to number of times at bat, which indicates the extra-base capability of the batter.

SLUGGING DUEL A game with many hits and many runs scored (SLUGFEST).

SLUMP A period of ineffectiveness for a team or an individual.

SMASH A powerfully hit ball.

SMOKING IT The throwing of pitches with top velocity—throwing "smoke."

SOFT LINER A line drive that is hit without much force.

SOFTLY HIT BALL A ball that is hit without much force.

SOLID CONTACT The act of hitting the ball and getting "good wood" or the fat part of the bat into contact with the ball.

SOLO CLOUT A home run with no one on base.

SOUTHPAW A left-handed pitcher.

SOUTHPAW SLANTS The pitching style of a left-handed pitcher.

SPEAR A LINER To catch a line drive by running it down and catching it with the arms fully extended.

SPIKE To inflict injury on another player with the spikes of baseball shoes—in sliding situations, for example.

SPIKES Metal projections on the bottom of the shoes worn by baseball players.

SPITTER An illegal pitch that involves a pitcher placing saliva or some other moist substance on the pitch to make it break oddly as it comes to the batter (SPITBALL; MOIST PITCH; WET PITCH).

SPOT STARTER A pitcher called into action to start games as the team needs him, as opposed to a regular starting pitcher.

SPRAY HITTER A batter who is able to spray the ball well.

SPRAY THE BALL To hit the ball to all fields.

SPRING TRAINING The conditioning and exhibition season of professional baseball teams, which generally starts in late February in a warm-weather climate and lasts until a few days before the start of the new season.

SQUARE AROUND TO BUNT A batter's movement out of a normal batting stance into a position facing the pitcher, with the bat extended parallel to the batter's feet, which point toward the infield.

SQUEEZE PLAY An offensive strategy move in which a team with less than two outs and a man on third base will have a batter bunt the ball, hoping the runner will be able to score. A SAFETY SQUEEZE takes place when the runner waits to see how effective the bunt is. A SUICIDE SQUEEZE takes place when the runner breaks the instant the pitch is released.

START An opportunity given to a pitcher to begin a game. To be the pitcher who begins a game.

STARTER A pitcher who starts a game (STARTING PITCHER).

STARTING ROTATION The order in which starting pitchers perform on a daily basis—every fourth or fifth day as a starter is the general rule, which would mean that a team has four or five starters.

STEAL To run from one base to the next, attempting to get there safely by catching the other team off guard.

STEP UP TO THE PLATE To get into the batter's box in preparation to hit.

STOLEN BASE A successful steal of a base by a runner.

STOP To bring a batted ball under control by knocking it down or slowing its movement so as to be able to play it.

STOPPER A consistently effective starting pitcher.

STRAIGHTAWAY To be lined up with an outfielder's position—a hitter can bat the ball to straightaway center field, and a fielder can play straightaway center field, for example.

STRANDED A term that describes a runner or runners left on base at the end of an inning, unable to be brought in to score by other hitters on their team (LEFT ON BASE).

STRETCH A modified windup used by a pitcher when runners are on base that enables the pitcher to keep closer check on runners.

STRIKE A pitch in the strike zone or one that is swung at and missed or fouled off. A highly accurate outfielder's throw.

STRIKEOUT The act of retiring a batter by getting three strikes on him.

STRIKE OUT The act of a batter being out on strikes.

STRIKE ZONE The imaginary area that extends over home plate from the batter's knees to his armpits; a pitch thrown in the strike zone will be a strike on the batter unless he hits it into fair territory.

STROKE To hit the ball smoothly, and usually well, to the outfield.

STUFF The movement and/or liveliness a pitcher is able to impart to the pitches he throws to a batter—a pitcher having his "good stuff" is throwing well.

SUNDAY BEST A term describing a pitcher throwing his most effective pitch(es).

SWAT THE BALL To hit the ball with power and for distance.

SWEEP A SERIES To win all the games in a series played with
another team.

SWING To move the bat in an arced motion to hit a pitched ball.

SWING AWAY To take a full cut (full swing) at a pitch.

SWING FOR THE FENCES To swing with maximum force in an
attempt to hit a home run. (SWING FROM THE HEELS; GO
FOR THE DOWNS.)

SWINGING BUNT A half swing, half bunt.

SWISH An expression describing a batter swinging hard at a
pitched ball and not making contact.

SWITCH HITTER A batter who can hit from either side of the
plate.

TAB To select a player for a certain performance—to "tab a pitcher
to start the first game of the World Series."

TAG OUT To touch a base runner with the ball as he is off base,
thus making him out (TAG).

TAG UP A situation where a runner stays on base until a fly ball is
caught and then has the option to run to the next base, attempting to beat the throw.

TAKE A PITCH To allow a pitch to come over the plate without
swinging at it.

TAKE OFF The opening move in the running of a player from one
base to another in an attempt to steal a base. A condition where
a pitch suddenly deviates in its motion as it comes to the plate
(usually refers to a ball that rises sharply).

TAKE-OUT PLAY A situation where a base runner slides into a
fielder, attempting to off-balance that player and prevent his
making a play.

TAKE SIGN A signal from a manager or coach to a batter to not
swing at a pitch.

TAP To select a player for a specific task.

TAPE-MEASURE HOME RUN An exceptionally long home run.

TEE OFF To hit a pitcher especially hard.

TEXAS LEAGUER A hit that is part fly-ball and part pop-up and that drops between the infielders going out for it and the outfielders coming in for it.

THIRD BASE The base on the left side of the infield, as viewed from home plate (THIRD).

THIRD BASEMAN The player whose position is third base and who defensively covers mainly the area between third and shortstop (THIRD SACKER; HOT SACK GUARDIAN).

THREAD THE NEEDLE A pitcher's ability to get a pitch in to a particular part of the plate where the batter is not able to effectively make contact with the ball.

THREE-BASE HIT A triple (THREE-BAGGER).

THREE-HUNDRED HITTER A batter who hits .300 or better.

THROWER A pitcher not distinguished by his thinking ability.

THROW OUT A BALL A situation where an umpire discards a ball that has become not playable because it is scuffed, marked, or dirtied.

THROW OUT A RUNNER The act of throwing a ball to a fielder who tags out a base runner.

TIME THE PITCH A situation where a batter swings at a pitch, making contact with the ball as a result of good timing.

TOOLS OF IGNORANCE Catcher's equipment.

TOP The first half of an inning. To hit a ball above its center line so that its flight or roll has topspin.

TOTAL BASES The adding up of the number of bases a hit is equal to: a single is one base, a double is two bases, a triple is three bases, a home run is four bases.

TRACK IT DOWN The running after and catching of a fly ball by an outfielder.

TRAP A BALL To catch a ball the instant after it touches the ground on a bounce.

TRIPLE A three-base hit (THREE-BAGGER).

TRIPLE CROWN The winning of the batting championship, home-run title, and RBI crown by one player in the same season.

TRIPLE PLAY Three outs recorded on one play.

TWIN BILL A doubleheader.

TWI-NIGHT DOUBLEHEADER Two games, usually for the same admission charge; the first game takes place in early evening, and the second game immediately follows.

TWIRL To pitch.

TWIRLER A pitcher.

TWO-BASE HIT A double (TWO-BAGGER).

UMPIRES Personnel who officiate at a game: the home plate umpire is stationed behind the plate and calls balls and strikes; other umpires are stationed near each base (ARBITERS; MEN IN BLUE; UMPS).

UNEARNED RUN A run scored as a result of a mistake made by the defensive team and not charged against a pitcher's earned-run average.

VELOCITY The speed of a pitched ball (ZIP).

WALK The receiving of a fourth pitch outside the strike zone by a batter, which allows him to move to first base (PASS; BASE ON BALLS).

WARMING UP The throwing of practice pitches in the bullpen by a relief pitcher who is readying himself to enter the game.

WARM-UP PITCHES Practice pitches allowed a pitcher each inning before the opposing side comes up to bat.

WARNING TRACK The area in front of outfield walls, composed of a surface different from the playing field, which serves to warn a player that he is nearing the wall.

WASTED PITCH A ball intentionally pitched out of the strike zone to get the batter to swing at it or set him up for the next pitch.

WEBBING Laces that connect a glove's (or mitt's) thumb and fingers.

WHIFF To swing at a pitch and miss it. To strike out.

WHITEWASH To shut out a team (BLANK).

WIDE A pitch outside the strike zone.

WILD PITCH A pitch far outside the strike zone that cannot be handled by the catcher.

WILD THROW A throw to a defensive player that is so inaccurate that it can't be handled.

WINDUP Arm and leg motions by a pitcher that serve as preliminary steps for the pitching of a ball.

WINNING PITCHER A pitcher officially given credit for a victory.

WINTER BALL Off-season, warm-weather baseball competition.

WORK THE COUNT A situation where a batter attempts to get the count in his favor by fouling off balls, taking pitches, etc.

WORLD SERIES The seven-game postseason championship between the winners of the National League and the American League pennants. The first team to win four games is declared the world champion.

WRIST HITTER A player who gets good wrist action into his swing at a ball.

WRONG-FIELD HIT A hit to the field opposite that which a batter is normally expected to hit to—a right-handed batter hitting to right field, for example.

BASKETBALL

AIR BALL An ineffective shot that completely misses the backboard and the rim.

ALLEY-OOP SHOT An acrobatic shot made by a player who goes
high in the air and shoots the ball as he is falling to the ground.

ANTICIPATION A player's ability to sense ahead of time what an
opposing player or team will do.

ASSIST A pass by one player to another that results in the second
player scoring a basket.

BACKBOARD The surface that the basket is attached to (GLASS).

BACKCOURT The part of the court that contains the basket. There
are actually two backcourts, as one team's backcourt is the
other team's forecourt, depending on whether the team is playing offense or defense.

BACKCOURT FOUL Foul against an offensive player in his own
backcourt.

BACKCOURT VIOLATION A professional rule that states a team
must move the ball out of its backcourt within ten seconds after
gaining possession. Failure to do this awards the ball to the
other team.

BACK DOOR A situation where an offensive player goes behind
the defense under his own basket to receive a pass.

BANK SHOT To use the backboard to make a shot via an angular carom of the ball into the basket, as opposed to shooting straight into the basket.

BASELINE The shorter boundary lines at either end of the court behind the basket.

BASKET An 18-inch-diameter metal ring from which a net is suspended and through which the ball must go for a field goal worth two points or a free throw worth one point (HOOP; HOLE).

BASKET-HANGER Also known as "hanger," a player who stays back under his basket while the other team is on offense; a quick pass to him from a teammate makes for a potentially easy basket. The problem with this strategy is that it leaves the basket-hanger's team shorthanded on defense.

BLOCKED SHOT A situation where a defensive player legally gets his hand on the ball held by an offensive player to hamper the shot.

BLOCKING Illegal movement of a defensive player into path of an offensive player to interfere with free movement.

BOMB A shot at the basket taken from long range.

BONUS (FREE THROW) An extra foul shot awarded when a team uses up its allowance of fouls in a quarter of play. A fouled player in pro basketball gets two attempts for a one-shot foul, three attempts for a two-shot foul. High schools and colleges award the bonus for one-shot fouls; if the free throw is successful, there is another free throw awarded (PENALTY SHOT).

BONUS SITUATION After a team has used up its allowable fouls in a period, the bonus or penalty situation is applied.

BOUNCE PASS The passing of the ball on one bounce from one offensive player to another.

BOX OUT To position the body in front of another player in jockeying for rebounding position.

BUCKET A field goal (HOOP).

BUZZER SHOT One that scores a basket just as time elapses in a quarter.

CAGER Another name for a basketball player.

CENTER Pivotman, generally the tallest member of a team, who usually plays with his back to the basket on offense.

CENTER CIRCLE A four-foot circle located in the middle of the court and intersected by the division line. This marked-off area is used for the center jump at the start of each half.

CENTER JUMP A procedure used to begin play in each half that involves opposing centers jumping at the ball tossed up in the air at the center circle by the referee. Each center attempts to tap the ball to a teammate.

CHARGING A personal-foul violation committed when an offensive player runs into a defensive player who has established his position on the court. If the defensive player had moved into that position to interfere with the offensive player, the defensive player is guilty of blocking, and there is no charging violation.

CHARITY LINE The free-throw line (CHARITY STRIPE).

COLD Lacking the ability to score points (COLD STREAK).

CONTINUATION A flowing movement into a shot by a player so that if the player was fouled in making the shot, he can be awarded a free throw for being fouled in the act of shooting. If the shot is missed, a player can be awarded two free throws.

"D" Defense.

DEFENSIVE BOARD The backboard guarded by the defense.

DEFENSIVE REBOUND A rebound off the defensive board.

DIVISION LINE The midcourt line that divides the court in half (TIMELINE).

DOUBLE DRIBBLE A violation that gives the ball over to the other team; it is caused by a player starting his dribble, stopping, and then starting it again.

DOUBLE FIGURES The scoring of more than nine points in a game by a player.

DOUBLE-TEAM The guarding of one offensive player by two defensive players.

DOWNCOURT The area of the court opposite that where the action is taking place.

DOWNTOWN Shooting at the basket from an area that is a long distance from the backboard.

DRAW A FOUL To deliberately maneuver oneself so as to be fouled; to be fouled.

DRIBBLE To bounce and control the ball with one hand and walk or run with the ball at the same time.

DRIVE To dribble with speed toward the basket in a scoring attempt.

DUNK To leap high in the air and, with hand(s) above the rim, drop the ball through the basket for a score (STUFF).

FADEAWAY JUMP(ER) A jump shot at the basket in which the body of the player falls backward in getting the shot off.

FAST BREAK A quick breakaway downcourt to their basket by the team on offense.

FEED To pass the ball to another player, who then shoots it.

FIELD GOAL A basket scored from the floor and worth two points (HOOP).

FIELD-GOAL PERCENTAGE Ratio of shots taken to field goals scored.

FIVE-SECOND RULE An amateur rule that bans players from holding ball in their forecourt for more than five seconds without making a move. Violation results in a jump ball at midcourt.

FOLLOW UP A situation where a player follows up a rebounded shot with another shot.

FORCE (FORCING) THE SHOT The act of a player shooting at the basket even though he is being defended effectively or does not have a good opportunity to make the shot.

FORECOURT The part of the court nearest the basket.

FORWARDS Two taller players who generally play in the corners on either side of their pivotman.

FOUL OUT To use up the allowed number of fouls and be forced to leave the game. In pro ball, six is the limit; in college the limit is five.

FREE THROW An unguarded shot worth one point taken by a player from the free-throw line for personal or technical fouls.

FREE-THROW AREA The part of the court that includes the free-throw line, the free-throw lane, and sometimes the free-throw circle.

FREE-THROW CIRCLE Located at either end of the court, these circles are bisected by the free-throw lines.

FREE-THROW LANE Bordered by the end line and the free-throw line, this lane is 19 feet long and 16 feet wide in pro basketball (THREE-SECOND LANE; THREE-SECOND AREA).

FREE-THROW LINE Parallel to the end line and 15 feet in front of the backboard, this 12-foot-long ''charity stripe'' is the line players must stand behind in taking free shots.

FREE-THROW PERCENTAGE The ratio of free throws made to free throws taken.

FRONT To attempt to deny the ball to a player by taking a defensive stance in front of him.

FRONTCOURT The area of the court closest to the basket for the team on offense.

FRONTCOURTMEN The two forwards and center.

FRONTLINE The three players who are frontcourtmen.

FULL-COURT PRESS Defensive guarding all over the court from the time the ball is inbounded by the team on offense.

GAME CLOCK The clock that indicates playing time used.

GARBAGE SHOOTER A player who specializes in taking and making easy shots close to the basket.

GET THE ROLL A phrase that describes a player's touch at the basket as the ball he has shot rolls on the rim and through the hoop.

GOAL Two points made on a shot from the field (BASKET).

GOALTENDING A violation caused by a player interfering with the ball before it begins its downward movement in an imaginary funnel over the rim.

GO BASELINE A phrase that describes a player on offense driving with the basketball along the baseline under the basket.

GUARDS Positions generally played by smaller players adept at ball-handling and dribbling; they usually operate on the perimeter of the offensive and defensive zones.

GUNNER A player who shoots the ball whenever he can (CHUCKER).

HACK To hit an opponent's arm with the hand—a personal foul.

HAND CHECK The action of a defensive player who places his hand(s) on the body of the ball handler.

HANGER A defensive player who stays back under his offensive basket while his team is on defense and awaits the opportunity for his team to go on offense so that he is positioned for an easy shot.

HANG IN THE AIR A phrase that describes a player's ability to remain airborne for a brief moment—while taking a jump shot, for example.

HANG ON THE RIM The act of illegally placing the hands on the rim of the basket and hanging from that position.

HELD BALL A situation where two opposing players simultaneously have possession of the ball, causing a jump ball.

HELPING OUT To assist a teammate in defensive coverage.

HOLE The basket. Also, an area deep in the pivot area under the basket.

HOOK PASS A pass made by a player who raises his arm high over his head and arcs the ball to a teammate.

HOOK SHOT A type of shot in which a player positions the ball high over his head in the outstretched hand of his outstretched arm and arcs the ball at the basket.

HOOP A basket.

HOT HAND A phrase that describes a player or team on a streak of effective shooting.

INBOUNDS PLAY A situation where the ball is put into play after it has gone out of bounds or play has been stopped.

INTENTIONAL FOUL A deliberate foul generally committed late in a game to stop the clock, giving opposition a chance at free throws in hopes that shots will be missed and the fouling team will gain ball possession.

JUMP BALL A situation where two opposing players leap up at a ball thrown by the referee and each attempts to tap it to their respective teammates; used at start of half and when disagreement as to who has the right to possession of the ball occurs.

JUMP PASS A type of pass where the player leaps in the air and passes the ball to a teammate.

JUMP SHOT A type of shot that involves a player jumping in the air and releasing the ball from a position over or behind his head.

KEYHOLE The free-throw-lane and free-throw-circle area.

LAY UP A close-in shot, usually after a drive to the basket.

LEAD PASS A pass ahead of a teammate, who runs for the ball.

LEAPER A player with top jumping ability.

LINE DRIVE A shot with no arc.

LOOSE-BALL FOUL In professional basketball, a personal foul by a player trying to get control of a loose ball. It is charged as a team foul, with the opposing team awarded possession of ball via a throw-in—except during a penalty situation, when two foul shots are given to the fouled player.

MAN-TO-MAN The guarding of one offensive player by one defensive player, as opposed to a zone.

MIDDLE The part of the court near the free-throw line.

MISMATCH A situation where a tall player by accident or missed assignment gets matched against a smaller player and gets a height advantage or vice-versa.

OFFENSIVE FOUL A personal foul committed by a member of a team on offense.

OFFENSIVE REBOUND A rebound taken off the boards the offensive team is shooting at.

ONE-AND-ONE A bonus shot given in amateur ball if first free shot is successful. In pro ball, the bonus shot is taken whether or not the first shot is made.

ONE-ON-ONE A man-to-man offensive and/or defensive action.

OPEN MAN An offensive player free to receive a pass with a good chance to take a good shot.

OPPORTUNITY SHOT A shot at the basket made available through luck or a defensive team's lapse.

OUTLET PASS A quick, long, downcourt pass generally made immediately after a rebound.

OUT OF BOUNDS A situation where a ball is no longer in play after touching or going over sidelines or baselines.

OUT-OF-BOUNDS PLAY A strategy used by a team in putting the ball back in play.

OUTREBOUND To rebound more effectively than another player or team.

PALMING Turning the ball over with a palm-twisting motion while dribbling—a violation that gives possession of the ball to the other team.

PASSING LANE An imaginary aisle between offensive players through which passes are made; the defense tries to protect against passes going through the passing lanes.

PENALTY SHOT A bonus free throw.

PENALTY SITUATION The condition of a team being in the bonus situation.

PENETRATION The ability by a player or team on offense to get in very close to the basket.

PERCENTAGE SHOT A shot at the basket that has a good chance to succeed.

PERSONAL FOUL Illegal physical contact by one player with another, such as charging, hacking, etc.

PICK A maneuver where an offensive player, by standing motionless, screens out a defensive player.

PICK-AND-ROLL A play where a pick is set and then the player moves off the pick and sprints toward the basket, anticipating a pass.

PIN To temporarily stop the ball on the backboard by pressing it there with a hand.

PIVOT To turn on one foot while keeping the pivot foot stationary.

PIVOTMAN A player who performs in the pivot or center position.

POINT GUARD A player who plays the guard position and directs his team's offense, generally from behind his team's offensive foul line.

POSITION The place on the court occupied by a player; good position is related to effective scoring, rebounding, and defense.

POST The pivot position: the high post is near the foul line for an offensive player; the low post is near the basket.

POWER FORWARD A strong rebounding and defensive forward.

PULL UP To drive to the basket with the ball, stop short, and, most times, shoot from this stopped position.

PUMP FAKE To feign shooting the ball up at the basket. A DOUBLE PUMP FAKE involves feigning a shot twice.

PURE SHOOTER A player who generally scores baskets cleanly and effortlessly.

PUSH OFF To illegally use the hands to push an opponent.

PUT THE BALL ON THE FLOOR To dribble the ball.

REBOUND To gain control of the ball as it comes off the backboard or rim after a missed shot.

REBOUNDER One who rebounds.

REFEREES The two or three officials who supervise all aspects of a basketball game. A TRAIL REFEREE is the one who follows the offensive flow of the game down the court. An ALTERNATE REFEREE is in attendance in pro basketball games to replace one of the three referees in case of an emergency or illness.

REVERSE DUNK The act of dunking the ball from an over-the-head or -shoulder position opposite that to which the body is leaning.

REVERSE ENGLISH Reverse spin put on a shot.

RIM The basket's circular metal frame.

RIMMER A shot that rolls on the rim (RIMS THE RING).

ROLL To turn the body and move toward the basket.

ROUNDBALL Nickname for basketball (CAGE SPORT; HOOP GAME).

RUN-AND-GUN A high-powered running and shooting offense.

SAG To position the defense around a particular player or area by moving defensive players from other positions.

SAVE To keep a ball from going out of bounds.

SCOOP SHOT An underhand (running) shot taken close to basket.

SCREEN A maneuver where an offensive player gets stationary position in front of a teammate, thus acting as a human barrier or screen for his teammate to shoot over.

SET PLAY Prearranged offensive move(s).

SHORT A shot that does not touch the basket, but may touch the rim.

SHOT CLOCK A clock that indicates the time left for shooting; in the National Basketball Association, players must shoot within 24 seconds.

SIXTH MAN The first substitute usually used by a team—generally an excellent player.

SLAM DUNK A dunk that is forcefully jammed into a basket (STUFF).

SLOUGH OFF The act of a defender(s) leaving the player being guarded to aid in coverage of another opponent.

SPOT A favorite mark on the court from which a player shoots well.

STALL A maneuver where an offensive team late in a game slows down the action, and sometimes does not even shoot the ball, in an effort to control the game and the time (this tactic is not too feasible in professional basketball, with the 24-second clock).

STEAL A situation where a defensive player legally takes the ball away from an offensive player.

STEPS Walking, traveling.

STREAK SHOOTER One who makes a high percentage of his shots in spurts.

STUTTER STEP A quick, switching movement by a player from one foot to the other to fake out his opponent.

SWEEP THE BOARDS Rebound effectively.

SWING MAN A player capable of playing more than one position well.

SWISH A term that describes the scoring of a basket by getting the ball into the hoop without it touching the rim.

SWITCH To quickly exchange defensive assignments in the midst of play.

TAP IN To tip a ball into the basket off a rebound from the rim or backboard.

TEAM FOUL A foul charged to a team's quota for a period, which, when exceeded, allows the other team the bonus or penalty shot. The National Basketball Association allows four of these fouls per period, one in the final two minutes of a period, three in an overtime period.

TECHNICAL FOUL A misconduct penalty for violations such as abusive behavior that gives a free throw plus possession of the ball to the other team ("T"). In the NBA, the offending team regains possession of the ball.

TEN-SECOND RULE A professional regulation that requires an offensive team, after putting the ball in play, to bring it over the midcourt line within ten seconds, or else lose possession of the ball.

THREE-POINT PLAY A situation where a player who gets fouled while scoring a basket has the opportunity to score a third point on the play via a foul shot.

THREE-SECOND VIOLATION A regulation that bans an offensive player from remaining in the free-throw lane for more than three consecutive seconds.

THROW-IN To put a ball in play.

TIP-IN A quick follow-up shot made when a player pushes or taps the ball into the basket without first gaining control of the ball.

TOUCH A good feel for shooting the basketball.

TRAILER An offensive player who trails the offensive flow and comes late into a play.

TRAP A situation where defensive players double-team a player with the ball in an attempt to gain control of it (TRAP PRESS).

TRAVELING A rules violation where an offensive player walks with the ball by taking more steps without dribbling than allowed (STEPS; WALKING).

TWENTY-FOUR-SECOND RULE A professional, and in some cases, a college basketball regulation that requires the offensive team to shoot within 24 seconds after gaining possession of the ball; failure to do so as indicated on the 24-second clock awards the ball to the other team.

WEAVE An arclike movement in a figure eight by offensive players aimed at freeing a player for an easy shot.

ZONE DEFENSE A condition that involves each defender guarding an area, not a player—illegal in professional basketball.

ZONE PRESS To press on defense in a particular area of the court.

BOWLING

AIMING The focusing of the roll of a ball by a bowler: a right-handed bowler will aim for the pocket of space between the 1 and 3 pins; a left-handed bowler will attempt to hit the 1 and 2 pins.

ALL EVENTS A reference to a bowler who manages the highest score in all three competition divisions.

ALLEY A lane 62 feet, 10 $^3/_{16}$ inches long and 41–42 inches wide down which a ball travels to the pins. Also, a building that contains many lanes.

APPROACH The 16-foot-long part of the lane that leads to the foul line, where the bowler moves forward to release the ball. Also, the stance, steps, and motion used by a bowler in releasing the ball.

AVERAGE The total number of pins plus bonuses credited to a bowler divided by the total number of games played during a specific time period.

BABY SPLIT A split where either the 2 and 7 pins or the 3 and 10 pins are left upright.

BACKUP A ball that veers to the same side as the hand that delivers it and hits the pins from the opposite side.

BACK WALL A surface that is used to stop the pins (BALL CUSHION).

BALK To cross the foul line without delivering the ball.

BALL-RETURN TRACK The surface the ball moves on as it returns to the bowler.

BEDPOST A split resulting in the 7 and 10 pins still standing.

BIG BALL A powerful enough delivery so that a strike can be accomplished virtually anywhere the ball hits the pins.

BIG FILL Following a spare, an effective pinfall on the first ball bowled.

BIG FOUR A split resulting in the 4, 6, 7, and 10 pins still standing.

BLIND SCORE Additional score granted a team for a game where a player has been disqualified or is absent—generally the non-competing player's average minus ten.

BLOW Inability to make a spare. Also, an error.

BONUS A spare bonus is the number of pins downed with the first ball of the next frame. A strike bonus is the number downed with the next two balls. Bonuses count in the frame in which they take place, as well as being added to the previous frame's spare or strike.

BOWLER'S THUMB Muscle strain in the thumb as a result of the stress on the thumb as it leaves the thumbhole on the ball.

BOX Score-sheet square that represents a frame.

BROOKLYN A strike made when a right-handed bowler's ball hits the left side of the headpin or a left-handed bowler's ball hits the right side of the headpin.

BUCKET Leaving the 2-4-5-8 or 3-5-6-9 pins in a spare cluster. The former is left by a right-handed bowler and the latter by a left-handed player.

CARRY Knocking down one or several pins.

CC A 200 game.

CHERRY An error that takes place when the ball knocks down only the front pins.

CHRISTMAS TREE A split that leaves standing the 3, 7, and 10 pins (by a right-handed bowler) or the 2, 7, and 10 pins (by a left-hander).

CINCINNATI A split that leaves the 8 and 10 pins standing.

CONVERT To use the second ball to successfully knock down the remaining pins and get credit for a spare.

COUNT After a spare or strike, the number of pins downed with the first ball of a frame; it is employed as a method for giving the bonus for the previous mark. Also, not knocking down the greatest number of pins in a frame.

CREEPER A ball that is rolled slowly.

CURVE A ball that sweeps in its roll to the other side of the alley from which it first made contact.

DEAD MARK The rolling of a strike or spare with the last ball in the tenth frame.

DEAD WOOD Pins that remain in the alley after being downed.

DODO SPLIT A split in which the headpin and either the 7 pin or the 10 pin are left standing.

DOUBLE Two consecutive strikes.

DOUBLE PINOCHLE A split that leaves the 4, 6, 7, and 10 pins.

DOUBLES Two players are paired against two other players.

DOUBLE WOOD Leaving one pin standing up behind another.

DUMP Impeding the hook of a ball by releasing with the thumb and fingers at exactly the same time.

DUTCH 200 A 200-point game during which the bowler alternates strikes and spares throughout the ten frames (DUTCHMAN).

ERROR Failure to convert a spare leave.

FAST A lane that is finished in such a way that before beginning to hook, the ball slides a greater distance than on another surface.

FENCE A row of pins standing after the first roll.

FILL The number of downed pins on the next ball after a spare.

FOUL LINE A ⅜- to 1-inch-wide line on the alley that is 60 feet away from the headpin. It separates the alley from the approach.

FOUNDATION A ninth-frame strike.

FOUR HORSEMEN A 1-2-4-7 or 1-3-6-10 leave.

FRAME One tenth of a game or a player's turn; or one of the ten squares on the scoresheet for indicating a player's continuing score.

FULL ROLLER A ball that slows up in its roll and the rotation placed on it makes it hook into the pins. The delivery is executed by a player holding his fingers at the side of the ball and giving a sharp lift to the ball when releasing it.

FULL SPINNER A ball that spins down the alley like a top because of the snapped-wrist release by a player.

GOLDEN GATE A double pinochle—the 4, 6, 7, and 10 pins remain standing in this split.

GRIP Most bowlers use the thumb, middle finger, and ring finger (three-finger grip). Some use a two-finger grip—thumb and middle finger. The CONVENTIONAL GRIP has the thumb and fingers placed in the holes to the second joint. The FINGERTIP GRIP puts the thumb completely in the hole, while the fingers are inserted only to the first joint. The SEMIFINGER GRIP is a compromise—fingers go into the holes halfway between the first and second joints.

GROOVE A path on the alley that has become slightly worn as a result of many balls rolling down it.

GUTTER BALL A ball that rolls into the alley and is dead (CHANNEL BALL).

GUTTERS Shallow grooves that run along each side of the alley that catch balls that are improperly aimed.

HALF WORCESTER A split in which the pins left standing are either the 3 and 9 or the 2 and 8.

HEADPIN The pin closest to the bowler; the 1 pin.

HEADS The first 16 feet of a lane, composed of maple boards.

HIGH-LOW-JACK A split in which the pins left standing are the 1, 7, and 10.

HOLDING A lane whose surface gives more than the usual amount of skid to a ball before it hooks.

HOLE Pocket: the spot most likely to create a strike.

INNING A frame.

KEGLER Another and more fancy name for a bowler.

KINGPIN The 5 pin.

LANE A wooden surface, generally 62 feet, 10 $^3/_{16}$ inches long and between 41 and 42 inches wide, that is the alley on which the bowler rolls the ball toward the pins at the far end. The surface is composed of pine wood, except for the first 16 feet and the last 3 feet, 10 inches, which are made of maple wood.

LEAVE Pins not knocked down after the first delivery of a frame.

LIFT A method of adding spin or special roll to a ball that is accomplished by a player releasing the ball with a quick snap up of the fingers.

LIGHT HIT Hitting the pins just off the pocket so that a strike is generally not possible.

LILY The 5, 7, and 10 pins are left standing after this split.

LINE A complete game of ten frames (STRING).

LOFT To throw the ball into the air and thus drop it onto the alley beyond the foul line.

MAPLES Pins.

MARK 10-point value for a strike or spare.

MATCH Direct competition between two bowlers.

MISS To not make a spare when there is no split (BLOW).

MIXER Rolling the ball so that the pins are hit in such a way that they will cause a chain reaction of spinning pins to make contact with and down other pins.

MOTHER-IN-LAW The 7 pin.

NOSE HIT Flush headpin contact with a rolled ball.

OFF-SPINNER A player who uses off-spin on the ball.

ONE IN THE DARK A condition where one pin remains standing obscured behind another pin.

OPEN BOWLING One person bowling alone.

OPEN FRAME When a bowler does not succeed in downing all the pins: a nonstrike, nonspare frame.

OUT AND IN A sweeping hook that goes toward the gutter and then hooks back to the pocket. This delivery is generally released near the middle of the foul line.

OUTROLL To triumph over the competition in a series.

PACER A noncompetitive bowler who varies bowling turns with a tournament participant to allow the latter to complete his string along with other players. The pacer's score is not counted and he also helps the competitive bowler obtain rest breaks between frames.

PERFECT GAME A score of 300 on 12 straight strikes.

PICK A CHERRY To be unable to down an easy leave's remaining pin(s) (LEAVE A CHERRY).

PICKET FENCE A split in which the 1, 2, 4, and 7 or the 1, 3, 6, and 10 pins are left standing.

PICK UP To turn over a spare.

PIN BOWLER One who generally aims at the pins.

PINCH To clench the ball too tightly.

PIN DECK The alley surface, made of maple boards, that the pins stand on.

PINFALL Those pins downed by one ball, or the aggregate total of pins downed by a bowler in any sequence of play.

PINS Made of maple, and either all wood or plastic-coated, they are 15 inches in height and are numbered from 1 to 10.

PINSETTER The method (or person) by which (whom) pins are set.

PIT The dropped section behind the pin deck into which knocked-down pins go.

PITCH The ball's finger-hole angle.

POCKET The space between the 1 and 3 pins or the 1 and 2 pins—for right-handed and left-handed bowlers, respectively—that is the best spot from which a strike may be scored.

POCKET SPLIT A split that includes the 5 and 7 pins or the 5 and 9 pins and that takes place after the ball hits the pocket.

PROVISIONAL BALL The rolling of another ball that results from an inability to immediately resolve differences about a previous pinfall.

PROVISIONAL FRAME The rolling of another frame that results from an inability to immediately resolve differences about a previous frame.

PUMPKIN Meager pinfall.

RAILROAD SPLIT A difficult split of two or more pins that are not close to each other.

RED-POSTS The 7-10 split (GOAL POSTS).

ROLL-OFF Playoff contest.

ROUNDHOUSE A curve that sweeps wide.

RUNNING An alley surface that causes an earlier hook or greater curve than on other surfaces.

RUNWAY The approach area.

SEMIROLLER (SPINNER) An effective and popular delivery that ranks between the full roller and the spinner.

SERIES Three straight games, the grand total of which figures in league play toward the team's score.

SETUP The arrangement of the pins, all ten in a triangular formation.

SHADOW BALL A practice ball rolled down a lane. Most times, there are no pins set up.

SHORT PIN A pin that rolls but does not knock down a standing pin.

SLEEPER PIN One pin hidden behind another in a leave (ONE IN THE DARK).

SLOW SURFACE A lane finish that slows the ball and creates a condition where a ball hooks earlier than on another surface.

SMALL BALL A relatively ineffective delivery of the ball because of limited action on it.

SOUR APPLE The 5, 7, and 10 pins are left standing in this split.

SPARE The knocking down of all ten pins with two balls in the same frame.

SPLIT The leaving of two or more pins standing after the ball is delivered. The pins are generally not close together (RAIL-ROAD).

SPOT Guide marks—dots, triangles—about 16 feet in front of the foul line in the lane, sometimes used to aim a delivery of the ball at the pins.

SPOT BOWLER One who uses the spots consistently to aim the ball, as opposed to aiming the ball at the pins.

SPREAD EAGLE A split in which the 2, 3, 4, 6, 7, and 10 pins are left standing.

SQUASH An ineffective, actionless delivery.

STIFF SURFACE A lane finish that holds the ball, is fast, and holds back the tendency of the ball to hook.

STRAIGHT BALL A ball that goes down the alley and does not hook or curve; the bowler's fingers are held behind the ball, which moves down the alley with a rotation toward the pins.

STRIKE To knock down all ten pins with the first ball delivered in a frame.

STRIKE OUT To complete a game with three straight tenth-frame strikes.

STRING A complete game (LINE).

SWEEPER An effective hook, downing most of the pins.

TANDEM A leave of two pins, one of which is positioned behind the other.

TAP An apparently perfect hit in the pocket that leaves a single pin standing.

THIN HIT A hit near the side of the pocket away from the headpin.

THREE HUNDRED A perfect game.

TOPSPINNER A player who uses a lot of topspin in his delivery.

TURKEY Three strikes in a row in one game.

WASHOUT Similar to a split, except that the headpin is left standing: the 1, 2, and 10 pins—and on occasion the 4 pin—are involved for a right-handed bowler. A left-handed bowler leaves the 1, 3, and 7 pins—and on occasion the 6 pin.

WOOD Pins.

WOOLWORTH A split that leaves the 5 and 10 pins standing.

WORCESTER A split in which all pins but the 1 and 5 are left
standing.

WORKING BALL A ball that has movement and action so that the
pins scatter on contact.

BOXING

APRON That part of the floor of the ring that extends out beyond the ropes.

BANDAGES Gauze; protective wrappings placed over the boxer's hands and taped at the wrist.

BANTAMWEIGHT A class division: maximum professional weight, 118; amateurs, 119.

BLOCK To ward off a punch by using the arms to receive a blow.

BOB AND WEAVE To shuffle from side to side and up and down in order to off-balance an opponent.

BOUT A contest or match.

BREAK To separate after a clinch.

BUTT(ING) Using the top of the head as a striking surface against an opponent; an illegal move.

CANVAS The floor (mat) of a ring.

CARDS Scoresheets used by officials to evaluate a fight. Also, the series of bouts slated for a specific day or night at a particular arena.

CLASS Weight divisions in which boxers traditionally fight.

CLINCH To hold an opponent's arms, making it difficult for him to strike a blow.

CLUB FIGHTER A local or neighborhood boxer; a fighter skilled in the ability to take punishment.

COMBINATION PUNCHES Blows delivered quickly, one after the other.

CORNERS Each ring has four corners: two are occupied between rounds by each fighter and his trainers; the NEUTRAL CORNERS are not occupied. When one fighter is knocked down, the other is required to move to the farthest neutral corner.

COUNT The act of a referee calling out numbers one through ten after a fighter has been knocked down.

COUNTED OUT When a fighter is unable to get back to his feet before the referee reaches "ten" in the calling of the count.

COUNTERPUNCH The throwing of punches by a fighter to counter those thrown by an opponent.

CROSS (RIGHT CROSS) A sharp blow that gets its power from a boxer quickly turning his waist and shifting his weight directly over a straight left leg.

CUT MAN An aide, stationed in the boxer's corner, who is skilled in taking care of cuts.

DECISION The awarding of a win to a fighter for taking the most rounds or getting the most points in a fight that goes the scheduled amount of rounds.

DOWN A situation that occurs when any part of a boxer's body, with the exception of his feet, touches the canvas or makes contact with the canvas; he is then subject to be counted out by the referee.

FEATHERWEIGHT A class division with a maximum allowable weight of 126 pounds for professionals and 125 pounds for amateurs.

FEINT A faked punch designed to fool an opponent.

5-POINT MUST SYSTEM A method of scoring that awards the winner of a round 5 points and the loser less than 5.

5-POINT SYSTEM A method of scoring where the loser is given any number of points less than the 1–5 awarded to the winner.

FLATTEN To knock out an opponent.

FLOOR To punch an opponent so that he is knocked down.

FLYWEIGHT A class division with a maximum allowable weight of 112 pounds.

FOOTWORK Movement of the feet for better offensive or defensive positioning.

FOUL An unsportsmanlike action, such as hitting an opponent below the belt or hitting an opponent who is down.

GLOVE A boxer's mitt which is padded as a protective cushion for both boxer and opponent, and which is laced at the inside of the wrist.

HANDLER A boxer's second; one who trains a boxer.

HEADGEAR (HEADGUARD) A protective covering over the ears and forehead of a boxer that is generally used in practice sessions.

HEAVY BAG A large stuffed training bag that is usually suspended from the ceiling and is used by a boxer to develop punching force.

HEAVYWEIGHT A class division with any weight over 175 allowed.

HOOK A short, powerful blow that has the weight of the entire boxer's body behind it; the elbow is bent and kept rigid and the blow is delivered in an arc.

INFIGHTING Boxing at close range.

JAB A stinging, straight blow generally delivered to the head.

KAYO Knockout: when a fighter takes the count of ten without being able to regain his feet (KO).

KIDNEY PUNCH An illegal punch at the small of the back.

KNOCK OUT To score a kayo, or knockout.

KNOCKOUT Kayo.

LAND A PUNCH To hit another fighter.

LEAD The first blow in a series of punches.

LIGHT-HEAVYWEIGHT A class division with a maximum weight allowance of 175 pounds.

LIGHT-MIDDLEWEIGHT An amateur class division with a maximum weight allowance of 156 pounds.

LIGHTWEIGHT A class division with a maximum allowable weight of 135 pounds.

LIGHT-WELTERWEIGHT An amateur class division with a maximum weight allowance of 139 pounds.

LOW BLOW A below-the-belt punch for which a boxer is generally penalized.

MANDATORY COUNT A regulation generally followed in amateur boxing that stipulates that, in the event of a knockdown, the fight does not continue until a mandatory count of eight has been called.

MIDDLEWEIGHT A class division with a maximum allowable weight of 160 pounds.

MOUTHPIECE A rubber guard placed in a boxer's mouth to prevent cut lips and damage to the teeth.

ONE-TWO A punching combination that generally consists of a left lead followed by a right cross.

OUTFIGHTING Boxing at long range.

OUTPOINT To win a decision on points.

PENALTY Loss of points or a fight by a fighter for illegal blows or behavior.

PRELIMINARY BOUT A fight by less experienced boxers that precedes a main-event match.

PUG Slang term for a boxer, derived from the word *pugilist*.

PULLING A PUNCH To deliberately soften the force of a blow.

PUNCHER A fighter known for slugging ability rather than for style and finesse.

PUNCHING BAG A term that applies to either a heavy bag used to develop power or a speed bag used to develop timing.

PURSE A fighter's share of the gate receipts.

PUT AWAY; PUT OUT To finish off an opponent via a knockout.

RABBIT PUNCH An illegal back-of-the-glove shot to the base of an opponent's skull or the back of his neck.

RING The area, generally 20 feet square, where matches are fought. Three ropes, placed at two-, three-, and four-foot heights, are supported by posts at each corner and form the surrounding boundaries of the ring.

RINGSIDE The area close to the ring.

RINGSIDE SEATS Seats close to the ring.

ROADWORK Outdoor running exercise done by a boxer as a form of conditioning.

ROPES Three or four strands of rope, covered with soft material, that surround the ring.

ROUND A three-minute period in professional competition during which the actual fighting takes place; each round is followed by a one-minute rest period.

ROUNDHOUSE A wide-sweeping hook punch.

SCORECARD The form used by a judge or a fan to keep a round-by-round score of a fight.

SHADOW BOXING A training procedure involving sparring with an imaginary opponent.

SPARRING PARTNER Another boxer whom a fighter trains with in preparation for a bout.

SPLIT DECISION A decision agreed to by a majority but not all of the officials.

STANCE The position a boxer takes in facing an opponent.

STOP To kayo an opponent.

STOP THE FIGHT An action by a referee that halts a bout in progress, generally because one of the fighters, in the referee's judgment, is unable to continue.

SUNDAY PUNCH A boxer's most effective punch.

TAKE A DIVE To fake being knocked out.

TECHNICAL KNOCKOUT The winning of a fight by a boxer as a result of a referee's decision that the victor's opponent is physically unable to continue the match (TKO).

TRAINER A person who conditions and cares for a fighter.

UPPERCUT A punch thrown up from the waist with a bent arm and generally aimed at an opponent's head.

WEIGH-IN The official weighing of two boxers who will compete against each other—in most cases, that same day.

WELTERWEIGHT A class division with a maximum allowable weight of 147 pounds.

DIVING

APPROACH The method of getting into position to dive.

ARMSTAND DIVE A dive accomplished from a starting handstand position, back to the water, at the platform's end.

BACK FLIP A backward somersaulting dive.

BACK HEADER A backward dive with the head hitting the water first.

BACKWARD DIVE A dive in which water entry is feetfirst facing the board, or headfirst facing away from the board; the starting position is facing the board (BACK DIVE).

BELLY WHOPPER A dive in which the front of the body (especially the stomach region) makes flat contact with the water.

CANNONBALL The act of jumping feetfirst off the board and into the water with knees tucked under the chin and arms wrapped around the legs.

COMPULSORY Mandated by the rules to be performed; a diver may choose from a list of compulsory dives.

DEGREE OF DIFFICULTY A method of determining a diver's final competitive score by assigning a number that indicates the relative difficulty of each of his preliminary and optional dives. The preliminary and optional dives are multiplied by this number.

DIVING WELL A deep area under a diving platform that has enough depth so that the diver cannot hit bottom as he or she dives.

ENTRY The moment of entering the water as a dive is completed.

FORWARD DIVE A dive in which water entry is headfirst facing the board or feetfirst facing away from the board; the starting position faces away from the board (FRONT DIVE).

FRONT HEADER A forward dive headfirst into the water.

HIGH BOARD A diving board positioned three meters (9.8 feet) above the water.

INWARD DIVE A dive in which water entry is headfirst away from the board or feetfirst facing the board; the starting position is toward the board, and the diver, by jumping away from the board, rotates his body forward to the board on his way to water entry.

JACKKNIFE A dive with the body positioned in a jackknife pose, hands touching or close to the ankles, head entering the water first.

LAYOUT A diving position with legs together and held straight, arms positioned up and to the rear, and back arched.

OPTIONAL A move left to the judgment of the diver.

PIKE A V-like diving position with arms held either straight out to the sides or in contact with the feet or the backs of the knees.

PLATFORM The diving board.

POINTS Ratings earned for approach, takeoff, maneuvers in the air, and entry.

REVERSE DIVE In this maneuver, the diver faces the water, jumps up, and rotates in reverse so that water entry is either feetfirst away from the board or headfirst facing the board (GAINER).

SWAN DIVE A dive with legs extended to the rear, back arched, and arms stretched out like a swan; water entry is headfirst.

TAKEOFF The method of leaving the diving board.

TOWER A platform for diving.

TUCK A diving position with knees bent, thighs pressed against the chest, and hands wrapped about the shins.

TWIST DIVE A dive in which at some point between the takeoff and entry the diver executes a twisting maneuver.

EQUITATION
(Horseback Riding)

AIDS Methods of controlling and communicating with a horse: natural aids are the rider's body and voice and use of weight; artificial aids consist of all mechanical devices.

BALANCED SEAT A riding position distinguished by a body-lean forward, well-bent knees, legs touching the horse; most often used for hunting or jumping events (FORWARD SEAT; JUMPING SEAT; MILITARY SEAT).

BALLAST The use of the rider's weight to give balance to the horse.

BASE OF SUPPORT That portion of the rider's body that makes contact with the horse or saddle; one of the four basic elements of the seat.

BETWEEN THE RIDER'S HANDS AND LEGS Control of a horse is accomplished by the rider's hands directing the forward part of the horse and the rider's legs directing that part of the horse behind the saddle.

BIT The portion of the bridle that fits into the mouth of the horse.

BRIDLE Headgear on the horse consisting of a headstall, a bit, and reins by which a horse is guided by the rider.

CADENCE The beat or rhythm of a horse's stride.

CANTER A slow, three-beat gallop, at about 10–12 miles per hour.

CHANGE OF LEG The changing of one lead foot for the other.

COLLECTION The moving of a horse into erect posture with hind legs and hocks positioned under him to make for a rearward center of gravity.

CONFIRMED The act of a horse having been placed on a desired gait and speed and maintaining them without additional effort by the rider.

DRESSAGE An event that demonstrates a horse's ability and training and the cooperation of the horse and rider as they perform a number of difficult maneuvers.

EQUILIBRIUM One of the four basic elements of the balanced seat; a means through which a rider helps the horse's balance by positioning his weight.

EQUITATION The act of riding on horseback; horsemanship.

EXTENSION To move the horse into a full stride.

FLANK MOVEMENTS Quarter turns made by a horse followed by riding straight forward in the new direction.

FLY SHEET A light blanket that fits over a horse's back to prevent flies from biting.

FREE SCHOOLING To work or train a horse without a rider.

GAIT Sequential moves by a horse whose hooves move forward, hitting the ground in a steady pace.

GALLOP A quick, three-beat gait in a leaping motion.

GIRTH A strap that is positioned under a horse's belly to hold the saddle in place.

HACKAMORE A bridle that exerts pressure on a horse's nose to aid in control.

HALTER A strap or rope and headstall used to lead or tie up a horse.

HEADSTALL The portion of the bridle that fits over the head.

HORN A knoblike projection from a saddle.

JUMP RACING Competition over hurdles or other obstacles.

JUMP RIDER A steeplechase-event rider.

LEAD The foot used by a horse to begin a gait.

LEG The rider's leg, broken down into the categories of active or commanding, assisting, and holding (the placement of the leg against the horse to hamper his moving in that direction).

LOWER LEG One of the basic elements of the balanced seat: that portion of the rider's leg not in contact with the horse. If needed, however, it can be brought into one of the three leg-positions.

NEAR SIDE The left side of a horse.

OFF SIDE The right side of a horse.

ON THE AIDS The responding of a horse to natural or artificial aids.

PACE A two-beat gait, a bit quicker than a trot, in which the legs on the same side of the body move at the same time.

RACK A fast, smooth gait in which each foot is lifted and put down separately (SINGLE FOOT).

RATE The act of making a horse decrease or increase his gait and remain at the new rate.

REIN-BACK The act of making a horse move backward.

REINS Narrow, long leather strips held at one end by the rider and attached at the other end to the bit.

SADDLE A padded leather seat on a horse. Also, the act of putting a saddle on a horse.

SEAT The rider's posture and stance in the saddle. Also, the flat part of the saddle.

SHOES Plates of metal fitted around the outside edges of a horse's hooves.

STEEPLECHASE A horse race conducted on a course with obstacles such as hedges and ditches.

STRIDE The horse's movement from the time a leg leaves the ground until it returns.

TACK Riding equipment.

TACTILE SENSITIVITY A rider's ability to sense what his horse is doing or will do.

TRAVERS A dressage position in which a horse is led near a wall, his body angled approximately 30 degrees from the wall, and his head close to the wall and pointed in the direction he is moving.

TROT A two-beat gait at about nine miles per hour with the horse's front and hind legs at opposite sides of the body simultaneously hitting the ground.

TURN A 360-degree turn by a horse so that he winds up moving in the same direction in which he began.

UPPER BODY One of the four elements of the balanced seat, involving all parts of the rider's body above hip level including the hands.

WALK A four-beat gait at about four miles per hour, with each foot touching the ground at different intervals.

FENCING

ABSENCE OF BLADE A condition in which the fencers' blades are not in contact with each other.

ABSTAIN The refraining from voting on the part of an official when he is unsure whether a touch or foul has taken place.

ACTION ON THE BLADE A maneuver that allows a fencer to make contact with the blade of an opponent.

ADVANCE To move toward an opponent by stepping out with the front foot and bringing the other foot close to the front foot.

ADVANCE LUNGE An advance followed without pause by a lunge.

ADVERSARY An opponent.

À PARTIE PRISE An attacking maneuver employed to disguise a defensive technique that an opponent is expecting to be used.

ASSAULT A contest between two fencers.

ATTACK Movement(s) designed to score a hit.

ATTACK ON THE BLADE Movement(s) designed to deflect or attempt to deflect the blade of an opponent.

ATTACK ON PREPARATION An attack just before an opponent has launched his attack; an attack while an opponent is preparing an attack.

ATTENTION A position taken by fencers just before the command to fence that involves the front foot pointed toward the opponent, a right-angled rear foot, and the sword held out and positioned at a 45-degree angle to the ground.

BACKWARD LUNGE An attack that ends up with the fencer in lunge position, but that is executed by sliding the rear foot directly backward.

BALESTRA A forward-jump lunge.

BARETTE An attachment to the lower front of the mask for protection of the throat (BIB).

BARRAGE A tie, or fence-off, in a qualifying round.

BEAT A sharp blow against the middle or weak part of the opponent's blade, designed to open a line of attack or provoke a reaction.

BEAT PARRY A parry that forces the opponent's blade out of line by giving it a quick beat.

BENEFIT OF THE DOUBT A cut or thrust so light that it is of questionable validity.

BENT-ARM ATTACK An attack executed without initially establishing right of way by taking a position in line.

BIND An attack that forces the opponent's blade up, down, or sideways from one line into another as a result of the pressure exerted by the binder's blade (*LÏEMENT*).

BLADE That part of the weapon (sword) that extends from the guard to the tip.

BOUT The personal combat between two fencers.

BREAK GROUND To retreat.

BUTTON Protective pad on the end of a foil.

CADENCE Fencing rhythm.

CAVATION A technique used during a thrust that directs the hand motion slightly to the side while angling the point at the target by wrist or finger action.

CEDING PARRY A parry against a thrust by yielding to its pressure, allowing the blade to be moved to a new line and then blocking the opponent's blade from this new line.

CHANGE BEAT A beat executed immediately after a change of engagement.

CHANGE OF ENGAGEMENT The act of engaging in a new line, of moving an opponent's blade into a new line.

CHANGE OF TIME The intentional breaking of the rhythmic pattern of action in an attempt to confuse an opponent.

CLASS Categories of fencers, including prep, novice, intermediate, and senior.

CLOSE IN To get into a clinch.

CLOSE THE LINE To carry the hand, at the conclusion of a thrust, far enough to the side to block a direct counterattack.

CLOSED STANCE A line that is blocked as a result of the arm or sword position of an opponent.

CLOSING IN An attacking or defending maneuver in which a fencer moves closer to an opponent to create problems for the opponent in executing a thrust.

COMPOSED ATTACK An attack made with an advance.

COMPOUND ATTACK An attack consisting of two or more movements.

COMPOUND PARRY A parry consisting of two or more movements used in combination.

COMPOUND RETURN A riposte consisting of one or more feints (COMPOUND RIPOSTE).

CONTRACTION PARRY A simple parry and a circular parry combined.

CONTRETEMPS A parry riposte created as a result of second intention.

CORPS-À-CORPS Torso contact between the contestants that cannot immediately be broken—results in a halt being called (CLINCH).

COUNTERATTACK The stop thrust and the time thrust—an attacking maneuver that responds directly to the attack of an opponent.

COUNTER-DISENGAGEMENT A simple disengaging action on

the attack in which the blade is moved around that of the opponent to deceive a change of engagement or counter parry by the defender.

COUNTER PARRY A parry that describes a circle, picks up the opponent's blade, and brings it back to the original line of engagement; a parry of a riposte.

COUNTER RIPOSTE An offensive action made immediately after parrying the opponent's riposte.

COUNTER TIME A planned move that uses a feint to draw an opponent into a counterattack, which is parried in anticipation of the scoring riposte.

COVERED A line of engagement is "covered" when the defender's weapon has closed the line to a straight thrust.

CUT A saber-fencing scoring blow that is accomplished by striking an opponent with the edge of the weapon.

CUTOVER A form of changing the line of engagement that is accomplished by passing the blade over the point of the opponent's blade (*COUPÉ*).

CUTTING THE LINE A phrase that refers to a parry that does not follow the normal lines of defense, but cuts across them.

DECEIVE To manipulate the blade so that a defender's parry is avoided.

DEVELOPMENT The complete lunge from arm-extension to completion.

DIRECT A term that refers to a riposte or attack delivered in the line of engagement.

DIRECT ATTACK An attack that involves one or more feints plus a final cut or thrust.

DIRECT CUT Ending with a blade-edged cutting move.

DIRECTOR The official who starts, stops, and supervises, who analyzes movements, and who awards the touches in a bout (PRESIDENT).

DISENGAGE An attack that changes the line of engagement by passing the blade under or over the blade of the opponent.

DISTANCE The space or distance between contestants at any given time.

DOUBLE An attack with two disengagements in the same direction followed up by a lunge.

DOUBLE TOUCH The act of two contestants making touches at the same instant.

ELBOW GUARD A protective leather cup that is strapped to the elbow of the sword arm.

ELECTRIC *ÉPÉE* An electrical device that automatically, via bell or light, records the touches in *épée* bouts.

END LINE Either line marking the extreme rear ends of the fencing area.

ENGAGEMENT A crossing of the blades covering any of the four possible lines.

ENVELOPMENT An attack that carries the opponent's blade into a complete circle.

ÉPÉE A sword similar to the foil except that the guard is larger and the blade is less flexible and heavier.

***ÉPÉE* INK** A red liquid that is placed on the *point d'arrêt* (a little point that catches onto clothing) of the *épée* to mark the spot of a hit.

FALSE ATTACK A simulated attack.

FEINT A blade movement designed to resemble an attack and aimed at drawing a reaction or parry.

FENCING STRIP The area where a bout takes place.

FENCING TARGET Those parts of the opponent that may be legitimately contacted with the weapon to score a touch.

FINGERING The act of controlling a weapon's movements through the use of the fingers and thumb without employing wrist, elbow, or shoulder.

FLECHE A running attack generally executed from beyond normal lunging distance (FLASH).

FORTE The strong section of the blade.

FRENCH STYLE The utilization of mainly the thumb and

forefinger in holding the weapon in attacking.

GAIN A lunge of more than usual length.

GLIDE An offensive action against the blade of an opponent in which pressure is applied laterally while the fencer is moving forward (GRAZE; *COULÉ*).

GRAND SALUTE A ritualistic mock or simulated combat that is done as the opening exercise of a competition.

HIGH LINES Lines of attack and defense located above the hand.

HIGH-LOW A 1-2 attack where the disengages are below the high and low lines.

IN DISTANCE Close enough to an opponent to score a hit just by lunging.

INFIGHTING Action so close that there is actual contact between the opponents.

IN LINE A condition where a fencer has his arm extended and the point of his weapon threatening his opponent's target.

INSIDE LINES The lines of attack and defense that are to the side leading to the front of the target.

INVITATION Any defending blade movement designed to prompt an opponent into an attack.

LA BELLÉ The final touch in a tie bout.

LINES The theoretical area of attack and defense; there are inside, outside, high, and low lines, all of which are related to the hand and weapon positioning.

LOW LINES Attacking and defending lines of attack located below the hand.

LUNGE The classical method of reaching an opponent on the attack that involves an extended sword arm, a stepping forward on the front foot, and a keeping of the rear foot in place.

MARCH ATTACK An advanced lunge.

METALLIC JACKET A highly conductive lamé jacket used in electric fencing that covers the torso or target area only.

ON DECK The act of being in position to begin a bout after the one in progress is finished.

ON GUARD The basic position of a fencer facing his adversary.

OPPOSITION Contact and pressure against the opposing blade to keep an opponent from scoring.

OUTSIDE LINES The lines of attack and defense that are on the side of the hand and blade nearest the back and forward flank.

PARRY A deflection of an opponent's blade. Parries are numbered one to eight. (They are sometimes referred to by their traditional French names: *prime* (one); *seconde* (two); *tierce* (three); *quarte* (four); *quinte* (five); *sixte* (six); *septième* (seven); *octave* (eight).)

PASSÉ A cut that misses and continues past its target.

PHRASE Interval of continuous action between contestants.

PISTE The surface fencers compete on (STRIP).

PRESSURE A lateral pressing upon the blade of an opponent, employed as a method of preparation for attack.

PRONATION A grip on the handle of the sword with the back of the hand facing up.

RECOVERY The return to "on guard" position after a lunge.

REDOUBLEMENT A renewed attack with a blade action.

REMISE A renewed attack that is generally a replacement of the point in the original line of attack.

REPRISE A new attack that takes place after the original attack does not work.

STOP THRUST A counterattack aimed at breaking up an attack just by thrusting into it.

STRAIGHT THRUST A direct and basic attack.

SUPINATION A sword-hand position with fingers facing up.

THROUGH STEEL A condition where a cut lands only because the flexible blade whips over the parrying blade.

TIME THRUST A closing of the line against an opponent by anticipating his final move and thus scoring.

UNCOVERED A position where a line is unprotected against a straight thrust.

WARNING LINE A warning-marker line parallel to and one

meter from each end of the fencing surface (piste) in foil competition and two meters from each end in saber and *épée*.

WHIRL A cut executed by swinging the blade through a complete circle. (*MOULINET* in French; *MOLINELLO* in Italian).

WIDTH OF GUARD "On guard" position distances between the feet.

WILLFUL BRUTALITY Intentional roughness.

YIELDING PARRY Intentionally giving way to an opponent with the aim of finally gaining control of the attacking blade.

FOOTBALL

AREA BLOCKING Blocking any opponent in a specific area instead of blocking a particular player (ZONE BLOCKING).

AUDIBLE Verbally changing a play at the line of scrimmage from the play originally called in the team huddle (AUTOMATIC).

BACK An offensive player who lines up most often one yard or more behind the line of scrimmage and whose duties include running with the ball, catching passes, and blocking (OFFENSIVE BACK).

BACKFIELD The four offensive backs: quarterback, two halfbacks, fullback. The names given to the various backfield members can change depending on the team formation.

BACKFIELD LINE A vertical plane one yard behind and parallel to the line of scrimmage that all backfield members except the quarterback must line up behind.

BACK JUDGE An official positioned in the defensive backfield on the same side of the field as the line judge; he mainly checks for infractions on deep plays and makes out-of-bounds and field-goal rulings.

BACKPEDAL A player's backing-up or running-back movements to receive a kicked football.

BALANCED LINE An offensive line positioned with an equal number of players lined up on either side of the center.

BALLCARRIER The player who runs with the ball.

BALL CONTROL Maintaining possession of the football for long periods of time without allowing the opposition to get its chance on offense.

BALL IS SPOTTED The placement of the football on the ground, from which "spot" play will resume.

BLIND SIDE The area a player (especially a quarterback) cannot see clearly; thus, if he is looking left, he may get hit on his right.

BLITZ A furious charge by defensive players against a quarterback—most often a gambling maneuver performed when the defense anticipates a passing play (RED DOG).

BLOCK A maneuver in which offensive players legally stop, interfere with, or off-balance the movements of defensive players by using the shoulders or body. Hands may not be used.

BLOCKER The player preceding a ball carrier who blocks to prevent the defense from tackling his teammate.

BLOWN ASSIGNMENT A mistake made by players in executing an assignment.

BOMB An especially long and generally spectacular forward pass.

BOOTLEG A situation where a quarterback takes the ball on a handoff, hides the ball at his side, and sprints to that area of the field generally unprotected by blockers.

BULLET A pass that is thrown exceptionally hard and fast.

BUMP AND RUN A defensive technique used by the cornerback who hits or bumps the receiver as he comes off the line of scrimmage.

BURN To badly beat a defender by scoring or getting away from him.

BUTTONHOOK An offensive maneuver in which a receiver runs downfield quickly and then turns sharply in to face the passer.

CADENCE The quarterback's signal-calling rhythm.

CAPTAIN'S MEETING A handshaking ceremony just before the start of the game during which the officials introduce the opposing team captains to each other.

CARRY The act of running with the ball.

CENTER An offensive lineman positioned in the middle of the line who snaps the ball to the quarterback.

CHAIN A ten-yard length of chain that measures the distance the football has to be moved forward for a series of downs. Both ends of the chain are fastened to a rod for easy movement.

CHAIN-CREW Officials' aides who move the chain and indicate the downs.

CHECK-OFF The act of calling an audible at the line of scrimmage to alter a play.

CHICKEN-FIGHT A situation where an offensive player on a passing play continually blocks a defensive lineman from an upright position.

CHIP SHOT An easy, short-yardage field-goal attempt.

CIRCLE A situation where a receiver runs a pass pattern across the line of scrimmage and circles toward the middle of the field for the reception.

CIRCLE PASS A pass thrown to a receiver running a circle route.

CLIP Blocking an opponent (except for the ballcarrier) by hitting or throwing the body against the back of his legs. This is a legal move within the clipping zone at the start of play.

CLIPPING A 15-yard penalty caused by a clip that takes place during a free-kick down or outside the legal clipping zone during a down from scrimmage.

CLIPPING ZONE A zone where an opponent may be legally clipped, extending approximately four yards on either side of the line of scrimmage and three yards in front and behind the offensive center.

CLOTHESLINE (TACKLE) To use the outstretched arm to strike and knock down an opponent; a tackle generally made with a forearm that contacts the head or neck area of a ballcarrier and stops him in his tracks.

COFFIN CORNER Any of the four corners on the field formed by the intersection of the goal lines and the sidelines. Punters aim for these areas to hamper a return and to give the other team poor field position.

COIN TOSS A procedure in which an official flips a coin at the start of a game or sudden-death overtime period, and the visiting team designee calls ''heads'' or ''tails'' to determine whether his team kicks off or returns the football, and which goal post his team will defend.

COMPLETE To throw a forward pass that is caught by a receiver.

COMPLETION A forward pass caught by a receiver that is credited in the statistics to the quarterback or the player who threw the pass.

CONVERSION One point awarded for a ball kicked over the crossbar after a touchdown; in nonprofessional play, two points are awarded if the ball is run or passed over the goal line.

CORNERBACK A defender who performs three–ten yards off the line of scrimmage, plays outside the linebackers, defends against the sweep, and covers the wide receivers.

COUNTER An offensive move designed to confuse the opposition in which the ballcarrier runs in the opposite direction of most of his blockers.

COVERAGE The way a defender or a defense as a whole guards; defensive responsibilities.

CRACKBACK An illegal blind-side block thrown by a pass receiver on a linebacker or defensive back; the receiver starts downfield and then ''cracks'' (cuts) back toward the middle of the line.

CROSSBLOCK Blocking a defensive lineman from the side— usually takes place when blocking assignments are switched.

CROSSBUCK The crossing of two running backs who have charged diagonally into the line of scrimmage; the quarterback fakes a handoff to one back, and gives the ball to the other.

CUT A quick change of direction by a ballcarrier to avoid a defender.

CUTBACK A ballcarrier's sharp, unexpected upfield move or cut toward the middle of the line after a lateral run behind the line of scrimmage.

DAYLIGHT Open space in a team's defense vulnerable to the offensive team's running.

DEEP BACK A member of the receiving team on a kickoff or punt return who is positioned farther back than other players on his team.

DEFENSIVE BACKS Generally, the two cornerbacks and two safeties, who usually play behind the linebackers and defend against the pass or the run.

DELAY A momentary hesitation by a running back or receiver prior to taking the ball or running with it.

DELAY OF GAME A five-yard penalty given to a team that does not play the ball within a certain period of time and thus stalls the progress of the game.

DOUBLE COVERAGE A situation where two defenders guard one offensive player.

DOUBLE REVERSE An offensive play which results in the final ballcarrier running in the original direction of play after a reverse with another handoff.

DOUBLE WING A situation where two halfbacks are placed wide on either side of the offensive formation; additionally, there is a split end, and one of the halfbacks plays a slotback position.

DOWN One of four chances given a team on offense to move the ball forward ten yards.

DOWN-AND-IN An offensive pattern in which a receiver sprints straight down the field, fakes, then cuts quickly to the inside.

DOWN-AND-OUT An offensive pattern in which a receiver sprints straight down the field, then cuts quickly to the inside.

DOWN INDICATOR A tall rod topped by numbered cards that is used at the sidelines to indicate the ball's position at the start of a down and the number of the down (1–4).

DOWNING Putting the ball on the ground to stop play.

DRAW (PLAY) A running play disguised as passing play; the quarterback at the last moment hands off to a back who usually has faked pass blocking and then runs straight ahead.

DRIVE A successful series of downs that generally results in a scoring play.

DROP BACK The action of a quarterback stepping straight back from the line of scrimmage to get passing room.

EAT THE BALL A phrase describing a quarterback's allowing himself to be tackled instead of throwing an intentionally bad pass.

ELIGIBLE RECEIVER A player permitted by the rules to catch a pass; ordinarily, only the two ends and the backs are eligible.

ENCROACHMENT Just before the ball is snapped, a player illegally places part of his body over the line of scrimmage or makes contact with an opposition player.

END AROUND A reverse play where an end comes into his own backfield, gets the ball, and runs to the other end of the offensive line.

ENDS Two players on each team who line up at the outer edge of the offensive and defensive lines.

END ZONES Goal areas, ten yards deep, located at both ends of the field between the end lines and the goal lines—where touchdowns may be scored.

EXTRA POINT A point after a touchdown is scored, accomplished by kicking the ball between the uprights of the goal posts.

FACE MASK (INFRACTION) A penalty imposed for grabbing the face mask (protective cage attached to the front of the helmet) of a player.

FADE BACK The action of a quarterback moving back a few steps from the line of scrimmage to throw a pass.

FAIR CATCH A catch of a punted ball in which the receiver raises an arm to signal he will not run after catching the ball.

FALSE START A violation that occurs when an offensive player, after getting into a set position on the line of scrimmage, moves before the ball is snapped.

FIELD GOAL A three-point score made by kicking the ball through the goal posts and over the crossbar.

FIELD JUDGE An official positioned in the defensive backfield some yards from the line of scrimmage; this official helps time the game and covers deep pass and punt situations.

FIELD POSITION The position of the offensive team's line of scrimmage relative to the goal line.

50-YARD LINE The midfield dividing line.

FIRING OFF THE BALL A maneuver in which the offensive line surges forward to block the instant the ball is snapped.

FIRST DOWN The first of a series of four downs; each time a team gets ten yards in four downs (tries) or less, a new first down is awarded.

FLAG A weighted gold or red handkerchief dropped by an official ("flags flying") to indicate a penalty.

FLANKER A halfback positioned wide in an offensive formation and generally used as pass receiver (flankerback).

FLANKS The ends of a formation.

FLAT The area directly to the left or right of the line of scrimmage in an offensive formation.

FLAT PASS A pass into the flat to a receiver.

FLEAFLICKER A play in which a quarterback throws a long pass after getting the ball on a double reverse.

FLOATER A pass that stays up in the air (floats).

FLOOD To get more pass receivers into a section of the field than there are defenders available to cover these receivers; to overload an area with players.

FLY The running of a straight downfield pattern by a receiver.

FORMATION The pattern (or set) in which offensive or defensive players line up from the line of scrimmage at the start of play.

FORWARD PASS A pass to an area that must be ahead of the passer; the passer must also be behind the line of scrimmage when he throws the ball.

FREE BALL A ball "up for grabs"; a live ball that is not in the possession of any player and that can be recovered by any player on the field.

FREE KICK A situation where a kicker is allowed to punt or place-kick the ball without interference; follows a touchdown, a safety, or a field goal.

FREE SAFETY A defender positioned generally about ten yards deep on the weak side who is not responsible for specific offensive coverage and who can retreat for specific offensive plays.

FRONT The defensive line.

FRONT FOUR The two defensive tackles and two defensive ends.

FULLBACK An offensive back who is generally stationed behind the quarterback.

FUMBLE An accidental loss of control or possession of the football by a ballcarrier, as opposed to a pass receiver not catching the ball.

GAINER A play that advances the ball.

GAME BALL A football given to a coach or player for contributing to a winning effort.

GAME BREAKER A player capable of making a big play that changes the course of a game.

GANG TACKLE A situation where a few tacklers gang up on a ballcarrier.

GAP An opening between linemen that a defensive or offensive player can "shoot" through.

GOAL LINE A line that runs the width of the field at each end of the playing field that marks off the end zone.

GOAL-LINE STAND An ordinarily furious battle close to the goal line, during which the defensive team tries to fight off the offensive team's scoring effort.

GOAL POSTS Two upright posts at each end line, approximately 20 feet high and crossed by a bar 10 feet off the ground. College goal posts are 23 feet, 4 inches wide and H-shaped. Professional goal posts are 18½ feet wide and in the shape of a squared **Y**.

GOAL TO GO A condition in which the attacking team is within ten yards or less of the goal line and can score a touchdown on the next play without getting a first down.

GRIDIRON A name for the football field, so-called because of the grid pattern formed by its numerous stripes.

GROUND GAINER A player who gains yards by running with the ball.

GUARDS The two blocking offensive linemen positioned on either side of the center.

HALFBACK An offensive backfield player generally positioned to the side of the fullback.

HANDOFF The giving of the ball to another player.

HANG TIME The amount of time a punt stays in the air.

HASH MARK An in-bounds line marker.

HEAD LINESMAN An official who supervises the chain crew, checks for offsides, marks out of bounds, etc.

HEAR FOOTSTEPS The losing of concentration by a player going for a pass as a result of anticipating that an opponent may be closing in.

HIKE The center's snap of the ball to the quarterback.

HITCH An offensive play where the receiver sprints downfield a bit and then turns quickly to receive a pass.

HIT LATE The act of making contact with the quarterback after he has thrown the ball, or with a kicker after he has kicked the ball, or with a receiver after he has caught the ball.

HIT THE HOLE The action of a ballcarrier who runs into an opening in the defensive line that was created by his blocker(s).

HOLDING A rules violation in which an offensive player uses his arms and/or hands to impede a defensive player, or a defensive player tackles or holds a player other than the ballcarrier.

HOLE A gap in the line, vacated by blocker, at which a play is aimed.

HOOK An offensive play in which a receiver runs a bit downfield and then cuts back to the scrimmage line.

HUDDLE A formation between downs in which players line up in a group to get signals straight for the next play; there is a defensive huddle and an offensive huddle.

I FORMATION An offensive formation in which two setbacks line up behind the quarterback and the third back is positioned as a wide receiver; the "power I" is a variation in which a fourth running back is stationed to the side of the other backs.

ILLEGAL MOTION A rules violation caused by line-of-scrimmage movement of lined-up offensive players before ball is snapped.

ILLEGAL PROCEDURE A violation of rules dealing with technical infractions.

INCOMPLETE A pass that is not caught.

INELIGIBLE RECEIVER A player who is not allowed to catch a forward pass.

INTENTIONAL GROUNDING A violation occurring when a passer throws the ball to an area where it can't be intercepted but where it is not possible for a member of his team to catch it.

INTERCEPTION The act of a defensive player catching a pass that the opposing quarterback aimed at his pass receiver.

INTERIOR LINE The portion of the line between the ends that consists of the interior linemen: tackles, guards, center.

JUKE To feint an opponent out of position.

KEEPER A deceptive offensive play where a quarterback fakes a handoff and then runs with the ball.

KEY ON To watch the moves of a specific opposing player to evaluate what he will do.

KICKOFF A ball kicked off by the offensive team—from the 35-yard line in professional football and the 40-yard line in college football—to the receiving team to start play in each half or after a field goal or touchdown is scored.

KICKOFF RETURN An effort made by the kickoff-receiving team to run the ball back for better field position.

KILL THE CLOCK To use up time via time-consuming plays; a team ahead late in the game often will use short running plays to kill the clock.

LATERAL An overhand or underhand pass in any direction except that toward the opponent's goal line. Also, a straight sideways movement by a runner.

LINEBACKER A defender usually positioned a couple of yards behind his line.

LINE OF SCRIMMAGE An imaginary line drawn through the spot on the field the ball was carried to in its last play and running parallel to the goal posts to either side of the field; the next play begins from this point.

LONG COUNT The action of a quarterback in making a longer signal count in order to off-balance the opposition.

LOOPER A short pass thrown in a fairly high arc.

LOSS OF DOWN A penalty for a violation that makes a team lose a down.

MAN IN MOTION An offensive back's movement parallel to or away from the line of scrimmage before the ball is snapped.

MAN-TO-MAN COVERAGE A defensive strategy in which specific defenders are assigned to specific potential pass receivers.

MARCH A long drive by a team toward the opposition's goal.

MIDDLE LINEBACKER A position in the middle of the defensive line.

MONDAY MORNING QUARTERBACKING The American custom of second guessing a football team's performance.

MOUSETRAP To lure a defensive lineman into the offensive team's backfield and then block that player from the side.

MOVE OFF THE BALL Quick movement by a player or players from a set position as the ball is snapped.

MOVING POCKET A protective screen of blockers for a quarterback that moves to shield him from opponents.

NEUTRAL ZONE An area that extends along the line of scrimmage for the width of the spotted football; no one except the center may be in the neutral zone when the ball is about to be put into play at the beginning of a down.

NOSE GUARD A defensive lineman who plays opposite the offensive center and between the defensive tackles (MIDDLE GUARD).

ODD FRONT An alignment of a four-man line in which one defensive tackle is positioned directly opposite to the center, as in a five-man line.

OFFSIDE A violation that involves having any part of one's body beyond the scrimmage line as the ball is put into play on a scrimmage down or beyond the restraining line on a free-kick down. The center, however, is permitted to be in the neutral zone while preparing for the snap during a scrimmage down, provided he is not beyond the neutral zone and his feet are behind the ball. The kicker or the holder in a free-kick down may have part of his body beyond the restraining line.

ONSIDE KICK An offensive strategy in which the kicking team intentionally kicks "short" in hopes of recovering the ball, which must travel at least ten yards to be in play.

OPEN FIELD The part of the field beyond the defensive line where defenders are spread and offensive players can run in the open.

OPTION PLAY An offensive play in which a player can choose to either run or pass; quarterback and halfback options are examples.

PASS-BLOCK Blocking protection for a passer.

PASSING GAME A strategy that uses a passing offense as opposed to a running offense.

PASS INTERFERENCE A violation caused by unfairly interfering with the attempt of a receiver to catch a forward pass.

PASS RUSH The charging of the passer by the defensive line.

P.A.T. Point after touchdown (EXTRA POINT).

PEELING TACKLERS A situation where a runner causes tacklers to fall off him as he runs with the ball.

PENALTY The loss of downs or yardage charged against a team that is guilty of a violation of the rules.

PENETRATION Movement into the opposition's portion of the field.

PIGSKIN Nickname for the football.

PILING ON Defenders jumping on a player after he has had his forward motion stopped on a play—an illegal move.

PIT A kind of war zone in the middle of the offensive and defensive line where the "battle in the trenches" takes place.

PITCHOUT An underhand lateral toss by one back to another, generally made behind the line of scrimmage.

PLACEKICK The act of kicking a ball that is in a stationary position on the ground, a technique used for kickoffs and attempted field goals.

PLATOON A unit trained especially for offense or defense.

PLAY-ACTION PASS A maneuver in which a quarterback fakes a handoff and then passes.

PLAYBOOK A team's strategy and play manual.

PLUNGE A back's lunge into defensive line for short yardage.

POCKET An imaginary zone behind the line of scrimmage where a quarterback usually stays for protection.

POP A short toss for safe yardage.

POST A pass route that sends a receiver downfield and then cutting toward goalposts (POST PATTERN).

POWER BLOCK A blocking maneuver in which an offensive lineman attempts to force a defensive lineman straight back or sideways.

POWER PLAY A play in which a ballcarrier follows blockers who attempt to power-block and clear a path for him.

PREVENT DEFENSE A defensive strategy usually used late in a game against a team that is trailing; the team that is winning puts in extra pass defenders to prevent a quick score, realizing that running plays will not be of much help to the opposition.

PRIMARY RECEIVER The main receiver on a particular play.

PULL Offensive blocking out led by pulling guards and tackles to create room for the ballcarrier; a line play that sees a guard (or tackle) pivot into his own backfield to lead a running play around an end of the scrimmage line.

PUNT A kick made by dropping the ball and kicking it before it reaches the ground.

PURSUIT The chasing effort of a defender against a ballcarrier.

QUARTERBACK An offensive back whose responsibilities include calling signals and directing the offense; he initiates the offensive action on a play from the line of scrimmage; positioned behind the center in the T formation, he receives the ball directly from the center.

QUARTERBACK DRAW A fake quarterback pass followed by a sprint past onrushing tacklers up the middle of the field.

QUARTERBACK SNEAK A situation in which, having the ball snapped to him, the quarterback immediately runs with it.

QUICK COUNT The opposite of a long count, a hurried and shortened signal-calling by a quarterback to off-balance the opposition.

QUICK KICK A surprise maneuver where a punt is made on a first, second, or third down from a passing or running formation, aimed at getting a team a better field position.

QUICK OPENER A situation where a running back heads straight at a hole in the defensive line after getting a quick handoff from the quarterback (QUICK HITTER).

READ THE BLITZ A situation where a defensive team's potential blitz is anticipated by the offensive team.

RECEPTION A pass catch.

RED-DOG The defensive charging of passer, usually via a linebacker blitz.

REFEREE The main official, positioned in the offensive backfield in plays from scrimmage; he oversees the game flow by starting the clock, placing the ball in play, etc.

RELEASE TIME The time needed by a quarterback to throw the ball.

REVERSE A play that is run in the opposite direction from the blocking pattern; a back moving in one direction hands the ball off to a teammate, who passes by him moving in the opposite direction.

ROLL OUT An offensive play in which the quarterback takes the snap from center and runs to one side of the field behind his line with the option to run, pass, or hand off to a running back.

ROUGHING THE PASSER A violation committed when a defender, after a pass has been thrown, runs into or manhandles the quarterback.

RUNNING GAME The offensive strategy of running instead of throwing the ball for yardage.

RUSH To charge a passer. Also, to get yards by running with the ball.

SACK The downing of a quarterback before he can throw the ball.

SAFETY Two points given to a defensive team for downing an offensive player carrying the ball in his own end zone.

SAFETY BLITZ A safetyman's charge through the line aimed at sacking the quarterback.

SAFETYMEN The two defensive backs who position themselves off the line of scrimmage to cover downfield passes and long runs.

SAFETY VALVE A secondary receiver, usually positioned in the backfield or just over the scrimmage line, who serves as an optional target for the quarterback if the other receivers are covered.

SANDWICHED A ballcarrier hit at the same time at different parts of his body by defenders.

SCATBACK A quick and tricky ballcarrier.

SCRAMBLE A technique used by a quarterback after a pass play has failed that involves running and dodging with the ball to avoid tacklers.

SCREEN PASS A pass into the flat to a receiver who has several blockers in front of him; accomplished by offensive linemen who allow defensive players to charge through the line and then create a screen ahead of the receiver.

SCRIMMAGE Any play that starts with a snap from the line of scrimmage.

SECONDARY The defensive backfield, composed of two cornerbacks and the two safeties, whose main task is pass coverage.

SETBACK A back lined up usually behind the quarterback.

SHANK To kick improperly with the wrong part of the foot so that the ball travels a short distance.

SHIFT The legal changing of position after lining up for the snap by members of the offensive team.

SHOOT The action of defensive men rushing through an opening between linemen to get at the player with the ball (RUSH; CHARGE; BLITZ; SHOOT THE GAP).

SHOTGUN OFFENSE A formation in which the quarterback gets the snap from center, not from a direct handoff, but from a position several yards behind the line of scrimmage, as in a punt formation.

SIDELINE PASS An offensive play in which the receiver goes straight down the field and then quickly sprints to the sideline for the pass reception; used to stop the clock many times, as the receiver can step out of bounds after he catches the ball.

SIDELINES Areas that are out of bounds, running parallel to the long sides of the field.

SINGLE WING An unbalanced-line offensive formation: the strong side of the line has a back just outside the end; the quarterback functions behind the line as a blocker; the tailback or fullback can get the center snap directly from their positions approximately five yards behind the line.

SLANT An angular run toward the goal line.

SLED A training device for blocking practice that has padding over a steel frame and slides on the ground as players push and pound against it.

SLOTBACK A player positioned behind the gap between tackle and end.

SNAP The act of a center passing the ball back between his legs to an offensive back.

SPECIAL TEAMS Squads that enter the game especially to make or return kicks and punts, to gain short yardage, etc.

SPIKE To slam the ball to the ground in an emotional manner, usually performed by a player in the end zone after scoring a touchdown.

SPIRAL A twisting rotation along the axis of an effectively thrown or kicked ball.

SPLIT END A receiver positioned at the end of line of scrimmage, some yards away from his teammates.

SPLIT THE UPRIGHTS An expression for making an extra point or field goal that describes what the ball in flight does as it passes over the crossbar.

SQUARE OUT An offensive play in which a receiver goes about 15 yards downfield, slants outside, and sprints to the sideline parallel to the scrimmage line.

SQUIB A kickoff that is purposely short and difficult to handle for the receiving team (SQUIBBLER).

STATUE OF LIBERTY PLAY A play in which the quarterback raises his arm, faking a pass, and has the ball taken by a teammate positioned behind him who then can run or pass.

STICKUM A type of glue placed on a receiver's hands to help him catch passes.

STOP-AND-GO A pass route in which the receiver stops short and then goes deep downfield for a pass.

STRAIGHT ARM The action of a ballcarrier using his extended arm as a way to shed a tackler.

STRIP To pull the ball from the hands of an opponent.

STRIPE Marking for a yard line.

STRONG SAFETY The tight defensive safety positioned opposite the strong side of the offensive line.

STRONG SIDE That part of an unbalanced line containing more players.

STUNT A maneuver that involves defensive players jumping in and out of line to off-balance the offense.

SUDDEN DEATH Professional football's extra period of play to determine the winner of a tied game; the first team to score wins (SUDDEN VICTORY).

SUPER BOWL The championship game of the National Football League that pits American Football Conference winner against National Football Conference winner.

SWEEP The act of a ballcarrier following his blockers around either end of the line, as opposed to going through the line.

SWING PASS A quickly thrown pass to a back on either side of the backfield positioned roughly parallel with the quarterback.

TACKLE ELIGIBLE A legal maneuver in which the tight end gets into the backfield before the snap and technically becomes a back, thus allowing the tackle beside him to function as an end and an eligible pass receiver.

TACKLES Offensive linemen positioned just outside the guards; defensive linemen positioned just inside their ends.

TAILBACK A running back positioned the greatest distance from the line of scrimmage.

T FORMATION Resembling the letter T, this formation has the quarterback positioned just behind center, the fullback about five yards behind the quarterback, and the halfbacks spread slightly ahead on either side of the fullback.

THREE-POINT STANCE Player position before the snap: legs spread wide and one hand touching the ground, body leaning forward.

TIGHT END A blocking and pass-receiving offensive end generally positioned close to the tackle.

TIGHTROPE The act of a runner gingerly straddling the sidelines, trying to avoid stepping out of bounds.

TIME OF POSSESSION The amount of time an offensive team controls the ball.

TOUCHBACK A downed ball in the end zone after a punt or kickoff is brought out to the 20-yard line for a first down for the receiving team.

TOUCHDOWN The scoring of six points awarded a team for getting the ball over the opposition's goal line.

TURN IN A receiver's pattern composed of a short downfield run followed by a cut to middle of playing field.

TURN OUT A receiver's pattern composed of a short downfield run followed by a sideline cut.

TWO-MINUTE WARNING A signal that stops play with two minutes left in each half for an official time-out.

UMPIRE An official stationed in the defensive backfield in plays from scrimmage who checks holding, the positions of linemen on passing and kicking plays, the equipment of players, etc.

UNBALANCED LINE An unequal number of players on either side of the center.

UNNECESSARY ROUGHNESS A penalty situation that takes place when one player uses undue force against another.

UNSPORTSMANLIKE CONDUCT Behavior that is contrary to the ideal of good sportsmanship, such as fighting, abusive language, unfairly assisting a player; generally it is penalized by a team's losing 15 yards.

UP BACK In the I formation, the ballcarrier closest to the quarterback.

WEAK SAFETY A safety positioned on the same side of the field as the offensive line's weak side.

WEAK SIDE That part of the unbalanced line with fewer players.

WEDGE A group of blockers set up in front of the man who receives the kickoff and who are positioned in a wedge-shaped formation.

WIDE RECEIVER A flankerback or split end in an offensive formation.

WISHBONE Resembling a wishbone in appearance, this formation, which is popular in college play, has the quarterback close behind the center, the fullback about five yards behind the quarterback, and the halfbacks behind and to the sides of the fullback.

GOLF

ACE To complete a hole with one stroke (HOLE IN ONE).

ADDRESS To take a stance and be positioned to hit the ball.

APPROACH SHOT A fully stroked shot hit from the fairway to the putting green.

APRON Close-cut grass area surrounding the putting green.

AWAY The ball estimated to be farthest from the hole and to be played first.

BACK NINE The last nine holes on an 18-hole course.

BALL A golf ball weighs no more than 1.62 ounces, is no more than 1.68 inches in diameter, and is covered with a rubber-dimpled surface.

BEST BALL A competition where the lower score of either one of two partners is counted for the match.

BIRDIE One stroke less than par for a hole.

BISQUE A handicap used by a player on a hole(s) that is put into effect as long as the player requests it before beginning play on the hole.

BITE The backspin on a ball that causes it to stop sharply.

BLAST To hit a ball out of a sand trap.

BLIND HOLE A hole that a player cannot see when attempting an approach shot.

BOGEY One stroke more than par for a hole.

BORROW The degree of swerve off a direct line of a ball on a sloping putting green; a method of putting to compensate for the slope of a green.

BRASSIE The number 2 wood club, useful for long fairway shots.

BREAK OF GREEN The slant or slope of the green.

BREAK PAR To complete the playing of a hole under par.

BUNKER(S) Sand trap hazard(s).

BUNKERED A situation where a golfer's ball is in a sand trap.

BYE HOLES In match play, the holes that remain after the match result has been decided; these holes are not played if a player has a lead greater than the number of holes left.

CADDY A person who helps a player with his clubs and otherwise provides assistance in accordance with the rules.

CALLAWAY SYSTEM A method used frequently by golfers who play infrequently and who have no established handicap; by applying the score a player makes to a predetermined formula, a handicap is arrived at.

CARD To get a specific score on a hole or a round.

CARRY The distance the ball stays in the air before it hits the ground.

CART A metal holder with wheels to carry clubs and golf bag.

CASUAL WATER A temporary collection of water not meant to be played as a permanent accumulation of water, such as a water hazard.

CHEAT SHEET Course diagram of the distances of holes.

CHIP SHOT A short and low approach shot to the green.

CLOSED CLUBFACE A stance in which the right foot is pulled back from an imaginary line across the toes and parallel to the line of flight.

CLUBFACE A golf club's face.

CLUBHOUSE A building where equipment is kept and where golfers can change clothing and relax.

CONCEDE The act of acknowledging in advance that an opponent will make a shot, which permits the opponent to get credit for making the shot without the bother of having to take it.

COURSE The playing area for golf.

CUP The hole in the putting green that the ball enters.

DESIGNATED TOURNAMENT A tournament that a golfing association requires all of its top players to perform in.

DEUCE Two strokes scored on a hole.

DIMPLE Little craters on a golf ball that aid the accuracy of flight and the roll of the ball.

DIVOT A piece of sod that a player's stroke dislodges from the ground.

DOGLEG A fairway bend that crooks in a similar manner to the hind leg of a dog.

DORMIE A player or a side leading in a match by as many holes as remain to be played.

DOUBLE BOGEY Two over par for a hole.

DOUBLE EAGLE Three under par for a hole (three strokes used to make a par 5 hole).

DOWN The number of holes or strokes that a player trails an opponent by.

DOWNHILLER A putt that has to roll down a green that slopes in the direction of the cup.

DRAW A shot that curves slightly from right to left with a slight hook.

DRIVER The number 1 wood club, used most often from the teeing-off area.

DROP To drop a ball in another spot away from an unplayable lie (FREE DROP).

DUB An ineffective golfer; a poor shot.

DUFFER A player lacking skill.

EAGLE Two strokes below par for a hole (except for par 3 holes).

EVEN PAR A score of par on a hole or round.

EXEMPT PLAYER One not required to qualify for a tournament.

EXPLOSION SHOT A forceful shot hit in a sand trap that powers the ball up and out of the trap and moves out quite a bit of sand.

FACE The flat contact surface of a golf club.

FADE A shot that curves in the air to the left or right.

FAIRWAY An area of short, mowed grass between the teeing-off area and the putting green.

FAT The putting-green area away from the shot.

FAT SHOT A swing in which the clubhead hits the ground before the ball, thus cutting down the distance of the shot.

FLAG A marker placed on the green to indicate the location of the cup; it consists of a thin pole with the number of the hole printed on a flap attached to its top (FLAGSTICK).

FLAT SWING A technique for swinging at the ball in which a less-vertical and more-horizontal swing than usual is used.

FLIGHT The path of the ball while in the air.

FORE A warning signal generally shouted before a golfer hits a ball, to alert others in the vicinity that the ball is coming in their direction.

FORM A player's stance.

FOURSOME Four golfers playing together, hitting their own balls and keeping their own scores. In match play, two partners on each side playing one ball per side and sharing turns hitting the ball.

FRONT NINE The first nine holes on an 18-hole course.

GALLERY The spectators at a tournament.

GIMME A putt so easy that it is conceded to an opponent.

GREEN An area of short, mowed grass at the end of a fairway that contains the hole the ball must go into (PUTTING GREEN).

GREENS FEE Monetary charge for playing a course.

GREENSIDE At or close to the green.

GRIP The position of the hands on the club. Also, the rubber or elastic material on the hand position of the club.

GROUND In addressing the ball, to touch the head of the club to the ground in back of the ball.

HANDICAP A certain number of strokes allowed to a golfer competing against a more skillful opponent; this handicap is deducted from the weaker player's final score.

HAZARD(S) Creeks, ditches, ponds, rivers, sand traps—features built into a course to offer extra challenges to a golfer.

HIT A BALL FAT To swing at a ball and get the clubhead low so that the shot goes high but short.

HOLE The cup: the 4½-inch-diameter, usually four-inch-deep target the ball is aimed at. The term also refers to the total playing area from the tee to the hole—the 18th hole, etc.

HOLEABLE An easy shot to make.

HOLE HIGH An approach shot that stops at one side of and generally even with the hole.

HOLE IN ONE Hitting the ball from the tee into the hole in one stroke (ACE).

HOLE OUT To hit the ball into the hole.

HOME HOLE The final hole in a round or on a course.

HONOR The right or privilege to tee off first.

HOOK To hit a ball that veers in the opposite direction (a right-handed golfer's hook would go left; a left-handed golfer's hook would go right).

HOOKER A golfer who has a tendency to hook the ball.

IRONS Clubs made of steel and numbered 2–9 that have thin, bladelike heads and in most cases provide greater accuracy and loft than do woods.

LAY UP Hitting a ball and getting it to stop ahead of time to avoid its going into a hazard.

LIE Where the ball comes to rest after being stroked. Also, an angle between the blade and the stick shaft.

LIKE AS WE LIE A term describing the playing of a hole or holes in the same amount of strokes as a competitor.

LINE The path a ball is going to travel as a golfer plays a hole.

LINKS A golf course with stretches of flat, undulating land along the seashore, covered with short grass.

LINKSMAN A golfer.

LIP The rim of the golf cup; to get the ball to hit the rim but not drop into the cup.

LOFT The angle of a club's face away from vertical. Also, the lifting of a ball into a high arc.

LOFTING IRON The number 8 club, which has characteristics that enable it to loft the ball.

LONG GAME Long drives and shots make up this playing strategy or need.

LONG IRON Long-distance irons: 1, 2, 3.

LOOSE IMPEDIMENT Not fixed or growing, or unnatural objects that can be removed in order that the ball may be played.

LOST BALL Competitive regulations state that after five minutes of search, a ball that is not found is lost; another ball can be substituted for it and the player takes a one-stroke penalty and replays his shot.

MARKER Scorer. Also, a coin or small, flat object placed on the ground to mark the position of a ball that is lifted by a golfer.

MASHIE The number 5 iron.

MASHIE-IRON The number 4 iron.

MASHIE NIBLICK The number 7 iron.

MATCH FOURSOME A competition where one ball is alternately shared by partners pitted against another set of partners who also share one ball.

MATCH PLAY Scoring in this competition is tallied after each hole; the winner of the most holes wins the competition.

MEDALIST Tournament medal play's low scorer.

MULLIGAN An extra or free shot granted in a friendly game to a player whose last shot was ineffective.

NASSAU Three matches in one: one point is scored for the first nine holes, another for the next nine, and another for the total 18.

NECK A position on a golf club's head close to the point where it leads into the shaft.

NET The score that remains after the handicap is deducted.

NIBLICK The number 9 iron.

OBSTRUCTION An artificial interference that may be legally removed.

ODD A stroke that, after a golfer hits it, becomes one more than his opponent needed to win a specific hole. Also, a handicap stroke.

OPEN A tournament open to amateurs and professionals.

OUT The first nine holes, as contrasted to the second (back) nine.

OUT OF BOUNDS Out of the area defined by the boundary markers; a ball hit here can be replayed with a one-stroke penalty from a spot as close to where the ball went out of bounds as possible.

OUTSIDE AGENCY One forbidden to give advice to a golfer during a match (partners and caddies are permitted).

PAR The number of strokes that course officials have judged necessary for a ball to be hit into a hole or for the total holes on a course. (BELOW PAR is to use less strokes than have been deemed necessary.)

PENALTY The adding of an additional stroke for a player who has to drop his ball from a hazard or put another ball in play.

PENALTY STROKE A situation where a violation of playing rules adds an extra stroke to the score of a player.

PIN Another word for the flagstick.

PITCH AND RUN To play a shot so that part of the desired distance is covered by the roll of the ball after it strikes the ground.

PITCH SHOT A lofting shot to the green, generally hit with backspin.

PLAY THROUGH The moving ahead of another golfer or group that plays slowly.

PRO-AM The pairing of a pro golfer with an amateur.

PROVISIONAL BALL A ball that is substituted for a "lost ball."

PUSH A straight-line stroke angled to the side of the player's dominant hand.

PUT A soft stroke of the ball with a putter on the putting green, usually aimed at sinking the shot.

PUTTER The last-used club, used for rolling short and accurate shots on the green and into the hole. Also, a player who is putting.

PUTTING FOR PAR A shot that if made assures par to the golfer.

PUTTING GREEN Close-cut grass that surrounds the hole where putting takes place.

RABBIT A nonexempt pro who must play qualifying rounds in order to be eligible for tournament competition.

READ THE GREEN The ability to evaluate the pitch and slope of a putting green to decide on shot strategy.

RECOVERY The act of shooting out of a sand trap or other hazard and stroking the ball into a more favorable playing position.

RELIEF A situation where a golfer can without penalty move the ball—for example, off an obstruction that is not a designated hazard.

RIM The cup's edge; to stroke the ball and have it go in the hole and out the cup's edge.

ROUGH A high-grass area bordering each side of the fairway.

ROUND The nine or eighteen holes of the course—a round of golf.

RUB OF THE GREEN A situation in which a ball's motion is influenced by a person on the course other than the caddie or a player and the ball then must be played where it is stopped.

RUN To stroke the ball in such a manner that it rolls forward after hitting the ground, as opposed to stopping short. Also, how far forward the ball goes after hitting the ground.

SANDIE Out of sand trap in one shot to sink the ball on the next.

SAND TRAP Low, moundlike areas filled with sand placed near the green or along the fairway.

SCLAFF To bounce the clubhead off the ground and then into the ball.

SCORECARD A card used by a golfer to keep his score.

SHANK To hit the ball poorly and get off a poor shot, generally as a result of the clubhead not making good contact with the ball.

SHORT GAME The putting and approach shots have significance in this type of game.

SHOT The stroke, or swing, that makes contact with the ball.

SLICE A shot opposite to a hook, one that curves to the right for a right-handed golfer and to the left for a left-handed golfer.

SOLE A clubhead's bottom part.

SQUARE Tied up, having the same score.

STROKE A swing at the ball that is charged to a player even if no contact with the ball is made.

STROKE HOLE A hole where the handicap stroke is awarded.

SUDDEN DEATH A method of breaking a tied match: the first player to win a hole wins the match.

TEE A wooden or plastic peg that raises the ball a bit off the ground to aid a golfer when he tees off (drives the ball).

TEEING GROUND The driving area from which a ball is hit at the start of play on a hole.

TEE OFF To start play on a hole by hitting the ball off the tee.

TEE SHOT A long shot; a shot hit off the tee.

TEE UP To put the ball on the tee.

THREE-PUTT Needing three putts before sinking a shot (the formula for par for a hole mandates two putts).

THROUGH THE GREEN The conditions affecting play from the time the ball is hit from the tee until it reaches the green; hazards, but not the rough, are exceptions.

TOP To hit the ball above its center.

TRAP SHOT A shot executed from a sand trap.

TRIPLE BOGEY Three strokes over par on a hole.

WAGGLE To move the club in a rhythmic manner back and forth over the ball to get coordination and concentration before actually hitting the ball.

WATER HAZARD A hazard with water in it.

WEDGE An iron effective for lofting the ball from an area near the putting green.

WOOD Clubs with hardwood heads that are numbered 1–5, used for long-distance shots.

YIP To hit the ball poorly when putting and have it not go into the hole.

YIPS Pressures (real or imagined) that affect a golfer's quality of play.

GYMNASTICS

AERIAL A procedure in which a gymnast turns over completely in the air and does not touch the floor with his or her hands.

AIR SENSE An awareness and a feel for position in the air.

ALL-AROUND GYMNAST One who participates in all events.

AMPLITUDE The maximum possible upward and outward extension or lift.

A-PART Lower-value movement.

APPARATUS Gymnastic equipment.

ARCH POSITION A position in which the body is bent backward in a curved and overextended position.

B-PART Intermediate-value movement.

CIRCLES A movement in which the gymnast keeps both legs firmly together while rotating his or her body around the pommel horse.

CODE OF POINTS International book of rules for gymnastic competition.

COMBINATION An exercise's construction; the correct sequence of moves and requirements throughout a routine.

COMPULSORIES Required routines that are prearranged and have specific moves.

C-PART Superior-value movement.

CRASH PAD A soft mat used in practice for safety.

DIFFICULTY A movement's difficulty and risk.

DIFFICULTY RATING A value assigned to a movement for its risk and effort.

DISMOUNT The movement from a piece of equipment to the floor; the final procedure in a routine.

DORSAL GRIP A movement executed with the high bar gripped behind the gymnast's back.

EMERY CLOTH A kind of sandpaper used to take off excess chalk that builds up on equipment.

EXECUTION The style of performing movements.

FALL An accidental or unintentional landing on the mat.

FLOOR MATS Soft and padded mats, generally one to two inches thick, used to cushion landing impact.

FORM A position in which the feet and toes are pointed and the legs are kept straight and tightly together.

FULL DIFFICULTY Meeting all the requirements in addition to risk.

GRIPS Handguards.

HANGING POSITION A position in which a gymnast hangs by his or her hands from the equipment.

HEIGHT How high a trick is performed above the floor or the apparatus.

HOP An action that takes place during the landing part of a dismount that involves stepping forward with two feet in an attempt to regain balance.

INTERMEDIATE SWING An extra swing of no value.

INTERNATIONAL STYLE The appropriate method of executing a maneuver.

INVERTED POSITION A position in which the feet are placed directly over the head.

KIP The movement from a hanging position (under the equipment) to a support position (above the equipment).

L-POSITION A condition in which the body is bent forward 90 degrees at the hips.

LANDING The final mat position after finishing a dismount.

LANDING MAT A mat approximately four inches thick, generally found in the landing area for dismounts from the apparatus.

LAYOUT POSITION A position in which the body during a movement is kept straight or arched to a degree; a still position.

LEG WORK The legs are kept apart during these movements on the pommel horse (SINGLE LEG WORK; SCISSORS).

LINEUP A list of participants for each event.

MOUNT The getting up and onto equipment; the first movement of a routine.

OPTIONALS Freestyle routines or movements chosen by a participant.

PARALLEL BARS A set of wooden bars, generally about 11½ feet long, 5½ feet high and 16 inches apart, upon which gymnastic movements such as balances, somersaults and swings are performed.

PART A single skill or movement.

PART OF NO VALUE A skill so basic and simple that it does not even deserve an A-part rating.

PASS Sequential floor exercise moves in one direction.

PIKE POSITION A position in which the body is bent forward at the hips, with the legs held still.

POMMEL HORSE A structure upon which swings and balancing feats are performed in men's gymnastics topped with two pommels (grips) approximately 16 inches apart.

POMMELS The wooden handles positioned on the top side of the pommel horse.

POSTFLIGHT An interval in the vault from the horse to the landing mat.

PREFLIGHT An interval in the vault from the springboard to the horse.

REPULSION The pushing of the hands to lift a gymnast off the body of the horse in a vault.

REQUIREMENTS Prescribed positions, skills, releases for a routine.

RIP Skin torn off the palm of the hand.

ROSIN A substance on slippers placed for improved traction.

ROUTINE The full set of skills executed in one event.

RUNWAY The approach aisle for running into a vault.

SEQUENCE A series of movements.

SOMERSAULT A complete circular movement of the body in the air.

SPLIT The movement of spreading the legs as wide apart as possible.

SPOTTER An aide stationed near the apparatus to guide or help a gymnast who falls.

SPRINGBOARD A takeoff board (RUETHER BOARD).

STOP POSITION A momentary hesitation in the performance of a movement.

STRADDLE POSITION Spreading the legs sideways as wide as possible.

STRENGTH PART A movement executed with strength.

SUPERIOR DIFFICULTY A rating assigned to a movement of extreme risk and tremendous effort.

SUPPORT POSITION A position in which the body weight is supported by a gymnast's hands and arms, which are positioned above the equipment.

SWINGING PART A movement executed with a swinging motion of the body.

TRAJECTORY The curving line of a vault.

TRANSITIONS The connecting parts linking men's floor-exercise tumbling sections.

TRICK Movement; skill.

TUCK POSITION Bent knees and legs held tightly against the chest with the hands characterizes this position.

VAULTING HORSE A structure which is used for vaulting feats in gymnastics; it is a leather-covered rectangular form and is vaulted from end to end by male gymnasts and side to side by female gymnasts.

VAULTING ZONES The three sections on the horse body indicated for hand placement.

HANDBALL

ACE A flawless serve that cannot be returned by an opponent.

AVOIDABLE HINDER Interference that is illegal because a player either gets in the way of another, not allowing him a shot at the ball, or positions himself so that he is struck by a ball hit by his opponent.

BACKCOURT An area between the short line and the back wall.

BACK-WALL SHOT A shot made off a ball that rebounds off the back wall.

BOTTOM-BOARD KILL A powerfully hit shot struck very low so that as it rebounds from the front wall it does not even bounce (FLAT KILL; ROLLOUT).

CEILING SHOT A shot that hits the ceiling before striking the front wall—a defensive tactic.

CENTER COURT A position near the short line in the middle of the court.

CHANGEUP A slow serve performed with a sidearm stroke at half speed.

CORNER KILL A shot hit with much force at one of the front corners that strikes two walls prior to bouncing on the floor.

COURT The playing area, which is 20 feet wide, 20 feet high, and 40 feet long, with a 12-foot or higher back wall.

COURT HINDER The striking of a court construction (a door latch, for example) by the ball, which constitutes an automatic hinder.

CROSS-CORNER KILL A corner kill shot hit on a diagonal across the court to the front corner opposite the hand that strikes the ball.

CROTCH BALL The striking of two surfaces by a ball at the same time.

CUT OFF To hit the ball as it rebounds from the front wall just before it bounces on the floor (FLY BALL).

CUTTHROAT A game of handball played by three players.

DEAD BALL A ball out of play without penalty.

DEFENSIVE SHOT A shot hit to move an opponent into a position near the back wall.

DIG To get to a low shot just before it bounces for the second time.

DOUBLES A game that involves two players on each side.

DOUBLES BOX An area next to the side walls in the service zone where a player must stay until the moment his partner's serve has crossed the short line.

DRIVE A powerful shot against the front wall that causes the ball to rebound quickly.

ENGLISH Spin given to the ball to make it hook.

ERROR A player's inability to legally return a ball after having gotten his hand on it.

FAULT A ball that is illegally served, causing a penalty.

FAULT FOOT A server's fault caused when one or both feet are outside the service zone during the serve.

FIST BALL A ball struck with a closed fist.

FOUR-WALL HANDBALL A game played inside an enclosed four-wall court—the most popular style of handball.

FREEZE OUT A doubles strategy that sees both players on one team attempt to get all their shots to one of the players on the other, thus keeping his allegedly more-skilled partner out of the action.

FRONT COURT The area of the court between the front wall and short line.

GAME The player or team that is the first to score 21 points wins the "game."

HANDOUT A doubles-team player who serves first and loses the service.

HINDER Accidental interference with an opponent or the ball that does not involve a penalty.

HIT To strike the ball.

HOOK The breaking to the left or right of a ball after it hits off the front wall and strikes the floor (HOP).

INNING The period of time service is held by a player or team.

INSIDE CORNER KILL A corner kill shot in which the ball strikes the front wall first.

IRISH WHIP A stroking motion in which the ball is hit close to the body with an underarm technique.

KILL A low scoring-shot against the front wall that prevents an opponent from making a legal return.

LEFT-SIDE PLAYER A doubles player responsible for the left side of the court.

LOB A shot that is hit high and softly against the front wall and then drops severely and takes a high bounce to the court's rear.

LONG A serve that initially strikes the front wall and then rebounds to the back wall before making contact with the floor (SHORT SERVE).

MATCH The winning of two of three games.

NATURAL HOOK A ball hit with the right hand that breaks to the left after rebounding from the front wall and hitting the ground; the ball will break to the right if hit with the left hand.

OFFENSIVE POSITION A stance taken by a player who is positioned with his feet set and is able to stroke the ball sidearm or underarm.

ONE-WALL HANDBALL A type of handball played on a court that has just one wall.

OUT Loss of service.

OUTSIDE CORNER KILL The ball strikes the side wall prior to hitting the front wall in this corner kill shot.

OVERHAND STROKE Generally a defensive shot in which a player hits the ball from a shoulder-high or higher position.

PASS SHOT A shot that scores as a result of being struck at an angle, causing it to rebound out of reach of an opponent.

POINT The serving side's tally.

RALLY The playing of the ball by both sides after the ball is served and until one of the sides is unable to make a legal return.

RECEIVER(S) The player or players the ball is served to.

REFEREE The official in charge of a tournament match.

REVERSE HOOK The opposite of a natural hook.

RIGHT-SIDE PLAYER A doubles player responsible for the right side of the court.

SCOTCH TWIST An angled serve aimed at striking close to the front-wall corner and then striking the side wall and rebounding diagonally toward the opposite side wall close to the back wall.

SEMIGLASS COURT Part of the side wall(s) and/or back wall is made of glass on this type of handball court.

SERVE To put the ball in play.

SERVER The person who puts the ball in play.

SERVICE LINE A line parallel to and 15 feet from the front wall.

SETUP An easy opportunity for a player to make a scoring shot.

SHADOW SERVE A ball that is illegally served because it passes too close to the server, making it impossible for the receiver to see the ball until it is too late for him to make a return; no penalty is involved.

SHOOT An attempt at a kill shot.

SHORT A serve that is illegal because of a "fault" or penalty by the server.

SHORT LINE A line on a one-wall handball court that is 16 feet from the wall and parallel to it.

THREE-WALL RETURN A defensive shot that hits three walls (side wall, front wall, side wall) before hitting the floor.

TRAP SHOT A ball that is struck very close to the floor immediately after it bounces.

HOCKEY

ALTERNATE CAPTAIN A player who is given the captain's duties when the official team captain is off the ice.

AMATEUR A performer in an amateur league who is paid and may also be given room and board.

ASSIST Credit for helping in the scoring of a goal, generally given to the two players who last handled the puck prior to a score.

ATTACKING ZONE The area of the rink that extends from the opposition's blue line to the goal line.

BACK-CHECK Quick maneuvering against an offensive rush by a player skating back to defend the goal.

BACKHAND Passing or shooting with the back striking-surface of the hockey stick; the name comes from the control exerted on the stick with the back of the lower hand.

BACK LINE Defenders.

BACK-SKATING Skating backward while facing an oncoming opponent.

BAD GOAL A score that results from a defensive lapse, generally by the goaltender.

BANANA BLADE A hockey stick's very curved striking surface.

BENCH PENALTY A penalty resulting from illegal behavior by members of a team's bench, including a coach; any team member may be designated by the coach to serve this two-minute penalty.

BLADE The hockey stick's striking surface.

BLIND PASS To pass the puck without looking.

BLOCKED SHOT An attempt to score that is blocked before it gets to the goal.

BLUELINER Defenseman.

BLUE LINES One-foot-wide lines 60 feet toward the center from each goal line; mainly used to determine offsides, they divide rink into the defensive, attacking, and neutral zones.

BOARD CHECK Illegally knocking an opponent into the walls surrounding the ring by hard checking (BOARDING).

BOARD PASS Using the boards to pass the puck off to a teammate.

BOARDS A continuous wooden wall 42 inches high that functions as a rink enclosure.

BODY CHECKING The legal use of the upper part of the body to block an opponent by hitting him above the knees from the side or front after using no more than two strides to reach the opponent.

BOX DEFENSE A formation used by penalty killers to defend against a power play.

BREAKAWAY A sudden rush at an opponent's goal before the defense has a chance to get set, leaving only the goalkeeper to beat for a goal.

BREAKING PASS A timed pass to a teammate who skates into position to receive it.

BREAKOUT Offensive strategy to move the puck from the defensive zone of a team.

BUTT ENDING An illegal move: hitting an opponent with the butt end of the hockey stick.

CARRYING THE PUCK Advancing the puck via stickhandling.

CATCHING GLOVE The goaltender's glove, used to catch high or on-ice shots.

CENTER(MAN) The position of center on the line.

CENTER FACE-OFF CIRCLE A 30-foot-diameter circle at mid-rink where the opening face-off and every face-off after a goal is scored takes place.

CENTER ICE The area between the blue lines; the neutral zone.

CHALLENGE THE SHOOTER A situation where the goaltender does not yield his position to a shooter.

CHANGING ON THE FLY Making player substitutions while the game is in progress.

CHARGING Illegally running into an opponent by taking more than two strides before hitting him.

CHECKING Close guarding of a player.

CHECKING LINE A defensive-specialist forward line that checks the highest-scoring forward line of the opposition.

CLEAR The act of a goaltender or a defenseman in passing the puck away from their defensive goal.

CORNER Any of the four rounded corners of the rink toward the back of the goals.

COUGH UP THE PUCK To lose the puck because of defensive pressure.

COVER THE POINTS To hinder the opposing pointmen's offensive maneuvers by close checking at the blue line.

CREASE A rectangular, four-by-eight-foot area in front of each net where goaltenders stand; it is off limits for offensive players without the puck.

CROSSBAR The goal net's metal-frame top.

CROSSCHECKING Illegally hitting an opponent with the stick held off the ice in both hands.

CROSSING PASS An across-the-ice pass.

CUPPING To place a hand over the puck to grip it.

CURVED STICK A stick that is concave in shape, not flat.

CUTTING DOWN THE ANGLE The movement of a goaltender out of the net to give a shooter less of a target.

DEFENSIVE DEFENSEMAN A defenseman whose main responsibility is defense, not offense.

DEFENSIVE FORWARD A forward whose main responsibility is checking rather than offense.

DEFENSIVE ZONE The area extending from either end of the rink to the nearest blue line in which a team defends its own goal.

DEFLECTION A pass or shot that bounces off a player, his stick, or his skate and may go into goal for a score.

DEKE A puckhandler's faking move.

DELAYED OFFSIDE The interception of puck by a defensive player immediately after it crosses the blue line into the attacking zone that causes a delay in calling an offside (when an offensive player loses control of a puck as he is crossing the blue line, an offside is called immediately).

DELAYED PENALTY If a penalty would result in a team's having fewer than four players on the ice, the penalty is temporarily put off. Also, a situation where the team that would benefit from a penalty has a good opportunity to score, in which case the referee will not call the penalty until a goal is scored or the team loses control of the puck.

DIGGING FOR THE PUCK Battling for puck control in a crowd of players, generally in a corner of the rink.

DOG A MAN To tightly guard an opponent.

DOUBLE SHIFTING To utilize a player on more than one forward line.

DOWN A MAN A situation where one or more of a team's players are in the penalty box and less than six men are skating.

DRAW A face-off.

DRIBBLE To use the end of the stick to control the puck while maneuvering it on the ice.

DROP PASS The leaving of a puck by the puck carrier for a teammate trailing the play.

DUMP THE PUCK To shoot the puck into the other team's defensive zone from center ice.

EAT THE PUCK A situation where a defenseman falls on a loose puck or throws his body at a shot at the goal.

ELBOWING The illegal use of elbows or arms to check an opponent.

EMPTY-NET GOAL A score made into a net that has been left empty because a goaltender has been replaced in the waning moments of a game by an extra skater, in hopes of providing his team with more offense.

ENDBOARDS The boards located at the ends of the rink.

ENDZONES The areas from blue lines to boards behind the goal that constitute the attacking or defensive zones.

ENFORCER The "policeman," a strong and tough player who inflicts punishment on opposing team members.

EXTRA MAN The extra player sent into a game to replace a goaltender.

FACE-OFF The dropping of the puck by the official between the sticks of two opponents to start or resume play (DRAW).

FACE-OFF CIRCLES Five circular areas centered on the face-off spots at center ice and in the end zones and inside which only the official and the two facing-off players are permitted during face-offs.

FACE-OFF SPOTS Nine round spots that serve as face-off locations when play is continued in a different zone of the rink or when the action has to be moved from where it was stopped to another point in the rink.

FAN ON THE PUCK To miss the puck with the stick in a scoring, passing, or defending move.

FEED THE PUCK To pass the puck.

FINISH-OFF PLAY Scoring a goal.

FLAT PASS The puck slides flat along the ice in this type of pass.

FLIP PASS The puck is lifted off the ice in this type of pass.

FLIP SHOT The puck is flipped through the air in this shot, which requires good wrist motion.

FLOATER An offensive player who slips into the center zone behind the attacking defensemen (HANGER).

FLOPPER A goaltender who frequently falls to the ice to make saves.

FORECHECK To check opponents in their own zone while attempting to regain puck possession.

FORWARDS The forward line: center, left wing, right wing.

FREEZE THE PUCK To attempt to stop play by pinning the puck against the boards with stick or skate and thus force a face-off.

GARBAGE COLLECTOR A player who looks for and gets easy goals.

GARBAGE GOAL An easy goal from right in front of the goal mouth.

GIVEAWAY Losing possession of the puck because of an error.

GLOVE To knock the puck down with the hand.

GLOVE SAVE The act of a goaltender stopping a shot on goal with his catching glove.

GLOVE SIDE The side of a goal cage closest to the glove hand of the goaltender.

GOAL A point scored when the puck is sent into the opposition's goal and passes entirely over the red goal line.

GOAL CREASE A rectangular, eight-foot-wide, four-foot-deep box outlined on the ice in front of the goals; it is off-limits to offensive players except when the puck is in the crease and/or the goaltender is not in the crease.

GOAL JUDGES Officials seated in the stands directly behind the goals who indicate when a goal has been scored.

GOAL LINE A red line that extends across the surface of the ice in front of the goals in the offensive and defensive zones.

GOAL MOUTH The opening immediately in front of the goal.

GOALTENDER A position played by a man who guards the net to prevent goals (GOALIE; NETMINDER).

GOOD GOAL A shot too effective to be stopped by goaltender.

GOOD PENALTY A wise penalty risked or sustained by a player to prevent an opposition score.

HANGING BACK The act of a player staying back, hoping an interception by a teammate will set him up with a breakaway pass.

HAT TRICK The scoring of three or more goals in one game by a player.

HEAD FOR THE HOLE The skating of a player into the open ice for a pass.

HEAD MAN To pass the puck to a teammate closer to the opposition goal during a rush.

HEADMANNING THE PUCK Offensive, never-retreating hockey; a combination of quick forward passes to teammates.

HEAVY SHOT A powerful and quick shot that sinks as it approaches the goal.

HEAVY TRAFFIC A battle for the puck in front of the goal.

HIGH STICKING Illegally hitting an opponent with a stick raised higher than shoulder level in professional play or four feet in amateur play.

HIP CHECK Bodychecking an opponent off stride through the use of the hip.

HIT A bodycheck that makes an opponent lose control of the puck or forces him out of a play.

HITTER A player highly skilled in bodychecking.

HOCKEY STOP A stopping maneuver in which a player rapidly turns both feet perpendicular to his angle of travel, causing his skates to scrape the ice and stop his motion.

HOOK CHECK Side-sweeping the stick close to the ice in an attempt to snatch the puck from the opponent's stick.

HOOKER A player skilled in hooking opponents.

HOOKING Illegally using the stick to hold or trip opponents.

ICE TIME The amount of time a player spends on the ice during a game or a season.

ICING THE PUCK Shooting the puck from behind the center (red) line to beyond the opposition's goal line—a legal maneuver only when a team plays shorthanded; at other times, a face-off is held in the shooting team's defensive zone.

IN ALONE A phrase describing an offensive player who slips behind the defense and has only the goaltender to beat for a score.

IN DEEP A phrase describing a skater with a puck who manages to get in close to the net.

INSIDE MOVE An attempt to stickhandle by a defender on the side toward the rink's middle, away from the boards.

INTERFERENCE A minor penalty for illegally impeding or checking an opponent who does not have possession of the puck.

INTIMIDATOR A player who is rough-and-tumble and poses a physical threat to opposing players.

JUMP STOP A stop from a jumping-and-sidewards turn that puts the skater's blades perpendicular to the line of movement.

KEEP THE PUCK IN A concentrated effort to play the puck in opponent's defensive zone.

KICK SAVE A goaltender's kicking away a shot heading for the net.

KILL To use up the time of a penalty.

KNEEING Illegally checking an opponent with the knee.

LIE The angle made by the shaft of the stick and the blade.

LIFT PASS A long pass that is flipped into the air.

LIFT SHOT A flicked-wrist shot that lifts the puck into the air; used most effectively against a goaltender sprawled in front of the net.

LINE CHANGE The replacement of a whole forward line with three new skaters.

LINEMATE A forward who plays on the same line with a teammate.

MAJOR PENALTY A five-minute penalty for a serious infraction, such as fighting, that mandates that an offending player report immediately to penalty box and that his team play shorthanded.

MATCH PENALTY A violation that suspends a player for the remainder of a game and leaves his team shorthanded for either five or ten minutes.

MATCH-UPS Offensive and defensive pairings in a game.

MID ICE The neutral or middle part of the rink.

MINOR PENALTY A two-minute penalty, the kind most often imposed.

MISCONDUCT PENALTY A ten-minute penalty for improper behavior that is charged against a player, not a team; substitution is permitted.

MISSING A CHECK A defensive lapse that allows an opponent to get free for a pass or a shot.

MOVING THE PUCK Effective offensive techniques that keep an attack flowing.

NETKEEPER Goaltender.

NETS The goal cage.

NEUTRAL ZONE Center-ice area between the blue lines; neither an attacking nor a defending zone.

OFFENSIVE DEFENSEMAN An offensively skilled defenseman who skates and shoots well and is a good puckhandler.

OFFENSIVE ZONE The area from the blue line to the goal a team is attempting to score into.

OFFSIDE An infraction caused when an attacking-team player crosses the blue line into the offensive zone before the puck; play stops and a face-off takes place in the neutral zone.

OFFSIDE PASS A forward pass by an offensive-team player to a teammate in another zone. Defending-team players are permitted to receive passes from their own defensive zone to the center red line.

OFF WING Reversing of positions by right or left wings during a play.

ONSIDE A player is onside when he is positioned behind a puck passed or brought into attacking zone.

OPEN ICE A section of the rink free and clear of opponents.

OUTSIDE MOVE An attempt by a player to stickhandle away from the middle of the rink and toward the boards.

PADS Bulky protective equipment worn by players, generally made of rubber and encased in fabric.

PAD SAVE The use of the leg pads by a goaltender to block a shot.

PASSING LANES Clear lanes on the ice for passes to teammates.

PASSOUT An attempt to set up a shot by passing the puck to the front of the net from behind the goal cage or from the corners.

PATROLLING THE WINGS Two-way hockey played by right or left wings on their side of the ice.

PENALTY A rules violation for which a player may be sent off the ice into the penalty box for two, five, or ten minutes, or for the duration of the game.

PENALTY BOX A small bench located in the neutral zone across from the players' benches and set off from the stands and the playing area by a partition (SIN BIN).

PENALTY KILLERS Players used mainly when their team is shorthanded on the ice who usually attempt to play defense and use up time.

PENALTY SHOT A rare free shot on a goal defended only by the goaltender; granted to a player fouled from behind while carrying the puck past the center red line on a clean breakaway.

PIN THE PUCK To stop the puck's movement by pressing it on the ice against the boards (FROZEN PUCK).

PIPE A goalpost; the goaltender plays "between the pipes."

PIVOT The offensive position of the center in front of the opposition's goal.

PLAY THE MAN To check an opponent, forcing him to lose possession of the puck.

PLUS AND MINUS Statistical evaluation of a player's team value; a plus is awarded a player who is on the ice when his team scores, a minus when the opposition scores.

POINTS Positions taken by defensemen just inside the offensive-zone blue line.

POKE CHECK A fast one-handed thrust of the stick by a defensive player aimed at knocking the puck away from an opponent.

POLICEMAN An aggressive and tough player who counterattacks if the opposition plays too rough.

POSITIONAL PLAY Skillfully positioned performances by the five skaters on a team, during which they avoid bunching together and execute plays effectively.

POWER PLAY The offensive thrust of a team that has a numerical advantage over the defending team because of a player or players in the penalty box. Generally, four forwards are put on the ice along with one defenseman to increase scoring ability during a power play.

PUCK A vulcanized rubber disc one inch thick, three inches in diameter, and approximately six ounces in weight.

PUCK CONTROL Similar to ball control: maintaining possession of the puck through good skating, handling, passing.

PULLING THE DEFENSE A faked shot by an offensive player in an attempt to draw a defenseman near him—then stick-handling around or passing the puck by the defender.

PULLING THE GOALIE Replacing the goaltender with a sixth skater when a team is behind late in a game.

PULL THE TRIGGER To quickly shoot at the goal.

RAGGING THE PUCK Maintaining puck possession by skating away from the opposition in center ice in circlelike moves (used especially when team is trying to kill a penalty).

REBOUND A shot on goal that bounces back into play.

RED LIGHT A light located above the boards behind each goal that is lit up by the goal judge to indicate a goal scored.

RED LINE The midrink, one-foot-wide dividing line.

REFEREE'S CREASE A ten-foot-radius semicircle where the referee consults with the penalty timekeeper; no one else is permitted there.

RISING SHOT A shot that starts at ice level but rises as it approaches the goal.

RIVER SKATER A strong, tireless skater.

ROUGHING Unnecessarily physical play that results in a penalty.

RUSH The attacking surge of a team on the opposition's goal.

SAVE A shot on goal stopped by a goaltender.

SCRAMBLE A close-range battle for the puck by several players from both teams.

SCREEN SHOT A shot on goal from behind a screen of players who block the goalie's line of vision.

SET UP To get the puck positioned so that a teammate may have a shot at the goal.

SHADOW To guard an opponent very closely throughout the game.

SHIFT That part of the game a player is on the ice without substitution.

SHINNY Poor and/or disorganized play.

SHOOT To drive the puck to the other end of the ice in a clearing attempt.

SHOOTING ANGLE The stance a player is in as he shoots from an angle at the goal.

SHORTHANDED A term describing a team that has a player or players in the penalty box and is thus at a disadvantage to the opposing team.

SHORTHANDED GOAL A situation where a shorthanded team scores a goal.

SHORT-SHIFTING Frequent changes in line-up by a team, aimed at keeping fresh players in action.

SHOT ON GOAL A shot that either enters the goal for a score or is saved by goaltender; used for statistical evaluation.

SHOULDER-CHECK The act of bodychecking with the shoulder.

SIDEBOARDS The boards along the sides of the rink.

SIN BIN Another name for penalty box.

SKATE-OFF To make continuous contact in skating against another player; to push him away from the puck and out of the action.

SKATING CLUB A team with excellent skaters.

SLAP PASS A pass made by a player of a puck he does not have full control of.

SLAP SHOT A maneuver in which a player raises his stick and shoots at the goal by bringing the stick down with force just behind the puck.

SLASHING Illegally swinging a stick at an opponent.

SLOT The area between the end-zone face-off circles where attacking forwards have good-opportunity shots at goal.

SMOTHERING A goalie's maneuver to stop the puck by falling on it.

SNAP PASS A quick pass made without backswing, accomplished by snapping the wrists forward to project the stick.

SOFT GOAL A slow shot that manages to get by the goaltender for a goal.

SOLO A breakaway of a player down the ice in an attempt to score.

SPEARING Illegally jabbing at a player with the point of the stick.

SPEED TEAM A club with swift skaters.

SPLIT THE DEFENSE A situation where a player skates between two opposing defenders for a shot on goal.

STALLING Delaying the game.

STANDING UP AT THE BLUE LINE Defensemen awaiting the opposition's rush at their blue line instead of retreating into their own zone to defend.

STAND-UP GOALIE A goaltender who remains erect in attempting the majority of his saves.

STICK A wooden device used to play the puck; the thin handle is connected to a blade, which is the part of the stick that hits the puck.

STICKHANDLING Controlling the puck with the stick while skating.

STICK MITT Goaltender's glove worn on the hand with which he grips his stick.

STICK SAVE A save executed by a goaltender with his stick.

STICK SIDE A shot at the goal directed toward the side of the net guarded by the goalie's stick.

STUFF To score a goal with a forceful shot from close range.

SWEEP CHECK To extend the stick virtually flat on the ice and sweep it toward the puck.

TAKE A CHECK To absorb a bodycheck from an opponent and not lose control of the puck or be put out of a play.

TAKING A RUN Intentionally skating from some distance away into an opponent's path.

TELEGRAPHING Looking directly at a teammate before making a pass.

TIE UP A PLAYER To effectively check an opponent and take him out of the play.

TRAILER An offensive player who lags behind a puck-carrying teammate, awaiting a backward or drop pass.

TRIPPING Illegally using the stick to trip a player.

UNASSISTED GOAL A goal scored by a player without receiving a pass from a teammate.

WANDERING GOALIE A goalie who often moves quite a distance from his goal cage to clear the puck.

WASH-OUT A hand signal by an official that can indicate a goal disallowed, no icing, or no offside.

WHEELS Slang expression for legs.

WIDE-OPEN HOCKEY Fluid and fast shooting, passing, and skating by both teams.

WINGER Positions of left and right wing.

WIN THE DRAW To win a face-off.

WRIST SHOT A quick shot resulting from a player's coordination of snapped wrists and a short backswing of the stick.

ICE SKATING:
Figure Skating, Freestyle, Ice Dancing, Pair Skating

ARABESQUE A position in which a skater balances on one leg, with the other leg raised horizontally, the body leaning forward, and the back arched.

AXEL A maneuver performed by a jump off the forward outside edge of one skate followed by 1½ turns in the air and a landing on the backward outside edge of the other skate.

AXIS An imaginary straight line around which skating curves are grouped in a symmetrical fashion.

BACK That part of the body which is pressing away from the direction the skating toe is pointing.

BACK INSIDE EDGE The curve created when a skater moves backward leaning over onto the blade's inside edge.

BACK OUTSIDE EDGE The curve created when a skater moves backward leaning over onto the blade's outside edge.

BACK OUTSIDE THREE A one-footed turn from a curve on a back outside edge to a curve on a forward inside edge.

BARRIER The structure surrounding an ice rink, usually 3–4 feet high and generally made of wood.

BLADE The thin metal strip on the bottom of a skate that glides on the ice.

BUNNY HOP A short jump from one skate to the toe of the other skate followed by a quick step onto the first skate.

CAMEL A spin executed with the body in the arabesque position.

CANASTA TANGO A dance on ice to a tango tempo.

CENTER The intersection of the long and short axes that constitutes the beginning and ending point of a figure.

CENTER A SPIN To keep a spin rotating on a fixed point (TRAVEL).

CHANGE OF EDGE To rock from edge to edge on one foot.

CHASSÉ A maneuver performed by bringing the free foot alongside the skating foot and shifting one's weight to the free foot while the skating foot is lifted slightly off the ground.

CHEAT To finish part of a turning jump after landing, instead of while still in the air.

CHECK A movement aimed at controlling the natural rotation of a turn.

CLOSED A position in which the body goes in the direction of the skating foot.

CLOSED POSITION An ice-dancing stance where partners face each other (WALTZ POSITION).

CROSSOVER A movement begun on the outside edge while the free foot crosses over the skating foot and lands on the inside edge.

CROSS ROLL A movement executed by crossing the free foot over the skating foot and positioning it to the inside of the roll.

CROSS STROKE An ice-dancing term for when the feet are

crossed and momentum is gathered from the outside edge of the foot that will become the free foot.

DANCE STEPS A freestyle term indicating a combination of edges and complex turns, skated to music, that forms a link between movements.

DEEPEN AN EDGE To cause the curvature to increase while skating an edge.

EDGE Either of the two sharp sides of the skate's blade. Also, the curve caused by a skater leaning so that an edge cuts into the ice.

EIGHT Two circles started and finished at a specific point on the ice and both having a diameter about three times the height of the skater.

FIGURE An officially recognized design based on two- or three-circle forms.

FIGURE SKATE A skate used for freestyle and figure skating that is slightly curved from front to back with small spikes (toe picks) at the toes.

FIGURE SKATING Skating that involves the tracing of geometric patterns on the ice: pair skating, freestyle skating, ice dancing.

FORWARD That part of the body that is either in front of the skating toe or pressing in the direction in which the skating toe is pointing.

FORWARD INSIDE EDGE The curve created when a skater moves forward leaning over the blade's inside edge.

FORWARD INSIDE THREE A one-footed turn from a forward inside edge to a back outside edge.

FORWARD OUTSIDE EDGE The curve created when a skater moves forward leaning over onto the blade's outside edge.

FORWARD OUTSIDE THREE A one-footed turn from a curve on a forward outside edge to a curve on a backward inside edge; the foot turns in the natural direction of the edge.

FREE That part of the skater's body on the side of the leg in the air.

FREE FOOT (LEG) That foot (leg) that has just completed the push and is in the air.

FREESTYLE Jumps, spirals, spins, dance steps, and other movements (FREE SKATING).

HAND-IN-HAND POSITION An ice dance position where both partners face front with arms extended and hands clasped (EXTENDED HOLD).

HIPPING A fault (common to forward-outside-edge skating) in which the skating hip presses into the circle.

HOCKEY STOP A stop favored by hockey players in which both heels are thrown to the right, the knees are bent, and the blades are turned at right angles to the line of travel.

HOLLOW The groove between a figure skate's two edges.

ICE DANCING A form of ballroom dancing on ice executed by a male and female duo that is classified as figure skating.

INSIDE EDGE The skating-blade edge closest to the body's midline; the curve skated on this edge.

KEY POSITIONS The four shoulder and free-leg positions that make up basic combinations.

KILIAN POSITION A dance-competition stance in which the partners face in the same direction, with the woman on the man's right.

KILIAN POSITION REVERSED A dance-competition stance in which the partners face in the same direction, but with the woman on the man's left.

LOBE A semicircle.

LOOP A movement performed on a single edge that starts with a semicircle, is followed by a quick rotation in the same direction, and is finished off with another semicircle, thus completing the circle.

LOOP JUMP A full-turn jump in which the skater takes off from a back outside edge, turns once in the air, and lands on the same back outside edge.

MASTER TOOTH A spike at the front of a figure blade generally used as a pivot for spins (MASTER PICK).

MATCHED SET A combination of a skate and a boot attached to each other.

MAZURKA A jump from a back edge that involves striking of the free toe into the ice, making a half turn in the air, and landing on the other toe and gliding onto a forward edge of the other foot.

MOHAWK A turn from forward to backward or vice versa, or from one foot to the other. Variations include the OPEN or INSIDE MOHAWK, in which the heel of the free foot is placed opposite the instep of the skating foot, the turn is made, the feet are changed, and the now-free leg is behind the heel of the skating foot; the CLOSED MOHAWK, in which the instep of the free foot is placed at the heel of the skating foot, the turn is made, the feet are changed, and the now-free leg is passed in front of the skating leg; the MOHAWK JUMP, which involves landing after the turn on the corresponding edge of the other skate and continuing the curve in the opposite direction; and the DROP MOHAWK, which is a mohawk followed by a change of feet, with the entire movement continuing in the original edge's curve.

NATURAL ROTATION A skater's normal body-flow created by the curve of an edge.

NEUTRAL POSITION A position in which the skater's body is squared in the direction of travel with neither shoulder, arm, nor hip ahead of the other.

ONE-FOOT SNOWPLOW A skating stop in which one foot is placed "pigeontoed" in front of the body.

ONE-FOOT SPIN A spin performed on one foot.

OPEN A position in which the skater's hips or shoulders are turned away from the skating foot and the free leg is a bit behind the skating foot.

OUTSIDE EDGE The blade's edge nearest the outside of the foot. Also, the curve skated on this edge.

PAIR SKATING A figure-skating category of lifts, spins, and free-style movements performed simultaneously by a pair of skaters.

PARAGRAPH THREE A figure eight pattern performed on one foot in which there is a turn within the circle so that the skater finishes in the direction opposite to that in which he or she began.

PATTERN An ice-dancing design for which edges and steps are laid out on the ice.

PICK A figure skate's sharp projection that functions as a grip on the ice in some spins and jumps (TOE PICK; TOE RAKE; TOOTH).

PIVOT A freestyle movement where the toe pick is positioned on the ice and the skater spins around it.

PREPARED POSITION The correct body position just before a turn.

PROGRESSIVE A movement where the free foot is passed in front of the skating foot, usually landing on an inside edge (RUN).

RADIUS The curve of a blade of a figure skate from front to back.

ROLL A half circle performed on the outside edge and generally followed by another half circle performed on the other foot's outside edge.

RUSSIAN SPLIT JUMP A straddle split leap in which the skater gets his legs slightly forward and extends his hands to his feet.

SALCHOW A jump from the back inside edge of one foot followed by a full turn in the air to the back outside edge of the opposite foot (named for Ulrich Salchow, a former world champion).

SCHOOL FIGURES A group of 69 distinct figures skated in two- or three-circle figure eight patterns (used in skating competition).

SCISSOR JUMP A jump in which the skating foot crosses behind the other foot in the air—a variation of the Mazurka.

SCULLING Movement off the heels and toes from an outer to an inner edge as a means of maneuvering oneself backward or forward.

SIT SPIN A squatting-position spin off one skate generally per-formed with the other leg extended in front of the skater (also known as the Haines or Jackson Haines spin for the U.S. skater who made it popular).

SNOWPLOW STOP A stop where both toes are turned in ("pigeon-toed") and cause the skater to stop by scraping the ice.

SPEED SKATE Designed for racing, this skate has a thin blade that protrudes a bit ahead of the toe's boot and has no curve from front to back.

SPIN To make several circular moves in the same place on one or both skates.

SPIRAL A freestyle body position generally taken in skating an edge: a woman approximates an arabesque, while a man stands up with his free leg crossed in back of his skating leg and held close to the ice's surface and with his arms outstretched; skating a circle in this position in a decreasing radius.

SPLIT JUMP A jump from the backward edge of one foot into a half turn in the air, with the legs snapping out almost parallel to the ice surface (splitting) and a return to the forward edge of either foot.

SPREAD EAGLE A gliding maneuver with arms positioned to the sides and skates positioned heel against heel in a straight line.

SPREAD-EAGLE MOHAWK A variation of the mohawk in which the free foot is placed on the ice just before the turn and lined up with the skating foot—an old-fashioned and cumbersome move.

STANCHION A supporting section of a skate connecting the blade to heel or sole plate.

STRIKE The act of moving body weight from one foot onto the foot that becomes the new skating foot. Also, a mark on the ice or a position on the ice where a strike takes place.

STROKE A thrusting push to move across the ice.

SUPERIMPOSITION In figure skating, the tracing of one figure on top of the preceding one in as exact a manner as possible.

SWING The moving of a free leg past the leg that is the skating leg. Also, body rotation.

SWING DANCE A basic ice dance to 4/4 tempo.

SWING MOHAWK Any mohawk in which the free foot is swung past the skating foot prior to its being brought back into place to make the turn.

SWING ROLL An ice-dancing edge position that is held for several beats while the free leg swings past the skating leg before its return into position before the new strike.

TAKEOFF The maneuver that enables a skater to leave the ice in performing a jump; the thrust in figures from one foot to the other to begin or sustain a figure.

THREE TURN A turn from backward to forward or vice-versa; the change to the opposite edge takes place along with rotation in the direction of the edge being skated (THREE).

THRUST Momentum gained by pushing the blade against the ice surface to start from rest or to pick up speed.

TOE LOOP JUMP A jump from a back outside edge that involves striking the free foot's toe into the ice and the execution of one turn in the air; the landing is on the original back outside edge (CHERRY FLIP; LOOP JUMP).

TRACE A white mark or figure made on the ice by the blade (TRACING).

TRACING FOOT The foot on which a skater is standing.

TRAVEL To move across the ice while rotating.

T STOP A stop that produces a skid because the free foot is placed behind and at right angles to the skating foot on the ice.

TUCK A slight crossing of the rear foot behind the skating foot on the final step of a forward progressive (TUCKING).

TURN A fast reverse of direction made in a flowing movement while skating an edge.

UPRIGHT SPIN A spin in a standing position.

WALLEY A jump from the back inside edge of one foot into a full turn in the air, returning to the back outside edge of that same foot; upon landing, the skater curves in the opposite direction from the turn's rotation.

WALTZ JUMP A jump from a forward outside edge followed by a half turn in the air and a landing on the back outside edge of the other skate (THREE JUMP).

WALTZ THREE A three turn from a forward outside edge in which the free foot is positioned on the surface and continues the curve (DROP THREE).

WILSON A jump from a back outside edge followed by a full turn in the air and a landing on the back outside edge of the other foot; it begins a curve in the opposite direction.

JUDO

ASHIWAZA Foot-throw techniques.

BLACK BELT A belt worn by an expert.

DAN Degree.

DOJO Practice or exercise hall.

GATAME Mat-work holding technique.

GI The judo or karate uniform.

IPPON One full point in a competitive match.

JIGO TAI A defensive stance or posture.

JUDOKA One who practices judo.

KAESHIZA Techniques for counterattack.

KAKE Technique application.

KAPPO A system of artificial respiration.

KATA Training techniques consisting of formal, prearranged movements.

KODOKAN The administration center of world judo, located in Tokyo.

KOSHIWAZA Hip-throw techniques.

KUZUSHI The moment of completely breaking an opponent's balance.

KWANSETUWAZA The art of locking an opponent.

KYU A degree for a pupil.

MATTAI A sign of submission; literally, "enough" or "I surrender."

MUNDANSHA A *judoka* below black-belt rank.

NAGE WAZA Throwing techniques.

NEWAZA Groundwork.

NIPPON DEN KODOKAN JUDO The formal and full name for recognized world judo.

OSAE KOMI WAZA Hold-down techniques.

RANDORI Free play; fighting practice.

REI Bow.

SAMURAI A feudal Japanese warrior.

SENSEI A teacher or instructor.

SHIAI A contest or competitive match.

SHIHAN A master.

SHINTAI Advancing and retreating.

SHUMEWAZA Strangulation or choking techniques.

SURI ASHI Sliding foot movements.

SUTEMIWAZA Sacrifice throws.

TACHIWAZA Techniques of throwing.

TATAMI A straw mat for practicing judo.

TECHI REI Bow from a standing position.

TORI One who applies judo techniques; the thrower.

TSUKURI The technique of breaking an opponent's balance.

UKE The person to whom techniques are applied; the one thrown.

UKEMI Breakfalls; the art of falling.

WAZA Technique.

WAZA ARI The half point in competition.

WAZARI AWASETE IPPON Two half points that equal an ippon (one full point) and determine a contest winner.

YUDANSHA A person who holds a black-belt degree.

ZA-REI A bow from the sitting position.

KARATE

BLACK BELT A belt worn by an expert.

BUDO The way of the warrior.

CHOSI Rhythm.

DO The way.

DOJO Karate school.

FUDO-DACHI An immovable stance.

GI Karate uniform.

HACHIJI-DACHI The natural stance.

HYOSHI Timing.

JIYU KUMITE Free sparring.

JUTSU Technique.

KAMAE Fixed position or stance.

KATA Set pieces and techniques; forms.

KEIKO Practice.

KEIREI Bow.

KERI Striking.

KI Vital energy.

KIME The point of focus; the maximum concentration of force.

KUMITE Sparring.

NAGEWAZA Techniques of throwing.

REI The ceremonial bow.

REIGI Politeness, courtesy.

RENSHU Training.

SENSEI A teacher or instructor.

SUKI An opening.

TSUKI Punching.

UCHI Striking.

UKE Blocking.

YOI The ready posture.

LACROSSE

ATTACKMAN A player with an offensive responsibility; there are three attack players and three midfielders (who attack and defend).

BALL A solid-rubber white or orange ball that weighs 5–5¼ ounces and has a 2½-inch diameter and a circumference of 7¾–8 inches. Also, a call by a teammate that indicates he is going to get the ball and that another player on his team should bodycheck the player from whom he is taking the ball.

BODYCHECKING The act of legally blocking another player with the body, if that player is in possession of the ball, is a potential receiver, or is within 15 feet of the ball.

BREAK A shout by a goalie indicating he has made a stop of the ball and wants his defense to break out for a clearing play.

BRUSH-OFF An offensive move that involves running an opponent into a teammate in order to gain freedom of movement (PICK).

CENTER A position occupied near midfield on both offense and defense by a player who usually participates in face-offs.

CHARGE A legal run into an opponent aimed at throwing him off balance.

CHECKING Hitting the stick of an opponent to dislodge the ball or hamper his passing or receiving of the ball.

CLEARING The mounting of an attack by the defensemen the instant they intercept or stop the ball in their defensive area.

CLOSE ATTACK The three attackmen: first attack, out home, in home.

CLOSE DEFENSE The three defensemen: point, cover point, first defense.

CRADLE To maintain the ball in the pocket of the stick, or crosse, by rocking the crosse in a backward and forward motion.

CROSSCHECKING Using the portion of the stick between the butt (bottom end) and the throat (the point at which the head of the stick begins) to stop an opponent with or without the ball; an illegal maneuver except when used against an opponent who is within 15 yards of the ball.

CROSSE The implement used to play lacrosse; it may not be less than seven inches nor more than 12 inches wide and must be between 40 and 72 inches long—except for the goalkeeper's crosse, which may be any length he wishes (STICK).

DEFENSEMAN A player assigned to the defensive zone or position other than the goalkeeper.

DODGING The act of an offensive player getting away from a defensive player by faking a move in one direction and then moving away with the ball in another direction. There are four main dodges: face, force, toss, and change-of-pace.

EEPH The act of scooping up the ball from the ground and passing it.

END ZONES Areas at either end of the field behind the goal.

EXPULSION FOUL A three-minute penalty and ejection from the game charged against a player who has tried to hit a member of the other team, an official, or a coach; the ejected player is replaced by a substitute after the three-minute penalty time is completed.

EXTRA MAN A situation where a team has an extra attacker, either as a result of a dodge or because the other team is shy a man because of a penalty.

FACE-OFF A method of putting the ball into play in the middle of the field at the start of the game, the start of each quarter, after each score, and when the official cannot decide which team caused the ball to go out of play. Two players face each other with their backs to their respective goals, their sticks flat on the ground, and the ball positioned between their sticks, and they attempt to gain possession of the ball or to pass it.

FLICK The act of shooting or passing the ball after a catch without stopping to cradle the ball.

FORCING The act of making an attacking player in possession of the ball retreat so that he is unable to execute a pass.

FREE PLAY The act of restarting play by the referee that involves his placing the ball in the stick of an opposition player at the point closest to where the ball was lost out-of-bounds by the other team.

HEN HAWK An underhand shot.

HOME The attacking players—two in men's play, three in women's play.

INDIAN CHECK A gambling check that is aimed at jarring an opponent's stick to spring the ball loose.

INDIAN PENDANTS The stick's-head end strings that can be manipulated to change the pocket's depth.

MIDFIELDERS The three players who perform on both offense and defense: second defense, center, second attack.

PENALTY BOX An area where players put out of the game because of infractions must stay until the expiration of their penalty time.

PICK-UP A goalie's call to a teammate, directing him to play a man.

POKE CHECK The act of keeping an opponent at crosse's length by poking at the butt of his crosse.

RIDING An action by a team after losing the ball or attempting a shot that is aimed at preventing the defense from clearing the ball to its attackers.

RIGHT BACK; LEFT BACK Calls by a goalie to indicate the position of the ball to his teammates when the ball is behind the goal.

SCOOPING THE BALL The act of getting the ball off the ground and into the crosse.

SCREEN A situation where the crease man positions himself between the goalie and the man with the ball, or where an attack player positions himself so that the goalie cannot see the shot on goal.

SHIFT A goalie's call that indicates a man has been dodged and that the entire defense should shift toward the ball.

SLASHING The illegal use of the crosse on the arm or hand of an opponent.

MOTOR SPORTS:
Auto Racing,
Drag Racing

AIR FOIL A device positioned on the rear portion of a car that utilizes wind to aid in handling.

ALTERED A drag-racing classification that describes a modified automobile body that generally does not have glass or fenders.

ANCHORS Drag-racing brakes.

AUTOCROSS A driving competition of timed heats through a twisting course (GYMKHANA; SLALOM).

AXLE A pin on which a wheel revolves.

BACK MARKER A vehicle positioned on the final few rows of the starting grid.

BACK OFF To slow down on the throttle.

BAD SCENE A not-too-pleasant situation.

BANK A turn's degree of incline (BANKING).

BEND A generally shallow turn. Also, to damage a racing car.

BIG BANGER A big engine, generally with more than 305 cubic inches of displacement (BIG BORE).

BINDERS Brakes.

BITE Tire traction.

BLACK FLAG A signal by racing officials that requires a driver to return to the pits the next time around the course.

BLEND The mixture of methanol and nitromethane used in some cars.

BLIP To race an engine in brief bursts.

BLOCK A car's cylinder block.

BLOWN ENGINE One broken down or supercharged.

BLUEPRINT To take apart an engine and rebuild it beyond the precision point of standard factory construction.

BODY IN WHITE A car body just off the production line in its natural metal color.

BOSS Outstanding.

BOX Transmission; gear box.

BRAIN FADE A driver's mental mistake.

BRAKE FADE The loss of effectiveness of brakes because of overheating as a result of continued use.

BRAKE HORSEPOWER A measuring instrument for evaluating the horsepower of an engine (B.H.P.).

BUBBLE A qualifying line-up's last position, in which a driver is vulnerable to being replaced by a faster driver.

BULL RING An oval track of a half mile or less.

BUY THE FARM To be killed in an accident (BUY IT).

CALIPER A clamping device that grips the disc in a system of disc brakes.

CAM A shaft formation that creates motion.

CAMSHAFT A rotating shaft that indirectly activates cylinder valves.

CATCH FENCES Fences positioned at different spots off the course to catch cars and minimize danger.

CC (CUBIC CENTIMETERS) A measuring unit used to calculate the amount of engine displacement; 1,000 cc. equals 1 liter.

CHAMPIONSHIP CAR A racing car built especially for major competition—similar to formula racers but possessing a larger engine displacement.

CHASSIS The understructure of a racer.

CHECKERED FLAG Composed of black and white squares, this flag is used to signal the end of a race.

CHICANE A manmade obstacle, such as a corner or turn placed where racing officials desire to reduce the speed of cars.

CHIEF STEWARD An individual who runs the race and is the leading official.

CHRISTMAS TREE The light system mounted on a vertical pole that is used to count down to the start of a drag race.

C.I.D. Cubic inches of displacement.

CLOSED COURSE A road designed only for racing.

CLUB RACING Amateur events.

COME-IN SIGNAL A signal (usually an arrow) used by a pit-crew member to call in the driver on his next lap.

COMINGMAN A rookie driver with great potential (British term).

CONSY Consolation race.

CRASH BOX A transmission that is not synchronized.

CUBES Cubic inches of displacement.

DICE A British term that describes very close racing between two or more cars with changes of position common; to engage in close racing.

DIFFERENTIAL Engine power comes from this unit to the drive wheels.

D.O.H.C. Double overhead camshaft.

DRAFTING Trailing close behind another car and literally allowing that car to break through the air (TOW).

DRAG RACE A race that is generally restricted to a quarter of a mile straightaway and based on acceleration speed.

DRAGSTER An auto used for drag racing, characterized by having the driver's seat set behind the rear wheels.

DRIFT A maneuver used in cornering in which all the wheels slide as the car is accelerated through a turn.

DRIVE SHAFT The drive-train part that sends power from the engine to the driving wheels.

DRIVE TRAIN The total system that carries power from the engine to the driving wheels.

ELIMINATED Beaten in a drag race.

ÉQUIPE French term for race team.

ESSES A sequence of continuous shallow left and right turns.

E.T. Elapsed time.

E-Z A signal from the pit to "take it easy," generally given to a driver well in the lead.

FACTORY TEAM A squad of drivers and cars entered in a race by an auto manufacturer.

FISHTAILING The weaving from side to side of the rear of a car.

FLAT-OUT At top speed (FULL BORE; FULL CHAT).

FLYING START The moving at high speed of a formation of racing cars as they take the starting line's green flag. In a ROLLING START, the cars move out at a relatively low speed.

FOOTPRINT The spot on the ground where a tire makes contact.

FORMULA Specifications detailed for open-wheel racing cars that have an open cockpit and a single seat.

FORMULA LIBRE Anything is possible; anything goes.

FOUR-WHEEL DRIVE (4-W-D) Engine power is transmitted in this system to all four wheels, rather than only to two.

FUEL INJECTION A technique in which fuel goes directly into the cylinders, as opposed to going through a carburetor.

GASSER A kind of drag racer.

GEAR BOX Transmission.

GET SIDEWAYS A spinning slide that moves the car on an angle to the traffic flow.

GO INTO THE COUNTRY To unintentionally leave the racing circuit.

GRAND TOURING CAR A sports car that blends passenger features with racing potential.

GRID The starting line-up in road racing (STARTING GRID).

GROOVE The best and most efficient racing route on an oval track.

GROUND CLEARANCE The space between the bottom of a car and the ground.

GT Grand touring sedan.

HAIRPIN A very sharp turn (SWITCHBACK).

HAIRY Exciting, wild, frightening.

HALF-SHAFT The axle shaft.

HEEL AND TOE The use of only the right foot on the brake pedals and accelerator—an almost mandatory technique for racers.

HILL CLIMB A race up a hill, with one car at a time racing against the clock.

HOBBY A novice-type stock-car racer.

HOMOLOGATION A manufacturing procedure that certifies a car for use in a given racing class.

HOT DOG A talented driver (HOT SHOE).

IMPOUND AREA Enclosed inspection area that is utilized after a race.

INFIELD The area enclosed by a road course or an oval track that is used for pits, parking, garages, and race watching.

KNOCK-OFFS A single-wing nut easy to put on and take off that is used to fasten a wheel to its hub; the nut is "knocked off" with a mallet.

KONI Type of shock absorber used in racing and sports cars.

LAP One complete circuit of the course. Also, to pass a slower driver by moving into the circuit ahead of that driver.

LAY IT ON To get a car to go exceptionally fast.

LINE The best and most efficient route in road racing around a circuit. Also, the manner or route in which a driver takes a specific turn.

LITER A metric unit measurement of liquid capacity—just a bit more than a quart.

LOSE IT To lose control of a car.

LOUD PEDAL The accelerator.

MAG WHEELS Magnesium-cast wheels.

MANIFOLD A distributing or collecting chamber: the intake manifold distributes the mixture of fuel and air to the cylinders from the carburetor; the exhaust manifold collects gases from the cylinders and sends them to the exhaust pipes.

MARK One of a series of cars or products (Mark II would be the second in a line of cars, etc.).

MARSHAL A road-racing communications individual, such as a flagman.

METHANOL A type of alcohol blended into the fuel in racing cars and in some drag racers.

MICKEY MOUSE Not to be taken seriously; a racing course with a great many turns.

MOD Up-to-date—as in a car with the latest modifications.

MONOCOQUE A chassis that lacks a frame.

MULE A car used for practice.

NERFING BAR A bumper that protects the wheels from making contact with each other.

NITRO An ingredient in the fuel blend used by racing cars and some drag racers (NITROMETHANE).

NOMEX A brand of flame-resistant fabric that is popularly used in the clothing of racing drivers.

NORMALLY ASPIRATED A nonsupercharged or turbocharged engine that gets air into combustion chambers via regular suction resulting from piston downstroke.

OUT OF SHAPE Any break or disturbance in the smooth line of movement of a driver's car.

OVERSTEER Inclination of a car to turn more sharply on a curve than the driver wishes.

PACE CAR A car, generally a flashy convertible, that is positioned ahead of the pack to set the pace prior to the start of a race.

PACE LAP An oval-racing quick circuit of the track by all the cars, which follow a pace car so that when the starting line is reached, the cars are virtually up to maximum speed.

PADDOCK A work and parking area for cars in road racing.

PARADE LAP A slow-moving formation of all the cars in the race, held prior to the pace lap for the benefit of the spectators.

PIECES Parts and/or engine components.

PIT(S) A service area for cars, generally located on the front straightaway and restricted to participants and officials (WORKING PITS).

PIT ROAD A path that leads in and out of the pits from the course (PIT LANE).

PIT STOP To get off the track for a stop in the pits in order to have the car serviced.

PLANING The floating on a film of water by a car whose tires are unable to provide much traction on a wet surface (AQUA-PLANING; HYDROPLANING).

POLE (POSITION) The number one position, because it enables a car to move flat-out without worry about banging into another car.

POP Methanol-and-nitromethane fuel blend.

PRODUCTION The manner in which a car is produced by a man-ufacturer.

PROTO(TYPE) A car that does not have to conform; one of a kind; a new car's test model.

PUMP GAS The same quality of gasoline used by the public (PUMP FUEL).

QUALIFYING Speed sessions before a race to determine the actual starting positions, with the fastest lap times resulting in the award of the pole position.

RAUNCHY Sloppy appearance of an individual or car, or improper behavior.

RED FLAG A solid red flag used to stop a race. Also, to stop a race.

REV COUNTER A tachometer, which indicates an engine's revo-lutions per minute.

RIDE A race-car driving assignment.

ROAD COURSE A partial or total road-racing course that uses public highways.

ROAD RACE A race held on a road course rather than an oval track.

ROLL BAR A safety device composed of tubular steel fastened to the chassis above the driver's head; it is designed to protect the driver if the car rolls over.

ROLL CAGE Tubular steel surrounding a driver in a stock car or Transamerican sedan and designed to protect him in a crash or turnover.

R.P.M. Revolutions per minute—the measurement of the speed at which an engine turns.

RUN OUT OF ROAD To go off course during a maneuver by using up all the track area.

SANDBAGGING To hold back on showing all the speed a vehicle is capable of and thus give the opposition a false sense of security.

SANITARY A clean race.

SCRUTINEERING A thorough inspection of a racing car for safety and conformity to the rules.

SCUDERIA Italian term for race team.

SHOES Tires.

SHUT THE GATE The blocking of a car that is attempting to move ahead on the inside of a turn (CLOSE THE GATE).

SHUT-OFF In road racing, the moment just before a turn that requires a driver to decrease speed; personalized shut-offs are a blend of the equipment, skill, and the courage possessed by a driver.

SLICKS Wide, flat-surface tires on drive wheels of drag racers.

SLIDE A skidding of the rear wheels.

SLINGSHOTTING A stock-car-racing technique that involves following in the slipstream of another car and then passing (slinging) by that car.

SPIN To lose control of a car by spinning out or spinning off the course.

SPOILER A device that enables a car to resist the tendency at high speed to lift off the ground—an air deflector.

STACK(S) Pipes affixed to the fuel-injection system or the carburetor to pull in air (VELOCITY STACKS).

STOCK BLOCK Mass-produced engine block that is adapted for racing.

STOCK CAR A racing car that is basically unmodified from a standard production model.

STROKE To drive a car at a speed lower than its potential. Also, the distance a piston moves inside a cylinder.

SUPERCHARGER A mechanical device that enables a car to have a more powerful fuel-air mixture than normal atmospheric pressure can supply.

SWITCHBACK A maneuver that is close to a U-turn.

T-BONE To smash broadside into another car.

TEN-TENTHS Ultimate performance, as opposed to nine-tenths (nearly ultimate performance), etc.

TIME TRIALS Solo competitions against the clock; speed competitions before a race to establish starting positions.

TORQUE A rotating shaft's twisting force.

TORSION BAR Suspension-system rod that operates like a spring.

TWEAK To attempt to get even more power out of an engine by tuning.

UNDERSTEER A tendency by an automobile's front to take control of the vehicle and drag it along and out of control.

UNREAL Exceptional.

YELLOW FLAG A signal that indicates there are dangerous conditions on the track (YELLOW LIGHT).

MOTORCYCLING

APE HANGERS Handlebars that rise up very high to the handgrips.

BACK IT IN A maneuver that turns a motorcycle into a sideways slide, making it corner so that it looks as if the rear wheel is ahead of the front wheel.

BERM A dirt bank created on an offroad-course corner as a result of the turns of a great many motorcycles.

BLOW OFF To skillfully pass another motorcycle.

BOINGER A rear shock absorber.

BUZZ IT To run an engine at an exceedingly high rpm.

CAFÉ RACER A personalized street bike with cosmetic features and, sometimes, performance features that resemble a road racer.

CAMBER The degree of bank in a turn.

CLIP-ONS Handlebars that are low and flat and attach directly to the motorcycle.

CROSSED UP An airborne jumping maneuver with the front wheel angled to the direction of flight.

DETUNED A term describing situations when things are going badly.

DNF Literally, "did not finish"; a condition where something was not accomplished.

DNS Literally, "did not start"; a condition where a performer or object was not able to function.

ELECTRICS Anything on a motorcycle involved with electricity.

ENDO The accidental going end-over-end of a bike and rider.

ENDOED To go end-over-end.

FACE SHIELD A plastic visor that is transparent and is attached to the front of a safety helmet.

FAIRING A streamlined shape that attaches to the front of a motorcycle to cut down wind resistance.

FISH OIL Fluids that do not function properly on a bike.

GETTING OFF Leaving a motorcycle that is still moving before the rider had planned to do so.

GETTING UNDER THE PAINT An extreme technique used to cut wind resistance in which the rider crouches down as low as possible on the tank.

GRAB THE BINDERS To brake a motorcycle.

GRID A competition event's starting area.

GROOVE The line tracked through a corner by a motorcyle.

HACKS Passenger-carrying sidecar motorcycles (SIDEHACKS).

HANGING OFF Reducing a bike's lean-angle by hanging off the seat in the direction of a turn.

HOLESHOT To seize the lead quickly as a race starts.

HOTSHOE A competent, quick rider.

LEATHERS Generally padded leather fabrics that make up the rider's protective outer clothing.

LIGHTWEIGHT A performer lacking skill or staying power.

MOTO One heat out of the two or three events that compose a complete motorcross.

MOTORCROSS Motorcycle competition conducted over all-natural terrain courses (MX; SCRAMBLE).

PEGS Footrests on motorcyles.

REAR SETS Pegs positioned farther to the rear of a bike than normal that accommodate laid-forward body positioning suitable for high speeds.

RED LINE The upper limit of rpms for a motorcycle engine; a red zone on the tachometer of a motorcycle indicates the limit.

SANO A sanitary machine in appearance and production.

SISSY BAR An upright metal bar fastened to the rear of the motorcycle seat that can be leaned against by a passenger.

SLICKS Tires lacking a tread pattern.

SMOKE To defeat someone convincingly.

SQUID A rider whose comments about his riding abilities far exceed his performance (STREET SQUID).

SQUIRRELLY Erratic riding ability.

TEAR-OFFS Disposable plastic sheets that can be attached to the face shield and removed when insects, mud, etc., cause reduced vision.

TOPPING OFF Filling a fluid tank or receptacle to the limit.

TRANNY Transmission.

TUCKED IN Buried into the motorcycle to cut down wind resistance.

TWO-UP Carrying a passenger on the motorcycle.

UP ON THE PEGS A riding position in which all the weight is placed on the foot pegs and the rider is standing up.

WFO Wide-open throttle.

WHEELIE Lifting the motorcycle's front wheel off the ground.

WIND IT OUT To get an engine revved up to its red line or best upshifting gear-point for each speed.

WOBBLY A rolling and turning of the machine virtually out of the control of the rider.

WRENCH A motorcycle mechanic.

ZAP To pass another rider with furious quickness.

MOUNTAINEERING:
Hiking and Climbing

ANCHOR ROPE The portion of a climbing rope that is tied from a belayer to a nearby anchor point.

AVALANCHE A snow- or ice-fall down a mountain slope.

BALANCE CLIMBING Movement up slopes and cliffs that are too steep to walk up.

BELAYING The braking action, playing, paying out, or taking in of a rope tied to a climber; the rope can run around a tree or rock or around a belayer (a climber who has secured himself to a rock or tree).

BELAY POINT That spot chosen by a belayer to secure himself or an object that is used for belaying.

CARABINER A round metal ring that can be linked to a stationary object and through which a rope can be run.

CHIMNEY A generally vertical opening through which a climber can move.

CHOCKSTONE A wedged stone that blocks a chimney.

CHUTE An opening that is usually wider than a chimney.

CLIFF A steep and high face.

CONTINUOUS CLIMBING Sequential climbing in distances of less than a rope length by two or more people connected by a rope; all climbers on the move at the same time.

CORNICE A snow mass that hangs over the side of a ridge.

CRAMPONS Strapped-on frames for shoes and boots that have spikes to facilitate moving along on ice or hard snow.

CREVASSE A glacier-surface opening.

FACE An unbroken vertical front on a cliff or mountainside.

FIXED ROPE Effective as a handline, a rope that is fastened to a secure object, such as a rock, that helps climbers in their ascending or descending movements.

FREE CLIMBING Climbing unaided by rope(s).

GLISSADING Skiing down a snow slope without skis by simply standing up and sliding.

GULLY A narrow ravine.

HOLD A support for a hand or foot on a rock.

ICE AX A picklike device that is used for cutting holds in ice and snow and as an aid to balance.

LEADER The first man in upward climbs; the person in charge.

MOUNTAIN WALKING The act of going across rocky terrain on foot.

PARTY CLIMB The act of several individuals roped to each other to climb a cliff.

PITCH A treacherous and steep part of a mountain.

PITON An iron spike that is hammered into cracks and used as an aid in climbing techniques.

PITON HAMMER A hammer that is used to hammer pitons.

RAPPEL The act of a climber sliding down a rope.

RAPPEL POINT The object a rappel rope is fastened to.

STATIC CLIMBING Climbing conditions where the belayer is always above the climber and where there is always one rope-length or less of height.

TENSION CLIMBING Climbing conditions where the climber is held by the belayer with tension on the rock.

TIMBERLINE The area or line above which trees do not grow.

TRAIL MARKERS Usually wooden markers positioned along a route for identification purposes.

TRAVERSING Zigzag pattern movement, as opposed to straight up-and-down movement.

PLATFORM
TENNIS
(Paddle)

ALLEY A two-foot-wide area between the side line and the alley line that runs the length of the court on either side.

ALLEY LINE The line that marks the inside of the alley.

ALLEY SHOT A shot straight down the alley area of the opposition's court.

BACKCOURT The playing court area between the service line and the baseline.

BACKHAND A stroke or grip in which the back of the hand faces the ball.

BACKSPIN A backward-spinning rotation applied to a ball (UNDERSPIN).

BASELINE The end lines of the playing court.

BLITZ A hard-driving shot by a player on defense followed up by movement into a position close to the net.

CARRY A condition where the ball fails to leave the paddle the instant it is hit.

CENTER LINE A line that divides the right-center and left-center courts.

CHOP SHOT A downward, oblique stroke used for backspin shots.

CORNER SHOTS Shots into the left or right corner of the screens that surround the court of the opponent(s).

CROSSCOURT SHOTS Diagonal shots.

DEUCE A scoring situation (when the game is at 40–40) where a team needs to take two straight points to win the game.

FAULT An improper serve.

FOOT FAULT A fault as a result of a server's foot crossing or touching the baseline before he or she has served the ball.

FORECOURT The area between the net and the service line, including the alley portions forward of the service line.

FOREHAND A stroke performed with the palm of the hand in the direction of the intended movement of the ball.

LET A point that must be replayed—for example, when a serve hits the top of the net and bounds into the proper service court.

LOB A stroke that lifts the ball high in the air into the opponent's playing area.

OFF-THE-SCREEN SHOTS Shots executed by hitting a ball after it has rebounded from the screens.

OVERHEAD A stroke employed to drive a high ball down into an opponent's court.

PLAYING COURT A marked-off area, 20 feet by 44 feet, where paddle takes place.

RALLY A series of shots in which both sides are able to keep the ball in play to the conclusion of a point.

RECEIVER The player positioned in the service court who receives the serve.

RUNNING AROUND ONE'S BACKHAND The action of a player who, in order to avoid making a backhand stroke, moves into a position to execute a forehand stroke (e.g., when a player moves to the left to avoid a backhand on a ball approaching on his left).

SCREENS Twelve-foot-high wire screening that surrounds the court.

SERVER The player who is serving.

SERVICE The stroke that starts each point in a game and is the means of getting the ball into play.

SERVICE BREAK The winning of a game by a receiver against the service of an opponent.

SERVICE COURTS The areas across the net where serving takes place, 12 feet deep by eight feet wide and marked off by the service line, the center line, the alley line, and the net.

SERVICE LINE The line that divides the service courts from the back court.

SIDE LINE The line that marks the outside of the alley.

SLICE A ball that spins sideways in its forward movement.

STRATEGIC SPOT A position on the court that enables a player to most effectively reach and hit the ball.

TOPSPIN The spin of a ball in the same direction as its flight, caused by hitting up and behind it.

VOLLEY To return a ball before it bounces.

RACQUETBALL

ACE A good serve that the intended receiver is unable to return and that thus scores a point for the server.

AMOEBA MAN A very slow-moving player.

APEX The highest point a ball bounces.

"A" PLAYER A highly skilled player in tournament competition.

AROUND-THE-WALL BALL A shot that strikes high up on the side wall, hits the front wall, then caroms to the other side wall, and finally bounces on the floor at three-quarter court.

AVOIDABLE HINDER Resulting in the loss of point or serve, an interference that causes problems in a rally's continuity.

BACKCOURT The area behind the short line.

BACKHAND CORNER The juncture of the side and back walls on the same side as the backhand of a player.

BACK-INTO-BACK-WALL SHOT A rear-wall drive that goes on the fly to the front wall.

BACK WALL The rear wall.

BLINKUS OF THE THINKUS To experience a mental lapse while playing.

BODY SURF A diving, sliding move onto the court floor by a perspiring performer.

BOTTOM BOARDER A flawless kill shot off the front wall's bottom board.

"B" PLAYER A player of average skills in tournament competition.

BULLSEYE A front-wall target that when hit results in a perfect serve.

BUMBLEBEE BALL Mishit ball that behaves like a wounded bumblebee.

BUMPER BALL A mishit shot on the bumper (the protective racquet-rim covering) that can cause a "bumblebee ball."

CONTROL The consistent ability to hit the ball to the intended spots.

CONTROLLER A player who relies on a defensive and passing game.

COURT HINDER An unavoidable hinder (a door latch, for example) that interferes with the ball and stops a rally, causing the point to be played over.

"C" PLAYER The least skilled classification in tournament play.

CRACK BALL A ball that is hit into the cracks between a wall and the floor.

CROTCH The intersection of two playing surfaces.

CROTCH SERVE A serve that lands in the intersection of the front wall and the ceiling or floor and is a side-out.

CROWDING Playing too close to an opponent and thus causing an avoidable hinder.

DIE A ball that just makes it to the front wall and rebounds with little or no bounce.

DIG To get to a low kill-shot just before its second bounce.

DONUT No points scored in a game.

DROP SHOT A softly lofted ball that hits low on the front wall (DUMP SHOT).

ERROR A misplay of the ball.

EXCHANGE The end of a rally that effects a point or a side-out.

FAULT An illegal serve.

FISHBOWL A court composed of one or more glass walls.

FLAT ROLL-OUT A kill shot in which the ball hits the front wall so close to the floor that it comes off with no bounce.

FLOATER A poorly hit ball or one with much backspin that floats toward the front wall.

FOOT FAULT Illegal move of a foot before or while serving.

FOUR-WALL RACQUETBALL Indoor play on a court with four side-walls and a ceiling—the most popular form of the game.

FREAK BALL A winning shot that is hit well from an unusual position.

FRONTCOURT The area in front of the short line plus the service box.

GAME Twenty-one points equals one game.

GARBAGE SERVE An off-speed serve that comes to the receiver at about shoulder-level and is generally returned to the ceiling (HALF LOB).

GARFINKEL SERVE A forehand crosscourt serve to the forehand of the opponent.

GUN HAND The hand that grips the racquet.

HALF-AND-HALF The doubles-team procedure of dividing the court in half, with coverage responsibilities understood.

HAND-OUT A loss of service in doubles play by the first partner.

HEAD The racquet surface that strikes the ball.

I FORMATION A doubles team procedure in which one player covers the front court and the other is responsible for the backcourt.

ISOLATION STRATEGY An effort in doubles play to hit the ball to one player while attempting to keep the other partner out of the game flow.

KILL A low shot hit off the front wall that rebounds so slightly as to make a return impossible.

LET A fault.

LONG SERVE A serve that hits the back wall on the fly.

MATCH The winner of two out of three games wins the match.

MERCY BALL Holding back on a swing to avoid having the ball or the racquet strike an opponent.

OFF HAND The hand that does not grip the racquet.

OUT An illegal serve that causes a loss of service.

PHOTON A powerfully hit shot (BULLET; POWDER BALL).

PLUM BALL A cinch set-up.

PUSHING OFF Illegal contact with an opponent.

RECEIVING LINE The five-foot line.

RIM A racquet's frame.

ROADRUNNER A player skilled in getting to the ball.

ROLLOUT A flat kill-shot that is impossible to retrieve.

SCREEN BALL The visual hindering of an opponent that results in the replay of the point.

SERVICE BOX The serving area, which is located between the front and short lines; the spot where the nonserving partner on a doubles team must be positioned when his partner serves.

SHOOT THE BALL To attempt a kill shot.

SHORT LINE The line that a served ball must pass before striking the floor; it is parallel to and midway between the front and back walls.

SHORT SERVE A serve that does not go beyond the short line.

SIDE-OUT Loss of service by one side dictating that points can be scored only by serving side; also, loss of rally dictates loss of service by serving side.

SKIP BALL A ball that strikes the floor prior to its getting to the front wall (SPLINTER BALL).

STRADDLE BALL A ball that comes off the front wall and goes through the legs of a player.

TARGET AREA The area that the server wishes the ball to go to after a front wall rebound.

THONG A strap affixed to the racquet handle that has a loop that goes around the wrist of a player.

THREE QUARTERS AND ONE QUARTER A diagonal division of court coverage by a doubles team in which the court is divided from one front corner to the opposite back corner.

TOUCH Fine control of the racquet.

TOUR OF THE COURT An extended rally dominated by one player who makes the other run all over the court.

V-BALL A pass shot that goes crosscourt.

WAFFLE FACE The act of a player hitting another player in the face with the racquet.

WALLPAPER BALL A side-wall-hugging shot (R.A.W. BALL—"RUN ALONG THE WALL BALL").

WINDSHIELD-WIPER PLAY A series of crosscourt drive shots hit by one player to another during a long rally.

Z-BALL Generally a defensive shot that strikes either corner high up on the front wall, rebounds to the near side-wall, goes to the opposite side-wall, and then hits the floor.

RUGBY

ADVANTAGE The referee's allowing of play to continue after an infringement if the nonoffending team gains a territorial or technical advantage.

BLIND SIDE Generally the side closer to the touch line—the side of the field where the fly-half (stand-off half) has positioned himself at line-out, ruck, maul, and scrummage.

CROSSKICK An across-the-field attacking kick.

DEAD BALL A ball not in play, blown "dead" by referee's whistle.

DEFENDING TEAM The team in whose half of the field the stopping of play takes place.

DRAWING YOUR MAN Getting an opponent to commit himself to tackling the ballcarrier instead of the man who is about to receive a pass.

DRIBBLING Ball control with the feet and the shins, a technique sometimes used by a pack of forwards who are advancing.

DROP KICK The kicking of the ball after it is dropped from the hands and just as it rebounds off the ground.

DROP-OUT A method of restarting play, either after an unsuccessful conversion attempt, or from behind or at the 25-yard line after an attacking player kicks, carries, passes, or knocks the ball into the opponents' in-goal area, but does not score. A dropkick is made by the defending team from within the 25-yard line.

DUMMY To fake passing the ball.

FALLING ON THE BALL By turning his back on the opposition, a player drops on the ball to stop the opposition's foot rush.

FIVE-YARD SCRUM After a defending player knocks, carries, passes, heels, or kicks the ball over his own goal line—and it becomes dead because it was touched down or went outside the playing field—the attacking team is given a scrum five yards from the goal line and opposite the spot where the ball went into the in-goal area.

FLY KICK A wild and unplanned kick (HACKING).

FOOT-UP A penalty given to any member of either team in the front row of a scrum who advances a foot before the ball has touched the ground.

FREE KICK If a score is being attempted, a free kick may be a dropkick or a place kick; if no score is being attempted, it is taken as a punt.

GROUNDING THE BALL Downward pressure applied to the ball by a player's hand(s), arm(s), or upper body to score a try.

GRUBBER KICK A punt designed to bounce along the ground.

KNOCK-ON Striking the ball with hand or arm toward the opposition's dead-ball line.

LINE-OUT A formation of at least two players from each team in single lines parallel to the touch line awaiting the ball thrown between them; it may extend from 5 to 15 yards from the touch line.

LOCKS Set-scrum second-row forwards.

LOOSE-HEAD A position that is the front row forward nearest to the referee in a scrum.

LYING DEEP A deep formation in an attack by the backs (halves and three quarters) to get enough running room.

LYING SHALLOW A shallow formation in defense by the backs (halves and three quarters) that is closer to their opposition.

MARK A fair catch from a kick, a knock-on, or an intentional throw forward executed by a player with both feet on the ground who shouts "mark."

MAUL A mob of players on both sides around a player in possession of the ball who shove and jostle each other to be able to get the ball when it is finally released.

NO-SIDE The end of the game.

OFFSIDE Generally, a player is offside when in front of the ball played by another member of his team.

PENALTY TRY A try granted by the referee to the attacking team if he judges that a try would have been scored if not for the defending team's foul play, misconduct, or obstruction; the try takes place between the posts and afterward a conversion may be attempted.

PLACE KICK A kick of a ball placed on the ground.

PLAYER ORDERED OFF A player ejected from the game who may not return to play again in that game.

PUNT A maneuver in which the ball is dropped from a player's hands and is kicked before it touches the ground—not a scoring kick, but one used to gain a tactical advantage.

PUSH OVER TRY A situation that occurs when the defending team is pushed from a scrum over its goal line into its goal-area by the attacking pack; a try is scored when an attacking member falls on the ball.

RUCK A loose scrum with the ball lying on the ground.

SCRUMMAGE A play in which the forwards on each team lock arms and crouch over, the two sides meeting head-to-head and the ball being put into play in the tunnel between the front rows; three players must comprise the front row of each side (SCRUM).

THE HANDLING GAME A phrase used to distinguish rugby football from association football (soccer) after 1823.

THE PACK The forwards.

TOUCH The ball is in touch after being carried on or over the touch line, or when it bounces on or passes over the touch line. A ball that passed over the touch line in the air and then is blown into play again by the wind is judged in-touch where it passed over the line.

TOUCH-DOWN A situation that takes place when a player first grounds the ball in his own in-goal area—not a score.

TRY A score worth four points accomplished by the grounding of the ball in the opposition's goal area by a member of the attacking team.

UP AND UNDER A timed high kick within the field of play hit so that the kicker's teammates are positioned under the ball as it comes down.

WHEEL A maneuver that takes place in a set-scrum, which is rotated when the ball is at the feet of the lock forwards; the players break to one side, advancing and dribbling the ball.

SAILING

ABAFT Toward the stern.

ABEAM At right angles to the boat's centerline.

AFT Toward the back of the boat; the stern.

AMIDSHIPS The center of the boat, midway between the bow and the stern and midway between the sides.

BACKSTAYS Lines from the mast to the stern which secure the mast.

BALLAST Weight at the lowest point of the boat for purposes of stabilization. OUTSIDE BALLAST is lead or iron weight in keels. INSIDE BALLAST is movable weight inside the boat.

BATTEN A strip of plastic or wood that stiffens the roach in a sail's leech.

BATTEN POCKET The pocket that holds the batten.

BEAM The width of the boat.

BEAR OFF Turning downwind, away from the wind.

BEAT To sail windward.

BEND To make a sail fast to a spar through the use of knots, hooks, grooves, slides, etc.

BILGE The turn of the hull below the waterline. Also, the area where water collects inside the hull.

BITTER END The free end of a rope, used for fastening.

BLOCK Pulley.

BOOM The spar at the bottom of a sail at right angles to the mast.

BOW The front end of a boat.

BRIDLE A length of wire fastened at either end and pulled at some point within its length.

BROACH To swing sharply toward the wind when running, because of poor steering, heavy seas, and heavy wind.

BUMPERS Protectors on a boat's side from docks, piles, other boats, etc.

BURDENED VESSEL A vessel that does not have right of way.

CENTERBOARD A device located on the boat's centerline which can be lowered to navigate in shallow waters for boats with permanent keels or to secure against a sideward slip.

CENTERLINE The center of a boat from bow to stern.

CHAIN PLATES Metal plates bolted to the side of a boat to hold shrouds and stays.

CHARTS Nautical maps that contain navigation aids, water depths, landmarks, etc.

CHOCK A casting of metal or plastic through which lines are led to other vessels or to shore and which guide these lines against chafing.

CLEAT A metal, plastic, or wood device that holds a line secure.

CLEW The lower aft corner of a triangular sail.

CLOSE-HAULED Sailing as close as possible to the wind with sails trimmed for beating (ON THE WIND; BEATING; STRAPPED DOWN).

COAMING A raised protection around the cockpit.

COCKPIT The portion of the boat for the crew to sail and sit in.

CRINGLE An eye of metal threaded into a sail for securing purposes.

DAGGER BOARD A movable, stiff device used to avoid side slip.

DECK PLATE A plate bolted to the deck, usually with an eye for shackles or blocks.

DOWNHAUL A rope or rope/block that pulls down the boom to tighten the luffs.

DRAFT The deepest point of a sail from the depth of its curve to an imaginary line drawn from its tack to its clew (its two bottom corners). Also, the distance from a boat's waterline to the bottom of its hull or keel.

EASE To relieve the pressure on a sail by letting out the sheet.

EYE SPLICE A splice in which the end of a rope is made into a loop.

FAIRLEAD An eye or casting that guides a line where a block is not needed.

FETCH *Verb:* to reach a goal without coming about. *Noun:* distance free from obstruction of tide or wind.

FLY A masthead pennant or piece of yarn in rigging, used to indicate apparent wind.

FOOT The lower edge of a sail.

FORE To the front (FORWARD).

FREE Sailing with the wind anywhere from abeam to directly behind.

FREEBOARD The vertical distance from the waterline to the deck.

FURL To wrap a sail to a spar.

GOOSENECK A joint-type fitting securing the boom to the mast.

HALYARD A line for raising and lowering the sails.

HARD A-LEE Short for "the helm is hard a-lee," which is the signal for the movement of the rudder incident to turning.

HEAD The upper corner of a triangular sail. Also, a boat's toilet.

HEADBOARD A wood or plastic stiffener used in the head of a sail.

HEADSTAYS Lines from the mast to the bow that secure the mast.

HEAD TO WIND Sails shaking as the boat heads into wind; luffing.

HEADWAY Forward motion.

HEAVE To throw or cast, to pull on a rope. As a noun, the rise and fall of a vessel.

HEEL To tip or tilt.

HELM The lever used as a rudder. Also, the tendency of a vessel to steer relative to the wind; WEATHER HELM means tending to steer toward the wind.

HULL The body of a boat exclusive of rigging, centerboard, etc.

IN IRONS A condition where the boat faces the wind and has lost all headway (IN STAYS).

JIB A triangular sail in front of the mast.

JIBE To change tacks by turning away from the wind toward the sail.

JIB-HEADED A triangular sail (MARCONI; BERMUDIAN).

JIBSTAY The stay that raises the jib.

JUMPER STRUT A device on the front side of the mast to increase stability of the upper part of the mast.

KEEL The backbone of a boat. Also, a fixed extension at the bottom of the boat for greater stability.

KNOT Friction devices to keep a line from slipping. Also, a nautical measure of speed: "one knot" means one nautical mile per hour. (A nautical mile is equal to one minute of latitude or longitude, and is 1.15 statute miles.)

LANYARD A short, light line for temporary ties.

LATERAL PLANE The hull, keel, or centerboard—the area designed to offset drift or slippage.

LAYLINE The line on which a boat can fetch a mark or buoy.

LEE Opposite to windward; the side of anything away from the wind. A lee shore is the shore at which the wind blows. "Leeward" means toward the lee side.

LEECH The aft edge of a sail.

LEEWAY The distance slipped to leeward.

LINES Ropes or wires used in rigging.

LIST The leaning of a vessel to the heavier side.

LUFF The fore edge of a sail. Also, the shaking of a sail when its head is toward the wind (luffing).

MAINMAST The sole mast of a small boat; the principal mast of a larger boat.

MAINSAIL A sail rigged on the back of the mast.

MAINSHEET A line used to control the mainsail.

MAKE FAST To tie up, secure.

MAST A vertical spar on which the sails are hoisted.

MOOR To secure to a mooring.

MOORING A means of securing a boat in water while it is not sailing so that it is free to move in a complete circle.

OFFSHORE Away from shore.

OFF THE WIND Sailing other than a close-hauled course.

ON THE WIND Sailing a close-hauled course.

OUTBOARD Beyond the hull.

OUTHAUL A line used to secure the foot of a sail.

OVERSTAND To go beyond the layline unnecessarily.

PAY OFF To ease out a length of line or to turn away from the wind with the bow (PAY OUT).

PENDANT A short piece of line used for securing.

PENNANT A length of line that fastens a boat to a mooring. A triangular flag.

PINCH To sail a boat inefficiently close to the wind.

POINT To head high, close to the wind.

PORT Left.

PORT SIDE To sail with the wind from the port side.

PRIVILEGED VESSEL A vessel with the right of way.

QUARTER The boat's side between the beam and the stern.

RAIL The outer edge of the deck.

RAKE The inclination of the mast toward fore and aft.

REACH Sailing a course between close-hauled and running.

READY ABOUT! A spoken signal to prepare for tacking.

REEF To make a sail smaller or reduce sail area.

REEVE To pass a line through a block or fairlead.

RIG A boat's sail-plan and mast arrangement.

RIGGING Spars, sails, lines, blocks, etc. STANDING RIGGING is permanent. RUNNING RIGGING can be moved about.

ROACH The curve in the foot, leech, or luff of a sail.

RODE The anchor line.

RUN To sail almost directly before the wind. Also, the aft underwater shape of the hull.

SAIL STOPS Lines used to tie a sail to a spar.

SEACOCKS Safety devices placed at or below waterline to control water flow in or out of a boat.

SEAWAY Sea area.

SHACKLE U-shaped metal fittings that join two objects.

SHEAVE The wheel in a block (pulley).

SHEET A rope used to control a sail.

SLIP A mooring or docking area between two small piers or floating booms.

SNAP HOOKS Hooks that spring closed.

SOLE The floor of the boat's cabin.

SPAR All poles.

SPINNAKER Large, lightweight sail used for reaching or running.

SPREADER A device used to spread rigging for increased strength in offsetting the tendency of a mast to bend.

STARBOARD The right side of a boat.

STAYS Lines that support the mast.

STEM The foremost part of a boat.

STERNWAY Backward motion.

STOPS Straps used to secure the sail to the boom.

TACK *Noun:* the forward corner of a sail; also, a forward course. *Verb:* to change from one tack to another.

TENDER Lacking stiffness; lacking a tendency to heeling. Also, a dinghylike craft used to transport supplies or people from shore to boat.

TILLER Wooden lever used to move the rudder.

TOPSIDES The sides of a boat above the waterline.

TRANSOM A broad, nearly vertical stern.

TRAVELER A track located near the stern and running horizontally. A slide runs on it that is fastened to the mainsheet. This enables the sheet to move from one side to the other when the boat is tacked, thus increasing sailing efficiency.

TRIM To adjust a sail relative to wind direction and course of boat. Also, the balance of a boat.

TURNBUCKLE A threaded link that pulls two devices together and is used to adjust tension in stays and shrouds.

WAKE Disturbances in the water caused by the drag or resistance of a vessel as it passes through water.

WATERLINE The dividing line between the topsides and the underbody of a boat.

WHISKER POLE A light pole used to hold a jib windward to allow it to fill with wind.

WINCH A small, drum-shaped device used to increase mechanical advantage for pulling in a line against tension; the line is wound clockwise, three turns or more.

WINDWARD Toward the wind; the opposite of leeward.

WORKING SAILS Ordinary sails, as opposed to light or storm sails.

SCUBA AND SKIN DIVING

ABSOLUTE PRESSURE The true pressure, which takes into account both air pressure at the surface and water depth.

ABYSS A depth of more than 1,000 feet.

AMBIENT PRESSURE At any depth, the surrounding pressure of water (LIQUID PRESSURE).

APPARATUS All the parts and materials that create a breathing device.

BAROTRAUMA Injury-producing pressure.

BREATHING AIR Compressed air inhaled by divers.

BUDDY BREATHING The sharing of air from the same cylinder by two or more divers.

COMPRESSED-AIR DEMAND REGULATOR A mechanism that gives off air to the diver whenever he inhales.

CYLINDER A container for compressed gas (BOTTLE; TANK).

DECOMPRESSION A technique that relieves a diver of pressure that has resulted from gases gathering in his body; the decreasing effects of water pressure felt by an ascending diver.

DECOMPRESSION SICKNESS The forming of gas bubbles in the tissues of a diver as a result of increased pressure.

DECOMPRESSION TABLES Tables that note where decompression should take place and how much time should be spent in decompression stops.

EBB TIDE A flowing out of the current from the shore.

EXPOSURE SUIT An outfit that is insulated to enable a diver to preserve body heat.

FINS Extensions attached to the feet of swimmers for more efficient speed.

FLOOD TIDE The highest tide.

GAUGE PRESSURE The difference between the surrounding atmospheric pressure and specific tank-pressure being measured.

HYPERVENTILATING Taking a series of deep breaths.

J VALVE An automatic shutoff valve on an air tank that is activated when pressure drops to 300 psi.

K VALVE A valve on an air tank that does not accommodate a reserve air supply.

MASK A diver's window that is equipped with an air space between the eyes and the water to facilitate underwater vision.

NITROGEN NARCOSIS A kind of intoxication affecting a diver exposed to the effects of nitrogen and other gases.

PNEUMOTHORAX A painful condition that results from the expansion of compressed air from a ruptured lung; the ascending diver's chest cavity is affected, and sometimes his lungs and heart.

RECOMPRESSION Treatment in a recompression chamber of a diver stricken with decompression sickness.

REGULATOR A device that enables a diver to receive the same amount of air which has the same pressure as the surrounding water.

RIP TIDE A powerful and dangerous current.

RUNOUT An undertow that follows an outgoing tide from the shore current.

SAFETY BUCKLE A device allowing the use of one hand to fasten straps.

SCUBA An ancronym for Self-Contained Underwater Breathing Apparatus, which is equipped with gas that can be breathed and is not surface attached.

SKIN DIVING A general term characterizing swimming on or under the water and using a snorkel or scuba equipment.

SKIP BREATHING A procedure involving the holding of breath or alternate breaths some extra time to conserve air.

SNORKEL DIVING Swimming with the use of a J-shaped rubber or plastic breathing tube that has a mouthpiece at the short end.

SPEARGUN An underwater hunting tool.

SURFACE INTERVAL The elapsed time between dives during which the diver is on the surface.

SURFACE LINE A line attached to both diver and boat that is useful in aiding a diver seeking to find his way to the boat when ascending.

VALVE A device that regulates air flow in one direction.

YOKE A device that connects regulators to cylinders or cylinders to other cylinders.

SKATEBOARDING

AERIAL SPIN A maneuver in which a leap off the skateboard is followed by a turn in the air and then a landing on the board.

AIR TACKING A display of balance that is executed by lifting the front end of the board while it is in motion and maneuvering it left and right (SPACE WALKING).

AIRPLANE A diamond-shaped downhill movement by four riders locked together and sitting on their boards.

ARABESQUE A stunt that positions a rider with his waist bent, one foot on the board and the other leg extended back, while his arms are extended forward.

BACKSIDE Moving or turning away from the front foot's direction; an outside turn.

BASE PLATE A plate that joins the board, the hanger, and the suspension bolt.

BEARINGS Small, round steel balls that reduce friction and make skateboard wheels turn smoothly.

BLANK The top of the skateboard, the riding surface (BOARD).

BONGO An injury or bruise that results from a fall from a skateboard.

BUDDY-BUDDY Two or more riders sitting on their boards and holding hands while going downhill.

BURGER A bad bruise.

BUSHINGS The rubber rings around the kingpin that aid spring and cushion shock (ACTION BUSHING; CUSHIONS; SHOCKS).

CAMBER An arch toward the board's rear wheels.

CARAVANNING A stunt that involves a few skateboarders riding down a hill in a line and holding onto each other, usually in a sitting position.

CARVING A TURN Turning sharply.

CATAMARANNING A stunt or trick that involves two skateboarders seated sideways with their feet on each other's boards.

CHASSIS A skateboard's board portion.

CHEW IT To fall badly.

CHRISTIE A move in which the skateboarder is crouched on one foot with the other foot extended to the side.

COFFIN The act of riding on a skateboard while lying on one's back.

COMPOSITION A name formerly associated with the material used in old wheels—roller skates.

COMPREHENSION The increased force felt on the body while making a turn.

DAFFY The act of riding with each foot on a separate board, legs are spread slightly forward and backward, while performing a wheelie on each board (nose-to-tail or tail-to-nose).

DOING A RUN Long-distance skateboarding, generally downhill.

FLEX The amount of flexibility in a board.

FREE EXERCISE Gymnastic moves associated with skateboarding.

FREESTYLE Competitive events involving solo tricks and movements that are judged on the types attempted and poise in performance.

GEEK An unskilled or clumsy skateboarder.

GLIDING Moving forward with few or no turns.

GO FOR IT Maximum effort, speed, or risk-taking.

GOOFY-FOOTING An unorthodox riding position; riding with the weaker foot forward.

GORILLA GRIP The act of jumping with the toes gripping the end of the board.

GREMMIE A clumsy skateboarder or a child who gets in the way.

HANGER The plate that joins the blank and the axle assembly of the truck.

HANG FIVE The act of hanging the toes of one foot over a board's front end.

HANG HEELS The act of extending both heels over a board's tail.

HANG TEN The act of extending the toes of both feet over a board's nose.

HAVING IT WIRED Being aware of precisely how a ride in a given area should be executed.

HEELIE A tail wheelie.

HODAD An amateur or novice.

HOP A jump made in a crouched position with both hands holding the ends of the board, taking the board along with the jump.

HOT A skilled rider or an excellent place to skate.

HOT DOGGING Trick skateboarding.

INERTIA The inclination of a moving body to remain in motion and of a body at rest to stay at rest.

JAM A gathering of skateboarders for fun and racing.

KICK A type of raised tail on a skateboard.

KICK-OUT The act of stepping off the board to the right with the left foot, so that the right foot, which is in back, kicks the board into the air in a flashy manner.

KINGPIN The main bolt that joins the truck to the base or hanger.

LEG LIFT A free-exercise movement in which one leg is extended straight up and supported by an arm, while the other is on the board.

LONG BOARD A board generally longer than four feet (SPEED-BOARD).

LONG-BOARDING Downhill racing.

MEMORY The tendency of a board to snap back to its original shape after flexing during weighting and unweighting.

NOSE A skateboard's front.

NOSE WHEELIE A wheelie where the tail is lifted off the ground.

ONE-EIGHTY (180°) A half turn that pivots one end of the board.

PEARLING Falling off the board (SPACING IT).

PIVOT The connector between the trunk's wheels that links up to the hanger or base.

PLANK RIDING Skateboarding (SIDEWALK SURFING).

POOL RIDING Skateboarding in empty swimming pools.

POWER SLIDE A parallel turn mainly done on banks or at high speeds from a crouch position.

PUMPING Side-to-side movements utilizing the skateboarder's weight for shifting from side to side—a means of moving along (WEDELING).

PUSHING ALONG Scooter-type movement that involves one foot on the board and the other pushing off the ground.

RADICAL Any exotic position, maneuver, or terrain.

ROAD RASH Scraped skin resulting from falls.

SEVEN-TWENTY (720°) Two or more complete spins executed without the lifted end touching ground.

SLALOM A competitive downhill event involving bobbing and weaving between cones.

SLIDE OUT A stopping maneuver executed by sliding the skateboard's rear end forward and skidding.

SPRING TRUCK A truck assembly that uses springs instead of bushings as shock absorbers.

STACKED BOARD Riding on two boards, one atop the other, while holding them together with the hands and executing different tricks.

STOKED Excited or psyched up.

SUPER SESSION A contest or exhibition.

SWITCHBACKING Skating zigzag, usually downhill.

SWITCHSTANCE The act of jumping from a regular stance to one where the weaker foot is positioned forward, or vice-versa, while in motion.

TACKING A zigzag, slowing-down motion.

TAIL The rear of a skateboard.

TAIL WHEELIE A wheelie where the nose is lifted off the ground.

TANDEM Two-on-one skateboard.

TERRAIN The land to be skateboarded; usually referring to its slope, curvature, and composition.

THREE-SIXTY (360°) A complete turn on a skateboard.

TIC-TAC-TOE Successive nose wheelies performed by touching the nose down to the left and the right, and variations of these moves.

TOE TAP A stopping maneuver executed by gently touching the toe of one foot to the ground repeatedly.

TRUCK Everything on a skateboard except for the blank and the wheels.

TUCK A deep crouch stance.

UNWEIGHTING Lightening weight on the board through lifting body weight off the board.

WALKING THE BOARD Taking small steps on the board while it is in motion (WALKING THE PLANK).

WEIGHTING Increasing weight on the board by crouching swiftly and slowly straightening up; more generally, the distribution of one's body weight on a board.

WHEELIE Lifting either end of the board while keeping two wheels on the ground.

WHEELIE STOP The act of stopping by executing a wheelie and lightly dragging the board's tail.

WIND SKATING Skateboarding with a sail and mast attached to the board.

WIPE OUT A bad spill.

WOBBLIES Severe vibrations caused by speed.

WONDER ROLLING Skateboarding.

YOKE That portion of the truck that contains the pivot, the kingpin, and the axle-support tube (the tube that joins the axle and the hanger).

SKIING

ABSTEM A turn that opens the tail of the lower ski into a **V** position.

ACROBATICS Ski stunts or tricks.

AERIAL TRAMWAY An uphill ski lift that uses two aerial cabin cars that move in opposite directions.

AIRPLANE TURN An airborne turn off a large bump.

ALPINE Concerned with downhill skiing.

ALPINIST A downhill skiier or one who competes in downhill events.

ANGULATION A body position that edges the skis into the hill with the knees bent toward the slope; the upper body is angled outward to compensate for this action (COMMA POSITION).

ANTICIPATION Upper-body rotation in the direction of the turn before unweighting and edge change.

APRÈS SKI Leisure-time activities after skiing.

ARBERG STRAP A leather strap fastened to the ski and wrapped around the boot to prevent the ski from running away when the binding releases.

ATTACK An all-out assault on a course.

AVALEMENT The ability of a skier to absorb the irregularities in the terrain (bumps, dips, etc.), or to be able to turn quickly at high speeds; this is accomplished via knee-flex movement and by pushing the feet forward a bit.

AXIAL MOTION Motion around the axis of the body that includes rotation and counterrotation.

BACKWARD LEAN Body positioning that places the skier's center of gravity behind the bindings.

BALACLAVA Protective knitted covering for the face and neck with openings for the eyes and sometimes the nose.

BANKING The leaning of the entire body in the direction of the imaginary center of a parallel christie turn.

BASE The running surface of a ski. Also, the amount of packed snow under the surface, a hill's bottom, or the bottom of a ski area.

BASKET A ring around the ski pole that prevents the point from going too deeply into the snow (SNOW RING).

BATHTUB A hole in the snow created by the body of a skier who has fallen down.

BENIGHTED Forced to return from a ski trek as a result of darkness descending.

BINDING A device that fastens the boot to the ski.

BITE To place pressure on ski edges to make them more effectively grip the snow.

BLOCK Contraction of rotary body muscles to transmit the turning power generated in one part of the body to another portion.

BOARD A ski.

BOILER PLATE A surface that is hard and frozen as a result of being exposed to a freeze after a warm period of rain.

BOMBER A speed skier, as opposed to a skier who prefers turning.

BOUNCE A motion utilized to unweight skis.

BREAKABLE CRUST A hard skiing surface that is nevertheless not strong enough to support a skier's weight.

BUNNY A novice female skier, generally overdressed and overly made up (SNOW BUNNY).

BUNNY HILL A gentle slope for beginners.

BURN IN Heating a base wax that was applied to a ski's running surface in order to make the wax into a liquid that will penetrate the wood.

CARVED TURN A turn in which the skier carves as finely as possible on the edges of the skis, making for a minimum of sideways slipping or skidding (CARVED EDGE).

CATCHING AN EDGE The accidental catching of the edge of a ski.

CHAIR LIFT Uphill transportation on chairs suspended from a moving cable.

CHANGE-UP An arm-resting technique employed by cross-country skiers in which they skip alternate thrusts of the poles.

CHATTER Ski-tip vibration as the ski turns on hard snow surface.

CHECK Any maneuver to slow down the skis.

CHRISTIE A contraction of the word "Christiana"—a turn that places skis parallel to each other as the turn is completed.

CHUTE A steep, narrow descent.

CONTROL GATES Sets of two flags positioned on a downhill course through which racers must pass; the purpose is to control and monitor potentially dangerous portions of the course.

CORN A type of snow occurring in spring or warm weather that is created from alternate freezing and thawing; easy turning is made possible for a skier by the honeycombed surface of this type of snow.

CORNICE A ledge of overhanging ice or snow.

COUNTERROTATION A turning motion of the upper part of the body that creates an equal but opposite action in the lower part of the body and takes place when skis are unweighted.

COURSE A racing route.

COVER A snow surface.

CRITICAL POINT The maximum distance point for a safe jump.

CRUD Snow conditions that are not desirable—breakable crust, etc. (JUNK SNOW).

CRUST Glazed surface atop snow caused by cycles of thawing and freezing.

DAFFY Separating the legs at the high point of a jump as a stunt in freestyle aerial competition: one leg is in front and the other is in back, both legs are straight, and the skis are virtually vertical.

DEEP POWDER A foot or more of soft, dry, light, powdery snow.

DIAGONAL A ski-touring striding technique that combines a kick by one leg with a push off from a pole gripped in the hand opposite that leg.

DIRECT PARALLEL An instruction method that stresses parallel placement of feet and skis.

DOPE Special wax preparations applied to skis, mainly used by California skiers.

DOUBLE-POLE To move forward by pushing off with both poles at the same time in ski touring.

DOUBLE STEM A running position in which both ski tails are pushed out into a **V** position (SNOWPLOW).

DOWNHILL The fastest and most dangerous of the three forms of Alpine racing—a race against time down a 1½-to-3-mile-long course.

DOWNHILLER A skier who participates in a downhill event.

DOWNHILL SKI The lower ski; the one that becomes the lower ski in a turn.

DOWNHILL SKIING Going down a slope after being towed to the top.

DOWN-UNWEIGHTING Reducing body weight on the snow by "dropping" the body sharply.

DROP Unweighting the skis by quickly lowering the body to make it easier for the skis to be turned.

EDGE A full-length piece of steel on the running edges of the ski that aid in gripping the snow when the ski is edged or turned.

EDGE CONTROL The ability to turn or to put skis on edge.

EDGE SET Edging the skis at the start of a turn.

EDGING Controlling the skis' sideward slippage by setting them at an angle to the snow and getting them to "bite" the surface.

EGG POSITION Downhill-racing maneuver of crouching tightly, with head near knees and poles tucked under arms.

EXTENSIONS Rising body motion to unweight skis and start a turn.

FACE The steepest part of a mountain; a slope's exposed front.

FALL LINE The steepest line of descent on a hill.

FLUSH Slalom-race combination of gates that forces a racer into a series of tight turns on the fall line.

FOOT STEERING Changing the direction of the skis by turning legs and feet.

FORERUNNER A skier who checks out a course by skiing it just before a competition to detect any problems and to insure that the course is ready.

FORWARD LEAN A skier's center of gravity is ahead of the bindings in this body position.

FREESTYLE A competition evaluated on individual style and execution in three different events: downhill over rough land (mogul); gradual-slope stylized moves (ballet); acrobatic moves (aerial).

FROZEN GRANULAR Snow condition in which frozen granules are compacted into a hard, sometimes solid surface.

GARLAND A momentary sidestep movement, performed while traversing a slope, that is followed by a straight traverse.

GATE Any arrangement of two poles or flags that a skier must pass through in the course of a race.

GELÄNDESPRUNG A jump over an obstacle or bump in which the skier uses both poles for support.

GIANT SLALOM A combination of a slalom and a downhill race.

GLISSADE To slide down a snow slope without the use of skis, by squatting or keeping the feet straight.

GLM "Graduated length method"—a method of teaching that begins with the using of short skis and the making of parallel turns as the opening learning procedures.

GODILLE Linked parallel turns executed in the fall line.

GONDOLA An uphill ski lift that transports several skiers in a series of enclosed aerial cars that are suspended from a moving cable.

GRADE The angle or pitch of a slope.

GROOM To get a slope ready for skiing by snow packing or crust breaking.

HAIRPIN A slalom figure composed of two consecutive closed gates.

HALF SIDESTEP Similar to sidestep climbing of a slope, except that the uphill ski is positioned ahead of the weighted one on each step and climbing takes place at an angle rather than straight up.

HELICOPTER A full-twisting freestyle aerial stunt.

HERRINGBONE Climbing a hill with skis in the V position and with pressure weighted against the inside edges of the skis.

HOGBACK A bump that is sharply ridged.

HOT DOG A freestyle skier.

INRUN The steep slope, many times set on a high scaffolding, from which a skier generates speed prior to jumping.

INSIDE The side of the body near where a turn is being made.

J-BAR LIFT A lift that carries a series of bars shaped like the letter J on a moving overhead cable; one bar is allocated to each skier.

JET TURN In this parallel turn, body weight is further back than normal as a result of pushing the skis forward.

JUMP TURN An aerial maneuver that is employed when a skier is going at slow speed; essentially a complete turn in the air.

KICK TURN A 180-degree turn executed while moving one ski at a time on level ground.

KLISTER A sticky running-wax employed by skiers on granular and crust surfaces in above-freezing temperatures.

LANDING HILL Jumping-competition landing site.

LEVERAGE A ski-turn effect created when a skier moves his or her weight forward or backward in relation to the center of the skis.

MINISKI A beginner's short ski.

MOEBIUS FLIP A full-twisting forward or backward flip in the air.

MOGUL A bump that generally has been created by many skiers turning on the same spot and pushing snow into a mound.

NORDIC Cross-country and ski-jumping competition.

NORDIC COMBINED Cross-country and ski-jumping event scores are totalled to determine the winner of this competition.

NORM POINT Landing-slope point in jumping competition where skiers are supposed to land.

OPEN SLALOM GATE A gate set with both poles perpendicular to the line of descent.

PARALLEL CHRISTIE An advanced, very graceful version of the skidded turn: the skis are pressed together and throughout the entire turn are kept parallel.

PASGANG A touring maneuver: a kick is done at virtually the same time as a push, with the pole on the same side of the body.

PISTE A ski trail.

PIVOTING Twisting the ski in a different direction by turning the ball of the foot.

POLING Using the skis to move along over flat terrain by pushing with them.

POMA LIFT A seat attached by a bar to an overhead moving cable.

PREJUMP The lifting of the skis into the air on the uphill side of a bump before a crest is reached.

RELEASE BINDING A binding that releases the boot under preset pressure, as in the case of a fall.

ROTATION Body motion around an imaginary axis in the direction of a turn.

ROYAL CHRISTIE An advanced turn executed on the inside ski, with the outside ski lifted off the snow.

RUADE A parallel turn performed by lifting the tails of the skis off the snow and pivoting around on the tips.

RUNNING WAX Wax that holds the ski in position but allows it to move forward when gliding.

SCHUSS High-speed, straight skiing down the fall line.

SIDESTEPPING Climbing by stepping skis sideways and at right angles.

SITZMARK A hole or indentation in the snow created by a skier's backward fall into the snow.

SKI LIFT OR TOW A mechanism that brings a skier to the top of a slope.

SLIPPED TURN A turn made with the skis relatively flat throughout most of the maneuver.

SNAKING The ability of the ski to follow variations in terrain fairly smoothly.

SNOW FARMING Maintaining and conditioning a ski slope's snow.

SNOW MACHINE A mechanism that sprays misted water and creates manmade snow.

SNOWPLOW To ski with the skis in an inverted **V** with tips close and heels apart in order to slow down or stop descent.

SNOWPLOW TURN To use the snowplow position while turning, by weighting one ski in the turn and winding up where that ski points.

SPRING CONDITIONS A cycle of freezing and thawing creating moist and sticky snow surfaces.

STEM Opening the tail on one ski into a **V** position.

STEM TURN To execute a turn by stemming one ski into the **V** position and keeping it there until both skis are moved parallel as the turn is concluded.

STEP TURN A turn executed by lifting one ski, positioning it to the sidewards direction of the turn, then weighting it; the other ski is then brought alongside.

SWING A parallel turn at high speed.

T-BAR LIFT Intended to accommodate two skiers, a lift in which a collection of bars, each shaped like an inverted **T**, is suspended from moving overhead cables.

TABLE POINT The most distant point a skier is expected to land on a ski-jumping landing hill.

TAIL The section of the ski behind the area where the boot is generally placed.

TAKEOFF To leave the ground, as in a jump.

TELEMARK The advancing of one ski ahead of another.

TOURING SKI A ski that is light and narrow and turned up at the front.

TRAVERSE Skiing diagonally across a slope.

TUCK Cutting down wind resistance in downhill skiing, for example, by squatting forward and placing poles parallel to the ground and under the arms.

TWISTING Turning the ski by pivoting the foot and lower leg.

UNWEIGHTING A method of reducing weight on skis just before turning, to make them move more easily.

UPHILL CHRISTIE A turn in which the skis are swung uphill from a traverse; generally used for stopping.

VORLAGE Forward body lean before a turn.

WEDELN A combination of close parallel turns made in the fall line with a minimum of edge set.

WEDGE A common stopping position or slowing-down maneuver accomplished by digging the inside edges of the skis into the snow with the backs of the skis apart and their tips together.

WIDE TRACK The act of skiing with skis parallel but feet positioned as much as 1–1½ feet apart.

SMALL CRAFT BOATING:
Rowing, Kayaking, and Canoeing

ABAFT Toward or at the stern of a boat.

ABEAM At right angles to the boat's centerline.

AFT Toward the back of the boat; the stern.

AMIDSHIPS The center of the boat, midway between the bow and the stern and between the sides.

BACKING (OF WIND) Directional wind change to a counter-clockwise motion.

BACKPADDLE To paddle in reverse, from stern to bow.

BAIL To scoop water out of a boat.

BANG PLATE A protective device for the upright part of a canoe (stem) affixed to the bow.

BEAM The widest part of a boat.

BEARING A direction in relation to a compass point.

BEAR OFF To push off or away from an object (BEAR AWAY).

BEAT To sail into or toward the wind (BEATING).

BEAUFORT SCALE A scale that measures wind velocity, named after the British naval officer who invented it in 1805.

BELL BUOY A buoy with a bell that rings as a result of wave movement.

BEND To secure one thing to another, usually ropes.

BLADE A paddle, or the flat or curved end of a paddle.

BOLLARD A heavy post on a jetty to which lines can be tied.

BOTTOM The underwater part of a boat.

BOW The front part of a boat.

BOWER The main anchor.

BOW PERSON The person who paddles from the front (bow).

BROACH To swing sharply toward the wind, usually in heavy seas and/or winds.

BULKHEAD Partitions that carry flotation.

BUOY A fixed marker in the water that indicates a chart point, navigable waters, danger, etc.

BUOYANCY Flotation, usually made of styrofoam blocks, and often built into canoes by the manufacturer.

BY THE HEAD A condition characterized by a craft more deeply loaded forward than aft.

BY THE STERN A condition characterized by a craft more deeply loaded aft than forward.

CABLE A rope or chain used for towing.

CANADIAN CANOE A craft powered by a person using a single paddle from a kneeling position.

CANOE A vessel with a pointed stern that is propelled by paddles.

CATCH A CRAB To unintentionally dip an oar into the water or have it struck by a wave on the recovery stroke in rowing.

CENTER OF BUOYANCY The center of underwater volume of a boat.

CENTER OF GRAVITY That single point of a vessel to which every other part is gravitationally attached.

CHART A navigational map.

CHINE The place where the sides and hull of a boat meet.

COAMING A raised frame for protection around the cockpit.

COCKPIT The hole cut into the boat for the paddler to sit or kneel in.

COURSE The route of a boat.

COXSWAIN A nonrowing crew member who directs the race and sets the beat (COX).

CREW A rowing team; the operators of a racing shell.

CREW RACING The sport of rowing.

DEAD RECKONING Calculation of the exact position of a vessel.

DEAD WATER The water near the stern of a boat, which appears to be flat.

DECK The upper surface of a boat, which has openings to admit the paddler into the cockpit.

DISPLACEMENT The amount of water displaced by the underwater volume of a craft.

DOUBLE BLADE A canoe or kayak paddle with blades at each end that are generally positioned at different angles (DOUBLE PADDLE).

DRAFT A boat's depth beneath the water (DRAUGHT).

DRAG Resistance to forward motion, especially in shallow water.

DRIFT The carrying along of a vessel by currents in the water. Also, the rate of a current, measured in knots.

EBB The tide falling.

EDDY A limited, circular movement of water.

EIGHT A racing shell with eight oars used in rowing.

ELITE A rowing oarsman in a winning boat in a major championship competition. Also, an event for elite oarsmen crews.

EVEN KEEL A craft that is evenly balanced.

FAIRING A structure designed to reduce drag.

FATHOM A measurement of the depth of water: one fathom equals six feet.

FEATHER To turn oars or paddles in such a way that there is a minimum resistance to their movement.

FEATHERED DOUBLE PADDLE Maximizing paddling efficiency by having one blade pull while the other one recovers water.

FERRY GLIDE The movement of a canoe or kayak from one side of a stream to another by angling the stern against the current and backpaddling.

FINISH The lifting of an oar from the water and the beginning of a recovery.

FLARE The upward curve of a craft's bow or its top overhang.

FLOOD The rising or incoming tide.

FORE Forward.

FOULED ANCHOR An anchor that has a turn of its cable caught around it or that is stuck on something.

FOUR A four-oared racing shell or its crew (in rowing).

FOURS Four-oared-shell competition (in rowing).

GALE A forceful and brisk wind of 32–63 mph.

GEAR Canoe or kayak camping-trip equipment.

GIRTH Generally, the hull's circumference at its biggest section.

GRP Fiberglass (Glass-Reinforced Plastic).

GUNWALE A general reference to the tops of the sides of a canoe (GUNNEL).

HEAD-OF-THE-RIVER RACE A rowing competition in which the shells begin at different intervals (HEAD RACE).

HEAVE TO To stop or maintain a minimum speed in a heavy sea.

HEEL To tilt or tip.

HITCH TO To make fast to another object by using a rope.

HOGGED A term referring to when the center of a boat is higher than its ends. If this condition results from intentional design, it is called REVERSE SHEER.

HOGGING A convex strain on a craft through its fore-and-aft axis.

HOG TO To thoroughly scrub.

HOLD A canoeing stroke that stops the craft's forward motion; reverse paddling or holding the paddle in the water with its blade perpendicular to the canoe's movement are two versions of the hold.

HULL The containerlike lower part of a canoe, kayak, or shell.

INBOARD To be within—generally near the center—of a craft.

J-STROKE A maneuver in canoeing that is used to adjust the trim or compensate for drifting sideways: a stroke that resembles the shape of the letter *J* is made as a variation after a normal stroke is completed.

KAYAK An Eskimo canoe composed of sealskins stretched over a wooden frame that cover the entire craft except for a little hole in the upper-center half, where the paddler sits.

KEDGE A small anchor used by canoes and kayaks.

KEEL The backbone of a boat. Also, a fixed extension at the bottom of a boat for greater stability.

KING PLANK A deck's center plank.

KING POST A deck's vertical post.

KNEES Angular pieces of frame or metal that frame a vessel (ELBOWS).

KNOT A nautical measure of speed: "one knot" means one nautical mile per hour. (A nautical mile is equal to one minute of latitude or longitude, and is 1.15 statute miles.)

LASH To secure with a rope (LASHING).

LATITUDE Degree measurements north or south of the equator.

LAUNCH To set a boat afloat.

LDR Long-Distance Racing.

LINE Small length of rope used to tie or tow a canoe (PAINTER).

LOA Length OverAll.

LONGITUDE Degree measurements east or west of the prime meridian at Greenwich, England.

LWL The Load Water Line, which notes the length of the waterline along the hull when either empty or loaded.

MOLD A method of manufacturing canoes through the use of two molds, one forming the hull and the other forming the deck; the mating of the two creates the craft.

OARLOCKS Square holes or U-shaped devices that hold the oars in place (ROWLOCKS).

OARSMAN A racing-crew member who pulls an oar (*female:* OARSWOMAN).

OPEN A boat without a deck.

OUTBOARD An auxiliary engine over the side of a craft.

OUTRIGGER A supporting frame that holds the oarlock out from a racing shell's side.

POOPED A condition in which large waves break onto a craft's rear.

PORT The left side of a boat.

PORTAGE A place where a canoe is carried over land to avoid an obstruction.

PORTAGED The act of carrying a canoe overland.

PRAM A dinghy of Norwegian style, generally with a flat bottom and square ends.

PUNT A long, flat-bottomed English boat.

QUADRUPLE SCULLS Four-man sculling competition (in rowing) (QUAD).

RACE Disturbed and generally fast-running water.

RAPIDS Swiftly moving stretch of water.

RECOVERY The raising, feathering, and bringing toward the boat's bow of the blade after a stroke is completed and just before the next one is begun.

REGATTA A series of rowboat, sailboat, or speed-boat races.

RIDE At anchor or on moorings.

ROWING The propelling of a boat by one oar with both hands.

ROWING TANK A big tank of water containing a simulated shell where rowing strokes and techniques are practiced.

SCULLING The simultaneous pulling of two oars positioned on opposite sides of the boat.

SHOOTING Going over falls and rapids.

SKEG The rear part of a keel; the metal socket that supports the rudder's bottom.

SKIN The outer covering of a hull.

SLAP SUPPORT A corrective stroke used to stabilize a canoe or kayak in which the flat of the paddle blade strikes the water.

SLIDING SEAT A racing shell's seat, positioned on wheels that slide on metal tracks attached to the shell's frame; this enables an oarsman to maximize the strength of his limbs and back.

SOUNDING A measuring of the depth of the water by paddle, pole, or weighted line.

SPRAY COVER A sealing device fitted around the cockpit's raised frame and the paddler's waist (SPRAY SKIRT).

SPRAY DECK An artificial canvas deck used to keep the spray out of the canoe's hull.

SQUARE A rowing maneuver in which the paddle blade is moved vertically at the beginning of a stroke in anticipation of entry into the water.

STARBOARD The right side of a boat.

STEM The upright part of the front of a canoe.

STERN The rear of a boat.

STERN PERSON The person paddling from the stern in canoeing.

STERNPOST The upright part of the back of a canoe.

STRIKE To put the oar in the water to start a stroke. Also, to row at a specific rate.

STROKE To push or pull a paddle or oar to propel a boat. Also, the person who paces the other crew members and sits in the sternmost seat in rowing.

SWEEP A long oar used by racing shells.

SWEEP STROKE A canoeing stroke that turns the craft by sweeping the paddle through the water.

TELEMARK A turning stroke executed when the boat is moving forward by leaning on the paddle and pivoting quickly about.

TIGHT Watertight.

TIPPY A condition of instability on the part of a craft.

TOPSIDES The sides of a boat above the waterline.

TOW To pull a canoe or kayak.

TRANSOM A broad, nearly vertical stern.

TRIM The balance of a boat.

TUMBLE HOME A feature that helps canoes stay dry where the beam is narrower at deck level than at the waterline.

UNDER WAY The condition of moving through the water.

VEER A clockwise wind change.

WAKE Disturbance in the water caused by the drag or resistance of a vessel as it passes through water (WASH).

WAKE HANG To surf on the bow wave or wake of a boat (WASH HANG; WAKE SURFING).

WASH To illegally move ahead of another rowing shell, making the other crew row in the wake of the offending craft.

WATERLINE The dividing line between a boat's topsides and underbody.

WHERRY A narrow exercise rowboat operated by one person with sculls.

SOCCER

ACTIVE RESISTANCE To use force in opposing another player.

ADVANTAGE RULE A regulation that mandates that play is not stopped for a violation if the offending team has not gained an advantage or if stopping play would place the offended team at a disadvantage.

ANGLE OF POSSIBILITY The angle created by imaginary lines drawn from the ball to each upright of the goal within which the ball must enter to score a goal.

ANTICIPATION Judging an opponent's action and moving into position to react accordingly and effectively.

ASSOCIATION FOOTBALL The British name for soccer.

ATTACKING TEAM The team in possession of the ball.

BACKFIELD Mainly defensive players: halfbacks, fullbacks, goalkeeper.

BACK FOUR In modern soccer, the four defenders.

BACK PASS A pass by a player to a teammate behind him.

BACK UP Playing behind a teammate to strengthen the defense or to receive a pass.

BANANA SHOT A forceful shot at the goal: the ball is kicked off center and curves in flight.

BEAT To reach a ball before an opponent does, or to outmaneuver an opponent through effective dribbling, or to get the ball.

BICYCLE KICK An acrobatic technique in which the ball is kicked overhead as the kicker lands on his back.

BOOK The recording in a book by the referee of the name or names of players guilty of unsportsmanlike behavior; this action is a warning to a player that he might be removed from the game if the unsportsmanlike behavior is repeated.

BOOT To kick the ball.

BOOTER A soccer player.

BOUNDING BOARD A goal-size structure used for kicking, passing, and ball-control drills (KICK BOARD).

BOX The ''18-yard box'' penalty area.

BULLY Frenzied and confused action with several players trying to gain control of the ball, generally in front of the goal mouth.

BUNCH A situation where two or more players from the same team move into the same area of the field as another teammate.

BYE A shot wide of the goal that crosses the goal line.

CAP To choose a player to compete for a national team in international competition.

CARRY(ING) A goalkeeper violation that involves his going beyond the four allowed steps without bouncing the ball.

CATENACCIO SYSTEM A line-up that has two strikers, three midfielders, and four defenders in the defensive side of the field, plus a sweeper positioned in front of the goalkeeper.

CAUTION A warning given by the referee to a player that involves the referee's holding up a yellow card and writing the player's name in a notebook.

CENTER The act of passing the ball in the air from a side-line position back toward the center of the field and, if possible, in front of the goal of the opposition.

CENTER CIRCLE A ten-yard-radius circle at the center of the field.

CENTER LINE A straight line dividing the field of play in half that runs from side line to side line.

CHARGE A legal move that results in the unbalancing of an opponent through shoulder-to-shoulder contact.

CHARGING Intentionally pushing an opponent away from the ball or throwing him off balance.

CHEST TRAP The act of trapping the ball with the chest in order to control the ball as it falls to the ground.

CHIPPING A short, raised pass made with the instep or inside of the foot. Also, the act of lifting the ball over the head of an opponent.

CLEAR (CLEARANCE) A throw or kick, usually by the goal-keeper, that sends the ball out of danger from his end of the field.

COMBINATION A play that involves two or more members of the same team who work together to outsmart the opposition.

CONTAINMENT The act of keeping the opposition restricted to a certain area of the playing field.

CONVERT To successfully make a penalty kick.

CORNER The small arc at each corner of the field from which corner kicks are executed.

CORNER FLAG A flag positioned at each corner of the field.

CORNER KICK A direct free-kick given the offensive team. The kick takes place from the corner of the field nearest the spot the ball went over the goal line after last being touched by the defending team.

COUNTERATTACK To begin an attack immediately after gaining possession of the ball.

COVER The act of staying very close to an opponent and hampering his ability to play the ball.

CROSS The act of kicking the ball from one side of the field to the other.

DANGEROUS PLAY A play that the referee judges capable of causing injury to a player.

DEAD BALL A ball no longer in play because it has gone out of bounds or the referee has stopped play.

DECOY PLAY A move designed to draw an opponent away from a certain area.

DEFENDER A defensive player, who aids the goalkeeper in protecting the goal.

DEFENDING TEAM The team that attempts to gain control of the ball while defending its own goal.

DEPTH An extra-man advantage that gives a player in possession of the ball several passing chances and additional support.

DIRECT FREE KICK A kick, awarded for major fouls, that is a free kick from which a goal can be scored directly by the kicker.

DISSENT Arguing with a referee, which may result in a player being booked or sent off (ejected from the game).

DRAW To cause an opponent to leave the player he is covering.

DRIBBLE To advance the ball past defenders through a series of short taps with one or both feet while keeping the ball within one stride.

DRIVING THE BALL A hard-hit shot at the goal or a long, well-hit pass.

DROP BALL A method of restarting play after temporary suspension of action whereby the referee drops the ball between two players who will both try to kick or otherwise gain control of the ball.

DROP KICKING The act of kicking the ball the instant it makes contact with the ground.

EJECTION The banishing of a player from the game by the referee.

ELEVEN A soccer team (XI).

END LINE The boundary line that marks the end of the field.

EQUALIZER A goal that ties the score.

EUROPEAN CUP Championship competition played by teams representing member nations of the European Football Association.

EUROPEAN CUP WINNER'S CUP Championship competition played by national champions of the European Football Association.

EXTRA TIME Additional playing time at the end of a game that is caused by unusual delays during the game and for which there were no time outs permitted (STOPPAGE TIME).

FA CUP The postseason championship tournament and trophy of the British Football Association.

FAR POST The goal post farthest from the kicker.

FEED Passing the ball to a teammate who can shoot for a goal.

FEINT A deceptive move to mislead or confuse an opponent (FAKE).

FIFTY-FIFTY BALL A loose ball that both teams have equal opportunity to bring under control.

FIRST-TIME KICK Kicking a ball without trapping or controlling it.

FISTING Punching at the ball with the fist(s).

FLICK Passing the ball with a strong, outside-of-the-foot movement (JAB KICK).

FORMATIONS Line-ups on the soccer field. Players today are broken down into three groups: defenders, midfielders, and forwards. The goalkeeper is omitted, for no matter what the formation, his position is always the same.

FORWARD Mainly an attacking player whose job is to create and score goals.

FOULING Illegally using the hands or body against an opponent, which can lead to a direct free kick for the opposition.

FOUL THROW An illegally executed throw-in.

FREEBACK A player not specifically designated to mark or guard an opponent (SWEEPER; LIBERO).

FREE KICK A unhampered kick of a stationary ball awarded a team when an opponent commits a foul.

FRIENDLY A game between two international teams before the beginning of regular international competition (British term).

FULL TIME The close of the game.

GARRISON FINISH A last-minute, surprising victory.

GIVE AND GO Passing the ball to a teammate and running to a position to receive the return (WALL PASS).

GOAL The target area, 24 feet wide by eight feet high. Also, the score made when the ball passes between the goal posts beneath the crossbar.

GOAL AREA A marked area in front of each goal that is 20 yards wide by six yards deep.

GOAL AVERAGE The difference between goals scored and goals allowed by a given team during a set period; this statistic is used to break ties of teams with the same won–lost record and to determine which moves ahead in competition.

GOALKEEPER The final line of defense and the only player permitted to use his hands within the field of play, with the restriction that this is done within the penalty area.

GOAL KICK A type of kick performed by a defender when the ball last touched by an attacking player passes over the goal line without going into the goal; the ball must be kicked from inside the team's goal area and must go beyond the penalty area of the team.

GOAL LINE The boundary line at the ends of the field.

GOAL MOUTH The area immediately in front of the goal, between the goal posts and the crossbar.

GOAL POSTS Usually wooden posts between four and five inches in width and depth.

HALFBACK A defensive player who usually plays in his defensive half of the field between the forward line and his goal and whose job it is to guard opposing forwards. Halfbacks are designated by the part of the field they occupy: left, right, center. The halfback is not restricted to defense, however, and may initiate an attack (MIDFIELDER; LINKMAN).

HALF TIME The end of the first 45-minute period of play.

HALF VOLLEY Kicking the ball just as it rebounds off the ground.

HANDLING Intentionally playing the ball with the hands, arms, or shoulders.

HANDS Illegal act of intentionally touching the ball with any part of the hands or arms.

HAT TRICK Scoring of three goals in one game by the same player.

HEADER A shot or pass made by hitting the ball with the head.

HEADING Hitting the ball with the front part of the forehead to pass, score, or control the ball.

HEDGING A stalling action where the player backs up while containing an opponent with the ball so that his defense can recover their position.

HOLDING Obstructing a player's movement with hand or arm.

HOOK TACKLE A tackle made by dropping down to one knee and at the same time extending the other leg to hook the ball away from the opposing player (SLIDING TACKLE).

INDIRECT FREE KICK A kick from which a goal cannot be scored directly unless touched by another player.

INDIRECT PASS A pass that requires a player to move to a certain position to receive the ball.

INDOOR SOCCER A version of soccer played in an indoor hockey arena. The ice is replaced with a floor, and walls surround the playing area to contain the ball. There are six members to a team, including a goalkeeper. The goals are 16 feet high and four feet wide. The game consists of three 20-minute periods. Fouls are penalized by suspension for 2–5 minutes of the guilty player, during which time his team plays shorthanded.

INJURY TIME Time added on to the end of a game to make up for time lost in the treatment and removal of a player who has been injured.

INSIDE FORWARD Either of the two forwards who usually play between the wings and center forward.

INSIDE-OF-THE-FOOT KICK A kick made with the inside edge of the foot, driving the ball to the side or diagonally forward.

INSTEP The part of the foot covered by the laces of the shoe, most often used for kicking.

INSWINGER A corner kick or cross that swings the ball in the air toward the goal mouth.

INTERCEPTION Gaining possession of the ball before it reaches the intended receiver of the other team.

JOCKEY The giving of ground by a defender in order to gain time.

JUMP KICK A kick made by jumping into the air and kicking the ball while it is two or three feet off the ground.

KICK IN Putting the ball in play when it goes out of play over the side line. In women's soccer, a free kick at a stationary ball on the touch line after the opposing team has driven the ball into touch.

KICKOFF A place kick executed from the center of the field at the start of the game, at the start of each period, and after each score.

KICK TO A STOP Kicking the ball to an open area where a teammate can reach it before an opponent.

LATERAL MOVEMENT Side line-to-side line movement.

LEAD PASS A pass aimed ahead of the intended receiver so that he can pick it up and drive on without breaking stride.

LINEMAN A forward.

LINESMEN Two officials who are assistants to the referee and who primarily aid in indicating when the ball has gone over the side lines.

LINKMAN Another name for a midfielder.

LIQUID CATCH Catching the ball with relaxed fingers and hands and arms drawn to the body.

LOFT (LOB) A high, soft kick taken on the volley; usually a kick over the heads of the defense.

LONG BALL A long pass.

LUNGE To execute a long stride, putting weight on the foot that is moved.

MARK(ING) Covering and guarding an opponent so closely that it becomes very difficult for him to receive a pass.

MARKER A score.

M FORMATION A formation resembling the letter *M* in which the five-man forward line assembles so that the outside forwards and the center forward play in a line relatively far from the goal, while the inside forwards play close to the goal. (Compare to a W FORMATION.)

MIDFIELDER A player with both offensive and defensive responsibilities whose main job is to link up forwards and defenders (LINKMAN).

MISKICK A poor kick.

MOVING Dribbling.

MOBILITY Constant movement by players to create and use space.

MULTIPLE OFFENSE The movement of players allowing the creation of several offensive patterns.

NEAR POST The post closest to the kicker.

NET Mesh fabric attached to and behind the goal, helpful in judging whether a goal has been scored.

OBSTRUCTING Intentionally blocking an opponent by standing in his path.

OFFSIDE A player out of position. In women's soccer, a player is offside when she is in the attacking half of the field and there are less than *three* defenders between her and the goal.

OFFSIDE LINE Either of two lines marked across the playing field parallel to and 35 yards from each goal line. These lines are used in American professional soccer in place of the halfway line to determine offsides, and are analogous to the blue lines in ice hockey.

ONE BOUNCE A delayed game (for example, stadium lights go out) is resumed by the referee dropping the ball at midfield between two opposing players, where it is played after bouncing once.

ONSIDE In a legal position with respect to the ball: being behind the ball when it is driven into the attacking part of the field, or having at least two defenders nearer the goal when the ball is being played by a teammate.

OUT OF BOUNDS A situation that takes place when a ball is completely over the end line or touch line.

OUT OF PLAY A situation that takes place when a ball goes off the field, the goal line, or the side line.

OUTSIDE FORWARDS The two forwards in a five-man forward line who usually play along the sides of the field.

OUTSIDE HALVES The two halfbacks who usually play near the sides of the field.

OUTSIDE LEFT The left wing forward.

OUTSIDE RIGHT The right wing forward.

OUTSTEP The outer surface of the instep.

OUTSWINGER A corner kick or cross that swings the ball in the air away from the goal mouth.

OVERLAP The attacking play of a defender moving down the touch line past his own winger.

OWN GOAL A goal that a defensive player accidentally knocks into his own goal.

PASS To kick or head the ball to a teammate.

PASS-BACK A pass made back to one's goalkeeper, usually in a pressure situation.

PASSIVE RESISTANCE Opposing with little effort.

PENALTY AREA A portion of the playing field in front of each goal; a foul by a defending player within this area results in a penalty kick for the opposing player. In men's soccer, the penalty area is 44 yards wide by 18 yards deep and centered on the goal. A ten-yard arc extending from the penalty kick mark beyond the far end of the area serves to extend the penalty area during a penalty kick, since no player except for the kicker is permitted to stay within ten yards of the ball. In women's soccer, the penalty area is a semicircle with a 15-yard radius centered on the goal.

PENALTY GOAL A goal scored on a penalty kick.

PENALTY KICK A direct free kick, taken from the 12-yard spot in front of the goal, that is awarded for fouls committed by the defending team within their own penalty area.

PENALTY MARK The spot 12 yards directly in front of each goal, usually indicated by a short line. It is from this mark that the penalty kick is taken.

PENALTY SPOT A spot 12 yards from goal from which penalty kicks are taken.

PENETRATION Accurate and quick advancing of the ball in a scoring attempt.

PITCH A British name for the playing field.

PIVOT INSTEP KICK A kick made by swinging the leg around in front of the body, hitting the ball with the instep, and driving it to the side rather than straight ahead.

PLACE KICK A kick at a stationary ball placed on the ground.

PLAY THEM OFFSIDE A method of making offensive players move away from the goal.

POSITION The area of the field occupied by a player.

PULL To remove a goalkeeper when trailing late in a game and replace him with an additional offensive player to increase the chances of scoring.

PUNT To kick a ball as it is dropped from the hands.

PUSH PASS A pass made by shoving the ball with the foot instead of kicking it.

READ Anticipating and getting set for action that may take place; understanding and reacting to the strategy of the opposition (READING THE GAME).

RED CARD A card used by the referee in international soccer to indicate that a player is being ejected from the game.

REFEREE The official responsible for the timing and control of the game.

RIDING A BALL A means of cushioning the impact of a ball, reducing its speed, and bringing it under control that is executed by a player giving at (or relaxing) the part of the body where the ball hits.

RUNNING OFF THE BALL Player movements into pass-receiving positions.

SAG OFF To move away from an opponent being marked.

SAVE The goalkeeper stopping an attempted goal by catching or deflecting the ball; any prevention of the ball from entering the goal.

SCISSORS KICK A kick made by jumping up and kicking first one leg into the air and the other, which sends the ball above the head, usually to the rear of the player.

SCORE To get the ball to pass over the goal line between the uprights and under the crossbar, without it being interfered with by the goalkeeper or another defensive player.

SCORING CHANCE An opportunity to take a shot at goal.

SCREEN Keeping possession of and protecting the ball by placing one's body between the ball and the opponent.

SENDING OFF The dismissal of a player from the game by the referee.

SET UP To kick the ball aloft and get it to land near the goal.

SHEPHERD To maneuver opponents into less dangerous positions while retreating.

SHOOTOUT North American Soccer League procedure used when teams are tied after playing two sudden-death overtime periods: the teams take five alternating shootout attempts at opposing goalkeepers in one-on-one situations.

SHOT An attempt to score by kicking or heading the ball toward the goal line.

SIDE FOOT A shot or pass made by kicking the ball with the side of the foot.

SIDE LINE The long side of the field-boundary line.

SKIED A ball kicked needlessly high into the air.

SLIDING TACKLE An attempt to take the ball away from the opponent by sliding on the ground, extending the leg, and hooking the ball.

SOLE KICK A kick in which the sole of the shoe is put on top of the ball and the ball is pushed forcefully to the rear (SOLE-OF-THE-FOOT KICK; SOLE TRAP).

SPACE Open areas on the playing field that can be used by the offense.

SPLIT TACKLE A tackle in which one foot is stationary and the other is aimed at the ball, as the tackler ends up on the field in a position resembling a split.

SPOT KICK A stationary-ball kick; another term for the penalty kick.

SQUARE BALL Passing across the field approximately parallel to the goal line.

SQUARE PASS A pass pushed laterally across the field to a player moving forward.

STALEMATE Two players facing each other, each waiting for the other to make a move (STAND-OFF).

STANCE The position of a player's feet.

STOP A catch or deflection of a shot by a goalkeeper.

STOPPER BACK The back who plays near the center of the field, usually the center halfback.

STRIKER A central forward position whose major responsibility is scoring goals.

STRONG FOOT The foot a player is more skilled in using.

SUSPENDED BALL A free-swinging ball that is employed as a training aid.

SWEEPER A defensive player who roams either in front or behind the defender-line to pick up loose passes.

SWERVE KICK A kick with the outside of the foot that makes the ball swerve in flight.

SWITCH The act of one player exchanging places (position) with a teammate, and vice-versa.

TACKLE (TACKLING) Attempting to kick the ball away from an opponent, to make him lose control of it, to cause him to hurry his pass. Tackling takes place when both players are playing the ball with their feet.

THROUGH PASS A pass that goes through two opposition players to a teammate.

THROW IN The means of resuming play after the ball has gone out of bounds at the sidelines: an opponent of the team that sent it out is given the ball to throw back in.

TOUCH Out-of-bounds area, outside of the touch lines.

TOUCH LINE Boundary lines on the side of the field; the side lines.

TOUCH-LINE KICK A free kick from the touch line performed from the spot where the ball left the playing field.

TRAP(PING) A method of controlling the ball by stopping it with the feet, chest, thighs, or head.

TRIPPING Intentionally throwing or trying to throw a player.

UNGENTLEMANLY CONDUCT Striking an opponent, etc., which can result in a player being dismissed from the game.

VOLLEY(ING) Kicking a ball while it is in the air.

WALL A lined-up barrier of 3–7 defenders positioned near the goal to help the goalkeeper in his defense against a free kick and to block as much of the kicker's view of the goal as possible.

WALL PASS A pass that is immediately kicked back to the passer so that it resembles a ball bouncing back from a wall (GIVE AND GO).

WEAK FOOT The foot a player is less skilled with.

W FORMATION A five-man forward line formation resembling the letter *W* in which the outside forwards and the center forward play in a line close to the goal, while the inside forwards play far from the goal. (Compare to M FORMATION.)

WIDTH The holding of wide positions on the field by players to facilitate passing over the entire width of the field.

WING The area of the field near the touch line.

WINGER A right or left outside forward; the forwards nearest the side lines.

WING HALFBACKS The halfbacks on either side of the center halfback.

WORLD CLASS Of the highest caliber in the world—"world class soccer," for example.

WORLD CUP A world championship competition held every four years. Each nation, generally represented by its best players, engages in regional competition until there is a final elimination competition of 16 teams. The World Cup trophy is won permanently by any national team that wins the World Cup three times.

YELLOW CARD A warning card held up by the referee to indicate that a player has committed a serious foul and is thereby being cautioned.

SQUASH

ACE A shot that an opponent cannot touch with his racket.

ALLEY SHOT A shot hit straight along the wall (RAIL SHOT).

BACKING ON THE BALL The backing up of a player to get a ball that has hit a side wall, then the back wall, and then breaks toward the middle of the court.

BOAST In the direction horizontally across the court.

BOAST FOR NICK A shot that is hard hit onto the side wall.

CORNER SHOT A shot that hits the corner and then returns.

COVERING A SHOT The position assumed by a player to physically block various returns by an opponent.

CROSSCOURT SHOT A shot against the front wall hit in such a manner as to land across the court (V SHOT).

DIE The failure of a ball to bounce.

DOUBLES Squash played by four people (two on a side) in a larger court than singles (45 feet by 25 feet, as compared to 32 feet by 18½ feet). A livelier ball with a red dot is used.

DRIVE A ball hit with power after it bounces.

DROP SHOT A ball hit softly to the front wall.

FAULT A service-rules violation that, if executed two straight times, results in loss of service and point.

GALLERY An area for spectators.

GET A scrambling return of a difficult shot.

HALL VOLLEY A ball that is hit the instant after it bounces.

LENGTH A term describing a ball that bounces twice or dies before it reaches the back wall.

LET A point that must be replayed.

LET POINT A point awarded to a player whom an opponent deliberately interfered with.

LOB A ball hit high on the front wall.

LOB SERVE An underhand serve.

MIDCOURT The midpoint between the front and back walls.

MONKEY DOUBLES Doubles played with a singles ball on a singles court with rackets whose handles have been cut down.

NICK A ball that hits the juncture of the floor and a side wall, or the floor and the back wall, in such a way that it rolls out and is almost impossible to retrieve.

NO-SET A call made optionally at 13–all or 14–all by the receiver (in both cases the game is won at 15), by a player who does not wish to lengthen a game by demanding that the player must win by two points.

OUT SIDE The receiving side.

PHILADELPHIA SHOT A trick shot; a boast in reverse (PHIL-ADELPHIA BOAST).

PUTAWAY A shot that cannot be retrieved (WINNER).

QUARTER CIRCLE An area where, when serving, a player places his foot (SERVICE BOX).

RALLY A series of shots.

REVERSE CORNER A crosscorner shot; a corner shot in reverse.

SERVICE LINE The line on the front wall that a ball that is served must hit above in order to be in play. The service line is 6½ feet off the floor for singles play and 8½ feet off the floor for doubles play (CUT LINE).

SMASH A hard, overhand swing at the ball that gets it to hit the wall with force.

T That area of the court just in front of the floor service-line and the center service-line—the best spot from which to hit returns.

TELLTALE A 17-inch-high rectangle of sheet metal positioned at the bottom of the front wall that gives off a ringing sound when hit by the ball (TIN).

TOUCH Finesse on the part of a player in hitting corner and drop shots.

TURNING ON THE BALL The act of turning around to get a ball coming off the back wall.

VOLLEY To hit a ball before it touches the floor.

SURFING

ABOVE THE PEAK Along the line of the highest point of a particular swell, to the left or right of the peak.

BACKWASH The water-flow off the beach incline that rushes back to the ocean after a breaker has washed up on shore.

BARGE A big and clumsy surfboard.

BELLY A surfboard bottom; sometimes, a surfback thicker than normal size is referred to as having a "belly."

BELLY-BOARD A board less than three feet long used in body surfing.

BELOW THE PEAK Along the line of the swell, southerly of the peak; to the left or right of the peak.

BIG-WAVE BOARD A board with a pointed tail whose maximum width is in front—a surfboard used for conditions where there are big waves (ELEPHANT GUN).

BLOWN OUT Choppy water that is not good for surfing.

BOARD A surfboard.

BODY SURFING Surfing down the face of the incline of a breaker by sliding along with the front part of the body.

BOUNCING THE BOARD Shifting the board's weight backward and forward to lift the nose of the board out of the water and then let it fall.

CHATTER The sound heard as the surfboard bends and slides over choppy water.

CHOP Rough water surface.

CLEAN-UP SET A set of breakers that brings all surfers to shore.

CLEAN-UP WAVE The biggest breaker in a set.

CLOSE OUT A condition where a wave or waves break along the beach without providing a shoulder for the surfer to ride on (CLOSED DOOR).

CORNER THE WAVE To be on the shoulder and away from the soup, or swirling water.

CRACK THE WAVE To ride the wave.

CRASHING SURF Fast surf: a breaking and rapidly changing condition in which the wave breaks all at once.

CRITICAL A wave with the potential to break at any instant.

CROSSOVER Walking the board by crossing one leg in front of another and moving either forward or backward on the board.

CURL The hollow part of a wave at the instant of its breaking (HOOK; TUNNEL; TUBE).

CUT-BACK To turn back into the hook, or breaking part of a wave.

DECK The top, or standing surface, of a surfboard.

DIG To paddle furiously (SCRATCH).

DOUBLE-ENDER A surfboard that is double-ended, with the fin able to be fastened to either end without changing the ability of the board to perform.

DROP The wave's steepest part.

DUMPER A plunging or crashing wave.

FACE OF THE WAVE The concave, steep part of a wave that faces the shore.

FAST A condition that affords fast surfboarding because the surf has a steep wave that forms a wall.

FEATHER A noncrashing or plunging wave that holds up, with only the top part breaking (SPILL).

FETCH The overall area in which the wind is able to catch the water to create swells; the length of the fetch generally has an effect on the height of the wave.

FIN A stabilizer on the bottom of the surfboard to prevent sideslipping.

FLAT A calm water condition in which there is little or no surf, making surfing unsuitable.

GLASSY A nonchoppy, smooth water surface.

GO-BEHIND To move past another surfer on the wave's seaward side.

GOOFY FOOT Most surfers stand with the left foot forward, but this term describes surfers who position themselves with their right foot forward.

GREEN BACK A swell that has not broken and is on the outside.

GREMLIN A phony surfer who engages in objectionable and improper behavior.

HAIRY A condition in which a surfer's ten toes project over the surfboard's nose while a wave is being ridden (HANG TEN).

HANG FIVE A condition where the toes of one foot project over the nose of the surfboard while a wave is being ridden.

HEAD DIP Showing off; dipping the head into the wall.

HOLD UP The holding together for a few extra seconds of a swell that is threatening to break at a critical point.

HOOK A wave's concave portion (CURL; TUBE).

HOOK A RAIL A situation in which the rail of the surfboard knifes into the water to tip or capsize the board.

HOT DOG A top surfer; a show-off.

HUMP A large wave; a peak; a swell.

INSIDE The wave's side that faces to the shore.

ISLAND To give up a ride by forcing the nose of the surfboard under the water (ISLAND PULL-OUT; NOSE PULL-OUT).

KICK Exerting force on the surfboard's rear by stepping down on it while simultaneously raising the lead foot; this lifts the board's nose out of the water and makes it possible to pivot the board on its tail (KICK OUT; KICK TURN).

KOOK A beginner or a surfer lacking skills.

LATE TAKEOFF Taking off when a wave is very critical.

LINE Fast surf: a condition when the wave walls up with an open door and does not crash; this enables the surfer to ride onto the wave's shoulder (LINE-UP).

LOCKED IN A condition in which a surfer finds a wave too steep to pull out from (HUNG UP).

LOG A big and clumsy surfboard that is difficult to maneuver.

MAKE THE WAVE To move across the wall (out of the hook) prior to its breaking on the surfer and board.

MALIBU BOARD The basic, highly maneuverable, small and lightweight, fiberglass-covered surfboard that is constructed of balsa wood (SIMMONS' BOARD).

NOAH A shark.

OPEN DOOR A breaking wave that allows the surfer to ride away from the peak, out of the hook, onto the shoulder.

OUT OF CONTROL An extremely big breaker or breakers; big surf.

OUTSIDE A breaker's far side; to the seaward side of the swell.

OVERSTRIDING To make an error by positioning weight too far forward on the surfboard and forcing its nose underwater.

PADDLEBOARD A hollow board that is intended for paddling with the arms and hands—not a surfboard.

PASS OVER To slide past another surfer by going high on the wave (GO-BEHIND).

PASS UNDER To go past another surfer while riding a wave on the shoreward side.

PEAK The highest point of a swell; the first part of the swell to break; a swell's steepest portion.

PICK UP A WAVE To catch a wave and get a ride.

PIG BOARD A narrow-nosed and broad-tailed surfboard (PIG SHAPE).

PITCH The rising and plunging of the surfboard's nose.

PLUNGING SURF Surf that is crashing.

POLY A surfboard composed of polyurethane.

PURLING The knifing of the nose of the surfboard under the water's surface (PEARLING).

RAILS Surfboard edges, or sides.

REVERSE A kick-out that sees the rider and the surfboard turn in opposite directions.

REVERSE (SKEG) TAKE-OFF A stunt performed by catching the wave when the surfboard is in a reverse position with the skeg (fin) pointing toward the shore; when the wave is caught, the board is turned about rapidly into the normal attitude.

ROCK DANCE A low-tide chore where surfers walk over rocks seeking to recover their surfboards.

ROCKER The amount of vertical curvature in the profile of the surfboard.

ROLL The rocking or tilting from side to side of a board.

SCRATCH To paddle with vigor.

SECTION A part of a wave that walls up to break in a section of several feet.

SEMIPIG Half as extreme as a pig board; a broad-tailed board.

SESSION A sequence of successive waves (SET).

SHAPE A surfboard's outline revealed when looking straight at the surfboard's deck, or belly.

SHOOT To ride a wave (SHOOT THE WAVE; SHOOT THE CURL).

SHOULDER A portion of the swell that is less steep than the part of the wave near the hook.

SHOWBOATING Hot-dogging, or showing off.

SHUFFLE Moving the feet along the surface of the deck and thus moving weight backward or forward without crossing the legs.

SKEG A fin.

SKIM BOARD A small disc-shaped or rectangular board, generally made of plywood, that is employed to skim over shallow water.

SLOW SURF Gentle, sloping swells; feathering-crest surf conditions that hamper fast rides.

SOUP Swirling and foaming water (SWASH).

SOUP OUT To ride out the soup by moving straight off in a close-out.

SOUTH BAY A squared-off-at-the-end surfboard tail.

SPILLING SURF Slow and/or feathering surf.

SPOOKY Surf conditions that are either hard to predict or difficult.

SPOON The surfboard's nose-upturn that functions in the same manner as the rocker.

STALL To throw the board out of trim and stop its sliding.

STRAIGHT OFF To ride the surfboard directly toward shore.

SURF SKI A wave-riding craft that is long and hollow.

THE AXE The breaking of a wave on top of a surfer that knocks him off his board (WIPE-OUT).

TRAIN A session; a set.

TRIMMING THE BOARD Effective distribution of a rider's weight on the surfboard, positioning it flat against the surface of the water.

TROUGH The depression in front of the breaker.

TUBE A wave's concave face (TUNNEL).

TURN-AROUND A showboat maneuver in which a surfer turns around 360 degrees on the board.

WALL The instant a large length of swell is about to crash all at once; an unsurfable beach (WALL UP; WALL OUT).

WAX The application of paraffin to a board's deck; paraffin.

WEDGE A type of board with stringers (wood strips) placed diagonally and joined at the nose.

WIPE-OUT "The axe."

SWIMMING

ANCHOR The final leg of a relay race.

ANCHORMAN The participant who swims the final leg of a relay race.

BACKSTROKE A swimming stroke in which the swimmer is on his or her back with legs alternately kicking and arms alternately pulling; one of the four primary competitive styles.

BREASTSTROKE A stroke executed face down, with the legs executing the frog kick while the arms move forward and out symmetrically and simultaneously; the oldest stroke, and one of the four primary competitive strokes.

BUTTERFLY A stroke in which the swimmer is face down, with the legs kicking in unison while the arms simultaneously move over and through the water; one of the four primary competitive strokes.

CIRCUIT TRAINING In-and-out-of-the-water training enabling a maximum number of swimmers to work out continuously without wasting time.

CRAWL Face-down swimming: the arms move independently of each other, and the legs kick individually; the most commonly used stroke in freestyle competition and the fastest competitive stroke (often synonymous with FREESTYLE).

DEAD MAN'S FLOAT The lying by a swimmer in a prone position on top of the water, with arms and legs extended.

DOLPHIN KICK The feet move up and down together in this butterfly-stroke kick that resembles the movement of a dolphin.

FLIP A tumbling turn in which the swimmer bends and twists his or her body, pushing off the wall with the feet in a corkscrew movement.

FLUTTER KICK A freestyle kicking maneuver in which the swimmer's knees bend and straighten as each leg and foot presses down underwater; the legs alternately move, two or more times per arm stroke.

FREESTYLE The last leg of a medley race, in which a swimmer may select his stroke; however, the crawl, being the fastest stroke, is almost always used and has come to be synonymous with freestyle; one of four primary competitive styles.

FROG KICK Similar to a frog's leg movements in the water, a kick in which the feet are drawn up behind the swimmer with knees bent and the legs then snap open wide and together; a kick used primarily in the breaststroke.

GET ON THE STROKE Shortening a stroke.

HEAT A qualifying competition.

INDIVIDUAL MEDLEY A competition that requires swimming each leg with a different stroke; the order is generally as follows: butterfly, backstroke, breaststroke, freestyle.

IN PHASE Touching the wall at the finish as part of the downward motion of a final stroke.

INTERVAL TRAINING Training procedure where participants swim prescribed distances repeatedly with specific rest intervals (generally equal to the time of the swimming period).

JAMMING THE PACE The intentional slowing down of the pace in the swimming of a portion of a race.

JUMP The leaving of the starting block too soon in a relay race by a swimmer who takes off prior to his incoming teammate's touching the wall; cause for a team to be disqualified.

LAP The length of a pool from one end to the other.

LEG One fourth of a relay swum by four different competitors.

MEDLEY A competition in which a different stroke is used for each leg.

METER A metric measure equal to 39.37 inches—a distance slightly longer than a yard (a 100-meter race is longer than a 100-yard race).

OVERDISTANCE TRAINING Techniques designed to build endurance in which swimmers swim longer distances than their normal racing-distance.

PACE Swimming rate.

PEAK A carefully planned procedure designed to round a swimmer's mind and body to top form before major competition.

PULLING Using only the arms while swimming.

RECOVERY A swimmer's sweeping arm movements over the water as they are placed in position to begin an underwater stroke (RETURN).

RELAY A competition in which four team members perform either the same stroke or one of four different strokes in a specific order; a combined time score for each team determines the victor.

SCISSORS KICK A sidestroke kick in which one leg is bent and both legs swing open and shut like scissors.

SIDESTROKE A stroke in which a swimmer lies on his or her side, legs performing the scissors kick, the upper arm thrust out and bent to the chin, while the lower arm is thrust forward and bent to the chin.

SPLIT A section of a race: that is, in a 200-meter race, for example, there are four 50-meter splits.

SPLIT TIME The amount of time used up in swimming a specific portion of a race.

SPRINT A short-distance competition.

STREAMLINING Stretching the body to minimize water resistance.

STROKE A particular combination of arm and leg movements and
body position.

TIME TRIALS Approximated racing conditions used to gauge
swimming speed and sometimes employed for the selection of
team members in a specific competition.

WASH A surge of water produced by a number of sprint swimmers
turning at the wall at the same time.

TABLE TENNIS

ANTISPIN A kind of inverted-sponge racket surface used to counter an opponent's spin.

ARC The curved path of a ball in the air.

BACKHAND A stroke or grip in which the back of the hand faces the ball.

BACKSWING The backward racket-movement that takes place before swinging forward into the ball.

BAT A racket.

BLADE The striking surface of the racket.

BLOCK A short, quick, forward defensive shot, generally performed backhand and very close to the table.

CENTER OF GRAVITY The place where a player's weight is evenly distributed—generally around the waist.

CHOP A very open racket-stroke applied to the underside of the ball, giving it reverse spin (CUT).

CHOP SMASH A combination of smash and underspin.

CIRCUIT TRAINING Basic exercise routines performed by a player for a set amount of time, generally 45 seconds.

CLOSED RACKET A racket position in which the top of the racket is closer to an opponent than the bottom.

COUNTERDRIVE A short and quick-stroked shot executed close to the table to respond to an opponent's driving shot.

DEUCE A situation when the score is tied at 20-all or above, in which case it is necessary for a player or team to take two straight points to win the game.

DROP SHOT A shot that just makes it over the net and whose purpose is to surprise an opponent.

DUMMY CHOP A fake chop.

DUMMY LOOP A fake loop.

EXPEDITE RULE A procedure to shorten games between advanced players that is generally put into effect after 15 minutes of play: a point is not allowed to last for more than 26 exchanges, and the point belongs to a receiver who gets the ball back for the 13th straight time.

FAULT A point to a receiver for an improper serve.

FOLLOW-THROUGH Arm, body, and racket movement after the ball is hit.

FOREHAND A stroke or grip with the wrist facing the ball.

FORWARD-DIVING LOOP A low loop, faster than the high-arcing kind.

FREE ARM The arm whose hand is not gripping the racket.

FREE HAND The hand that does not grip the racket.

GET-READY POSITION A stance that is used to await an opponent's serve or return and that provides free movement in any direction.

HANDLE The part of the racket that is gripped.

HIGH-ARCING LOOP Slower than the forward-diving type, this loop goes high in the air.

INVERTED PIPS A racket surface on which pimplelike projections face inward.

INVERTED SPONGE A racket surface on which a sponge layer is covered by inward-facing pips.

LET A situation where no point is scored for either side.

LOB A very high topspin shot—generally a defensive maneuver.

LOOP An exaggerated overspin or topspin shot (OVERSPIN).

LOOP DRIVE A shot with a great deal of topspin (SUPER LOOP).

NEUTRAL POSITION The get-ready stance or position.

NEUTRAL RACKET A racket position in which the racket is virtually perpendicular to the table.

NORMAL BALL A regular shot with no spin on it.

OPEN RACKET The opposite of closed racket: the top of the racket is angled further away from an opponent than the bottom.

PADDLE A racket.

PENHOLD A popular grip with Oriental players: paddle's head is down, the handle extends up between forefinger and thumb which are placed over the front with the remaining fingers braced against the back.

PIMPLES Tiny racket-surface projections that face in or out (PIPS).

PING-PONG A popular synonym for table tennis that sometimes is used to comment negatively on a poorly played game.

PIPS-OUT A sponge-layer surface covered by a rubber surface on a racket; the pips face out.

PUSH SHOT A shot performed with a slightly open racket in which the ball is pushed as opposed to being fully stroked.

RALLY Shots exchanged until a point is won.

RECEIVER The player who returns the serve.

ROBOT A training or practice machine that can be set to serve a ball as quickly and as fast as a player wishes it to.

SANDWICH The designation for compositions of layers of wood, sponge rubber, and pimpled rubber that make up rackets.

SERVE To put the ball into play.

SHADOW STROKING Practicing stroking without a ball.

SHADOW TRAINING Practicing a series of shots and simulating game conditions without the ball.

SHAKEHANDS The racket-grip style popular with many Americans and Europeans in which a player, in essence, "shakes hands" with the racket by gripping it between the thumb and all four fingers.

SIDESPIN A sweeping forehand or backhand shot that makes the ball spin sideways.

SMASH A powerful, quick hit that usually wins a point (KILL; PUT-AWAY).

SPOTTING POINTS A handicap of several points given to an opponent before beginning a game in order to make for a more equal match.

THIRD-BALL ATTACK A server's planned strategy to win the point after the return of service by the receiver.

TOP To lift the ball over the net with a short stroke by snapping the wrist in slightly in an upward direction.

TOPSPIN A stroke in which the ball is rotated back at an opposing player top-over-bottom.

UNDERSPIN A shot in which the ball turns bottom-over-top in its movement toward an opponent (BACKSPIN; REVERSE SPIN).

VOLLEY A ball hit before it bounces.

TENNIS

ACE A point earned by serving a ball that cannot be returned.

AD-IN Advantage to the server.

AD-OUT Advantage to the receiver.

ADVANTAGE A point won by a player after deuce. If the player wins the next point, he wins the game; if he loses the next point, the score returns to deuce (AD).

ADVANTAGE COURT The left-handed service court, where the ball is served when an advantage belongs to one side or the other.

ALL A tie or equal score: "30-all," for example, refers to a tie at 30 in the game.

ALL-COURT GAME A player's ability to perform well from all over the court with all types of strokes.

ALLEY An area on each side of the singles court used to make the court larger for doubles play; the alley is out of bounds for singles play.

AMERICAN TWIST A serve in which the ball is struck with an upward motion, causing it to spin in flight and bounce to the left of the receiver when it hits the ground.

ANGLE GAMES A playing style that uses the angles of the court; specifically, the short angle at which a player hits a forehand shot crosscourt in order to land the ball inside his opponent's forehand side line.

ANGLE VOLLEY A volleying strike angled by an opponent.

ANTICIPATORY POSITION A position a player takes while awaiting the opportunity to serve or return the ball.

APPROACH SHOT A hard, deep shot into the opponent's court that gives the hitter a chance to move up to the net while putting the opponent on the defensive.

AUSTRALIAN FORMATION A positioning of players in a doubles game in which the server's partner stands on the same side of the court as the server (I FORMATION; AUSTRALIAN DOUBLES).

BACKCOURT The area between the baseline and the service line.

BACKHAND A stroke made with the playing arm and racquet across the body and the back of the hand facing the direction the ball will be hit to; a stroke played on the left-hand side of a right-handed player.

BACK ROOM The space between the baseline and the court's backstop or fence (RUNBACK).

BACKSPIN Rotation on a ball resulting from a player hitting down behind it, making the ball spin in the opposite direction from its flight; when the ball hits the ground, it will stop short or bounce backward (UNDERSPIN).

BACKSTOP A behind-the-court obstruction preventing the ball from rolling away.

BACKSWING The initial swinging of the racquet backward in preparation for a forward stroke (RACQUETBACK POSITION).

BAD BALL A ball that does not land in the playing area.

BALL The tennis ball: a hollow rubber sphere with a cemented, fuzzy, white or yellow cloth covering. Also, the word used for the effect of a stroke—for example, a "good-length ball" refers to a stroke that gets the ball to hit the ground near the baseline.

BALL BOY; BALL GIRL One who retrieves the ball for the players.

BASELINE The back line at either end of the court behind which a player must stand while serving.

BASELINE GAME A playing strategy in which a player stays close to the baseline and seldom moves into the forecourt.

BASELINER One who plays a baseline game.

BEATEN BY THE BALL Arriving too late to have a good position from which to return the ball.

BIG GAME A type of play emphasizing a big service and a net attack.

BIG SERVER A player who has a powerful serve.

BLOCKED BALL A ball returned by meeting it with a stiff wrist and stationary racquet (STOP VOLLEY).

BOUND The rising action of the ball off the surface of the court; the rising angle from a first and second impact on the court surface.

BREAK The unnatural bounding action of a ball as it leaves the ground after being hit with a cut or twist stroke.

BROKEN SERVICE A game won by the server's opponent.

BULLET A ball hit with great force.

BYE A player in an elimination tournament who does not have to play in a round and automatically advances to the next round.

CALL The score at a given time in a game.

CANNONBALL A serve that is extremely flat and fast.

CENTER MARK A short line projecting inward from the middle of the baseline that indicates the edge of the area a player must be standing in when serving.

CENTER SERVICE LINE A line that divides the service court in halves and separates the right and left service courts.

CENTER STROP Used on some playing surfaces, a two-inch-wide piece of canvas that fastens the net at the center of the court.

CHALK White-material marking lines on some tennis surfaces. A ball striking a chalked line will often raise white dust, and tennis players talk of "seeing chalk"—indicating their feeling that a disputed ball was in play because it hit the chalk.

CHALLENGE CUPS Trophies offered to winners of lawn tennis competition. The current holders are challenged by other entries for the right to hold the cup. Generally, the holder must compete against the winner of an event annually; a trophy won three times by the same player passes into his or her permananent possession.

CHALLENGER The team or player that wins a preliminary competition for a challenge cup and thus has the right to challenge the champion for the trophy.

CHALLENGE ROUND The final round in a challenge-type tourney. The champion nation, for example, of the previous year awaits the results of the challenging nations' elimination tournament. The winner of the eliminations automatically becomes the challenger pitted against the champion in the championship round.

CHANGE OF LENGTH Shots made with varying lengths—a short shot, a deep shot, etc.

CHANGE OF PACE Changing speeds on shots and/or reversing spin on the ball.

CHANGING COURTS A procedure followed by players at the end of every odd game in a set, in which they change their positions, moving to opposite sides of the net (CHANGE OVER; CROSSOVER).

CHIP A short, angled shot, generally sliced and used to return a serve in a doubles match.

CHOKE To grip the handle of the racquet nearer its head, as opposed to toward the end.

CHOP To give the ball a sharp backspin or underspin by chopping down and under the ball with the racquet.

CIRCUIT The different competitions and tournaments on a player's schedule (TOUR).

CLOSED-FACE RACQUET A racquet that has its face inclined in the direction of an oncoming ball.

CLUB PLAYER One who plays regularly at a club as opposed to on tour.

CONTINENTAL GRIP Using the same grip for forehand and backhand (SERVICE GRIP).

COURT A 78-foot-long by 36-foot-wide rectangle that forms the playing area of the game of tennis. A three-foot-high net divides the court in half. Running parallel and 4½ feet inside the side lines are the service side lines, which function as the boundary lines for the service courts and the side lines for the singles courts. Parallel to the net and 21 feet on each side are the service lines, which are connected by a line that marks two service courts on each side of the net.

COURT MATERIAL The playing surface: grass, clay, hard, synthetic, etc.

COVERED COURT An indoor court, generally used for winter play, that has a synthetic surface and a roof.

CRACK Slang expression for an expert player.

CROSSCOURT A diagonal stroking of the ball from one side of the court to the other.

CURL Spin, cut, or twist placed on the ball as a result of a sharply cut stroke.

DAVIS CUP An international tennis tournament that involves singles and doubles competition between men. The tourney was named for Dwight Davis, who donated the large silver trophy in 1900.

DEAD A ball out of play is dead—when a ball has struck the ground twice anywhere on court or once out of the court; when the ball has fallen into the net; when a player through a rules infraction has lost the point.

DEAD BALL A nonlively ball or one that has lost air pressure and lacks rebounding ability. Also, a ball that has been smashed out of the reach of an opponent—a killed ball.

DEEP A ball that is hit near the opposition's baseline or deep into his or her playing area.

DEEP-COURT GAME A playing style that positions a player deep in the backcourt.

DEFAULT The losing of a tournament match by a player who fails to play; the opposition moves into the next round (WALK-OVER).

DEFENSIVE VOLLEY A volleying stroke made from below the level of the net (LOW VOLLEY).

DEUCE An even score after six points of a game.

DEUCE COURT The ball is served into this right-handed court whenever the score is deuce.

DEUCE SET After each side has won five games in the same set, a tie results; unless a tie-breaker is used, one side must win two consecutive games to win the set.

DIE A term that describes the movement of a ball that scarcely bounces at all.

DINK A softly hit ball that falls just beyond the net (SOFTIE).

DIPPING BALLS Balls barely clearing the net that drop quickly and short.

DOUBLE ELIMINATION TOURNAMENT A competition in which a player is eliminated after losing two matches.

DOUBLE FAULT Two successive misses (faults) in serving.

DOUBLE HIT To stroke the ball twice on the same play—an illegal play.

DOUBLES A game for four players, two on each side.

DOWN-THE-LINE SHOT A ball that hits close to and parallel to the side line.

DRAFT The roster of players entered in an event written out and bracketed in the order they will play.

DRAW The organization of entrants in a tourney. For example, a traditional single elimination tournament will have each competitor's name placed on a separate card. The cards are then selected at random and the names on the cards are entered in the tournament chart as they have been selected. Seeded entrants are not involved in the process, since their positions have been determined beforehand.

DRIVE A hard-hit ball that usually travels quickly from one end of the court to the other.

DROP SHOT A softly hit ball with backspin that just clears the net and lands with a low bounce close to the net.

DROP VOLLEY A shot that resembles a drop shot, but instead of being executed as a ground stroke, it is executed as a volley.

EARNED POINT A point won because of skills of a player rather than because of the error(s) of an opponent.

EASTERN GRIP Generally the most popular tennis grip in the United States: the palm is to the side of the handle when the racquet's face is held in a vertical position, making a **V** between the thumb and forefinger at the top of the handle; in the backhand stroke, the **V** of the hand is toward the front edge of the handle as a result of the hand being placed forward.

EVEN COURT The right court; whenever play is started here, an even number of points has been played in the current game.

FACE The strings of the racquet; the hitting surface. A closed-face racquet indicates that the top edge is turned forward, positioning the hitting surface down toward the ground. An open-face racquet indicates that the top edge of the racket is positioned backward, making the hitting surface face upward.

FALL A shot that bounces twice without being returned.

FAULT A serve that lands outside the proper service court; two straight faults cause a player to lose a point, but not the service.

FIFTEEN (15) The first point won by a player in a game.

FLAT A racquet-head position with the face perpendicular to the court and squarely facing the net (SQUARE FACE).

FLUB To miss an easy shot.

FOOT FAULT A violation that takes place when a serving player steps on or over the baseline; illegal movement of the feet is also a foot fault.

FORCING SHOT A powerful attacking shot that is generally well-placed, deep, and quickly delivered; it is designed to create a weak return or an error on the part of the opposition.

FOREHAND A stroke performed with the palm of the hand facing in the direction of the intended movement of the ball.

FORTY (40) The third point reached in a game. If both players reach this score, deuce is called.

GALLERY The spectators watching a game. Also, an area for spectators to watch the game.

GAME POINT A point that, if won, can clinch a game victory.

GRASS A grass tennis court.

GRIP The way a racket is held in the hand.

GROOVED STROKE A familiar stroke that a player performs automatically.

GROUND STROKE A stroke in which the ball is hit after it has bounced.

HACK To take a clumsy swing at the ball.

HACKER An ineffective player (DUFFER).

HALF VOLLEY A defensive stroke in which a player hits the ball immediately after it has bounced.

HEAD The frame and strings of a racket.

HOLD SERVICE A situation where the server wins a game; holding service each time makes it impossible to lose a set.

KILL A shot hit so hard that it is almost impossible to return (SMASH; PUTAWAY).

LEFT COURT (PLAYER) The partner on a doubles team who is served to in the left court; this court is also called the odd court, or backhand court, because a player with a stronger backhand generally positions himself or herself there.

LET A serve that is done over again—for example, a serve that hits the top of the net before landing in the proper area. Also, a point interrupted by interference that is played over.

LINE BALL A shot that hits the line.

LOB A ball hit high in the air and deep into the backcourt of the opposition.

LOB VOLLEY A shot similar to the lob but more advanced, since a player hits the ball just as it has bounced.

LOOP A ball hit with topspin, making it dip sharply.

LOVE A scoring term that represents zero.

LOVE GAME A game in which the losing player does not score.

LOVE SET A set in which the losing player wins no games.

MATCH A game of tennis.

MATCH POINT A point that will win the match if won by the player who is leading.

MISS To fail to hit the ball, as in a missed swing.

MIXED DOUBLES A match in which a man and a woman form a team for a game of doubles against another man and woman team.

NET BALL A ball that hits the net and goes over, to remain in play (except on a serve).

NET GAME A playing strategy in which a player stations himself in the forecourt.

NET MAN The partner of the server in a doubles game, who positions himself in the forecourt near the net.

NETMAN A tennis player.

NET PLAY Action near the net.

NO-MAN'S LAND Midcourt area where players are especially vulnerable to balls bounced at their feet, forcing them to attempt demanding half-volleys.

NOT UP A ball that bounces twice and cannot legally be played.

ODD COURT The left court: when play is started in this court, an odd number of points in the current game has been played.

ON THE RISE An aggressive playing style in which the ball is returned by a player before it reaches the high point of its bounce; playing the ball "early" cuts down the reaction time for the opposition.

OPENING A good offensive opportunity that if capitalized on, will enable a player to score a point.

OVERHAND A stroke in which the racquet is positioned above the shoulder.

OVERHEAD SMASH A hard overhead stroke that resembles a serve and is used to counteract the lob (SMASH; OVER-HEAD).

OVERSPIN Topspin.

PACE The degree of speed placed on the ball.

PASSING SHOT Hitting the ball either down the line or crosscourt out of the reach of a net player—a technique used by a back-court player when an opponent rushes the net.

PAT BALL DELIVERY A service that is soft.

PLACE To accurately hit the ball to a desired location.

POACH An advanced technique in doubles play that involves a net man vacating his position and crossing in front of his partner to take a ball that would have normally been played by the partner.

POP-UP A high lob to the baseline that is made from close to the net.

POWER GAME A style of play that features hard smashes and serves.

PUSH To stroke the ball with the racquet held flat so that no spin is placed on the ball.

PUT AWAY A shot hit so well that it is virtually impossible for an opponent to return it (KILL; WINNER).

QUARTERFINALS The round in which eight players remain in a singles tournament, or eight teams in a doubles tournament (ROUND OF EIGHT).

RALLY Play after a serve to the conclusion of a point. Also, a series of shots during which both players are able to keep the ball in play.

RANKING The order players are ranked in by associations, based on their quality of play.

RECEIVER The player who receives the serve.

REGISTERED PLAYER A player allowed to keep his or her amateur status even though he or she may register in an open tournament and keep any prize money won.

RETRIEVE To make a long run to return an effective shot made by an opponent.

RETURN To hit the ball back to an opponent; in general, this term applies to the return of a served ball.

RIGHT COURT The doubles-team partner who gets service in the right court (EVEN COURT; FOREHAND COURT).

ROUGH/SMOOTH Trimmings strings wound around racquet strings near the tip and throat; a hitting surface can feel "smooth" or "rough" depending on the type of string winding.

ROUND Single-elimination tournament rounds are numbered up until the quarterfinal round: the first round is the first set of matches played; half the players are eliminated, and the others move into the second round, etc.

ROUND-ROBIN A competition in which each player or team plays every other player or team; the entry that wins the greatest number of matches is the victor.

RUSH THE NET A playing style in which a player, after hitting an approach shot, rushes the net to position himself or herself more effectively to win a point.

SEEDING Ranking teams and/or players on the basis of their ability or potential.

SEMIFINALS The round in which four players remain in a singles tournament, or four teams in a doubles tournament; semifinal winners move ahead to the finals.

SERVER The player who is serving.

SERVICE The served ball.

SERVICE ACE A good serve that cannot be returned by the receiver.

SERVICE BREAK The winning of a game by a receiver against the service of an opponent.

SERVICE COURTS The two areas on both sides of the court that lie between the half-court line and the service side line and extend from the net back to the service line.

SERVICE LINE The rear boundary of the service court—a line 21 feet away from and parallel to the net.

SERVICE SIDE LINE That part of the singles-court side line between the net and the service line that defines the side boundary of the service court in both singles and doubles play.

SET One of the major units into which a match is divided.

SET POINT A point on which the player leading a set can win the game and the set both at the same time.

SET UP An easy shot that an opponent can hit very well and usually score a point on.

SHORT-ANGLE SHOT A crosscourt shot directed near the juncture of an opponent's side line and service line.

SIDE LINE The line at either side of the court that marks the outside edge of the court's playing surface.

SIDESPIN The vertical spinning of a ball like a top.

SINGLE ELIMINATION TOURNAMENT A competition in which the loss of one match eliminates a player or team.

SINGLES A contest between two players.

SLICE A groundstroke or volley hit with backspin; a ball that is served hit with sidespin.

SMASH A powerful overhead swing at a dropping ball.

STOP VOLLEY A stroke aimed at dropping the ball just over the net (BLOCKED BALL).

STROKE To strike the ball with the racquet.

TAKE THE NET To move in close to the net.

TAPE A canvas strip attached to the top of the net (BAND).

TEAM TENNIS Tennis performed by teams; a match equals five sets.

TENNIS ELBOW A painful injury to the elbow.

TENNIS GRIP The (Eastern) grip used to hold a racquet.

TENNIST One who plays tennis.

THIRTY (30) The second point reached in a game.

THROAT That part of the racquet just below the head.

TOPSPIN The spin of a ball in the same direction as its flight, caused by hitting up and behind it.

TRAJECTORY The flight of the ball, which varies according to the stroke used.

TWIST The spin applied to curve a service ball; topspin.

UNDERCUT To hit the bottom of the ball to create reverse spin.

UNSEEDED A nonseeded player—one who is not favored to get through the early rounds of play.

UP AND BACK A doubles-play strategy in which one player positions himself or herself near the net while the other stays in the backcourt.

VOLLEY Return of a ball before it bounces.

VOLLEYER A player who is skilled in volley play.

WESTERN GRIP A grip in which the racquet is placed on the ground face down and the player simply picks it up with the "V" between the thumb and forefinger on the back plate. The player's palm is toward the bottom of the handle, and there is generally no hand shifting for a backhand stroke.

WIDE-BREAKING SHOT A slice service with so much spin on it that the receiver is pulled into or beyond the alley.

WOOD SHOT A stroke in which the ball is hit off the wooden portion of the racquet.

TRACK AND FIELD

AMERICAN HOP A body-positioning technique used for throwing the javelin.

ANCHOR The final or fourth leg (or runner) of a relay team.

ANGLE OF DELIVERY The angle to the ground at which an implement is released.

APPROACH The adjustment(s) or run just prior to executing a throw or jump.

BATON A hollow cylinder passed from one member of a relay team to another.

BLIND PASS A pass of the baton by a relay-team member who is looking forward (NONVISUAL EXCHANGE).

BOX The container in which vaulters place their poles before taking off.

BREAK To leave the starting block before the gun sounds.

BREAKING FOR THE POLE Running to get the inside-lane position.

BREAK MARK A mark made in the landing pit by a performer.

CIRCLE Competitive area for the discus, shot, hammer, and weight throws.

CLEARANCE The space by which a performer clears an object such as a crossbar or a hurdle.

CLOSED POSITION The positioning of a shot or discus to the rear of the right shoulder and hip to get maximum power into the throw.

CROSSBAR A bar about 16 feet long made of wood, plastic, or metal that functions as an obstacle for high jumpers or pole vaulters.

CURB A running track's inside border.

CUT-DOWN The dropping of the lead leg in clearing a hurdle.

DEAD HEAT A tie between two or more runners.

DECATHLON A 2-day, 10-event competition consisting of the following: day 1—100 meter dash, long jump, shot put, high jump, 400 meter dash; day 2—100 meter hurdles, discus throw, pole vault, javelin throw, 1500 meter run. Competition is judged on the basis of points deducted from a maximum score based on an arbitrary standard of time.

DRIVE LEG The leg that provides power for takeoff or stride.

EXCHANGE ZONE A 20-meter-long area in which the relay baton must be passed (PASSING ZONE).

FALSE START A runner illegally leaving the starting block before the gun is fired.

FINISH POSTS Uprights to which the finish tape or string is attached.

FLAT Ground that is level.

FLATS Nonspiked track shoes, generally used by field-event competitors.

FLIGHT A hurdles lane. Also, a round of trials.

FLOP A high-jumping procedure that involves going headfirst and backward over the bar and landing on the back.

FLYAWAY A pole-vaulting procedure that consists of leaving the pole at the peak of a vault.

FOUL LINE A line that a contestant must remain behind in order to have his jump or throw qualify.

FOUL THROW A throw that violates the rules; it is counted as a trial but is not measured.

GATHER Composure intentionally created to generate increased effort, before a long-jump takeoff, for example.

GUIDE MARK A mark on the track made by relay runners to assist them in recognizing the baton-exchange zone.

GUN IS UP A verbal warning that the starter is about to begin the race.

GUN LAP The final lap in a race.

HAMMER THROW A field event throw where a performer hurls a hammer with both hands from a throwing circle 7 feet in diameter; the throw is aimed for distance and the hammer must land in a throwing sector which is bounded by 2 lines extending at a 60-degree angle from the center of the throwing circle.

HANDOFF The baton exchange between the incoming runner and outgoing runner in a relay race.

HEAD WIND A wind blowing against an athlete's or runner's course.

HEAT A preliminary contest that qualifies contestants for the final competition.

HIGH-JUMP STANDARDS Supports that hold the crossbar for the high jump.

HURDLE An obstacle that runners must leap over in a hurdle race or steeplechase. As a verb, to leap over a barrier that is made of wood or metal.

INSIDE LANE The inside part of the track (POLE POSITION).

JOG To run at a slow and even pace.

KICK To accelerate near the end of a race.

KICKER A runner who relies on his "kick" to win a race.

LANES Generally a 4-foot-wide course marked out on a track on which a trackman runs.

LAP A complete circuit around the track.

LEAD LEG The first leg over a hurdle. Also, the first or kicking leg in jumping.

LEAD-OFF RUNNER A relay team's first runner.

LEG A specified distance that must be run by a member of a relay team.

MARATHON A race generally run over public roads—from which traffic has been banned—that is, 26 miles, 385 yards long.

MARK A starting point for a race. A point of check during approach. The point where the long jumper, shot, or discus lands.

MEDLEY A relay race in which the team members run different distances.

ON THE MARK A position taken by a runner directly behind the scratch line that is assumed at the command "on your mark," prior to the "set" command.

ORDER A relay team's running sequence.

PACE A generally predetermined and consistent rate of speed used by a runner.

PASS A decision made by a contestant to decline attempting a jump or throw. Also, the exchanging of a baton in a relay race.

PENTATHLON A 5-event contest that is usually part of women's track and field competitions consisting of the long jump, high jump, 200 meter dash, discus throw and 1500 meter run. Points are awarded according to participant's positions on a scale based on arbitrary standards.

PICKUP ZONE An area 11 yards long in front of the passing zone in which the receiving runner in a relay race may begin running.

PIT A jumper's landing area, composed of cushioning material.

POLE VAULT A field event where a competitor uses a pole to vault over a horizontal bar that is supported by 2 upright bars; each contestant must clear the bar in 3 opportunities, it is then raised to a higher position. The winner is the last contestant to clear the bar in its highest position.

PUSH-OFF A push up and away from the pole at the top of a pole vault.

PUT The technique of pushing the shot in the air.

RECALL The calling back of runners after a false start.

RECEIVER The relay runner receiving the baton.

RECOVERY LEG A runner's nondriving leg.

RELAY A race in which several runners compose a team and each runner runs one leg of the competition.

REVERSE The follow-through after a throw or put that involves reversing the feet.

RUNWAY The approach area to the takeoff board in long jumping, or the scratch line in field competition.

SCRATCH LINE A line that jumpers or throwers may not go over during a trial or that runners may not pass before the gun is fired.

SECTOR LINES Markings that section off where a fair throw must land in the discus throw or shot put.

SHIFT Moving the vaulting pole from the carry position to the vaulting box.

SHOT A sphere made of iron or brass used in the shot-put competition that weighs eight, twelve, or sixteen pounds and is approximately five inches in diameter.

SHOT PUT To heave a shot.

SHUTTLE A relay in which the legs are run back and forth.

SPRINT A race up to 400 meters (DASH).

STAGGERED START Generally used in races around a curve, a starting alignment in which runners are positioned in a staggered manner in order to equalize the distance each must run.

STANDING BROAD JUMP A jump for distance attempted without a running start.

STANDING HIGH JUMP A jump for height attempted without a running start.

STARTING BLOCKS Mechanisms generally anchored to the track against which runners place their feet as an aid in starting a race.

STEEPLECHASE A race in which runners encounter hurdles and a water jump.

STOPBOARD A shot-put mechanism, usually a curved wooden block, anchored to the front edge of the throwing circle that acts to restrain the performer from stepping out of the circle. Also, a board that catches a vaulting pole at the start of a vault.

STRADDLE A high-jumping style in which the performer crosses over the bar on his stomach.

STRAIGHTAWAY The straight area of a track, as opposed to the curved portion.

STRIDE A step in running.

TAKEOFF The act of leaving the ground in a jump or vault.

TAKEOFF BOARD A board used for the takeoff by a running long jumper.

TAKEOFF FOOT The foot that provides drive off the ground.

TAKEOFF MARK (SPOT) The spot from which the takeoff is performed in such competitions as the high jump and the long jump.

THROWING SECTOR The specific arc where a thrown object must land.

TIEING UP The developing of an inability to compete in a track and field event due to nervousness, muscle tightness, etc.

TRAILING LEG The rear or takeoff leg.

TRIAL An abbreviated term for field trial—an attempt made in a field event.

TRIATHLON A women's competition, consisting of three events.

TURN The portion of the track that is curved.

VISUAL EXCHANGE A baton exchange in which the receiver has his eye on the incoming runner until the baton is passed.

WEIGHT MAN A competitor who throws or puts a weight.

WEIGHT THROW A throw in a field event where a specific weight is thrown with both hands from a throwing circle 7 feet in diameter. The weight must land in a throwing sector bounded by 2 lines extending at a 45-degree angle from the center of the throwing circle.

WESTERN ROLL A high-jumping style in which the jumper clears the bar while lying on his side.

WIND SPRINT A short-distance sprint.

TRAMPOLINING
AND TUMBLING

ARABIAN HANDSPRING A handspring made with the legs positioned evenly or together throughout the technique.

ARCH A bowlike position executed with hips thrust forward, spine bent backward, and toes pointed.

ARCH DOWN A chest roll executed downward from a hand balance.

ARM HOOK A quick bending of the elbow that snaps the arm across the chest in an upward-slanting manner.

ARM SWING A quickly raised arm, generally with a straight elbow position.

BACK BEND A backward arch that positions the hands below the head on the mat.

BACK FLIP A 360-degree turn backward from a springing start accomplished without the hands touching anything (BACKWARD SOMERSAULT).

BACK HANDSPRING A springing movement off both feet into a backward arch with a pullover into a handstand that is completed with a spring to the balls of the feet (FLIPFLOP; FLIC-FLAC).

BACKOVER A variation of the flipflop that is executed slowly, with the legs allowed to move apart during the maneuver but not at the start or completion of the technique.

BACK ROLL A tuck off a backward roll that enables the body to perform a 360-degree turn and wind up positioned vertically (BACKWARD ROLL).

BARONI A half-twisting somersault that uses forward-to-backward momentum; a body-whipping somersault aided by a twist to the side to reverse the landing direction (BARANI; BROWNY).

BRIDGE Support for the body by the head and feet, or head, hands, and feet—only in the positions of forward bent or backward arch.

BUCK A diving stunt to the hands followed by a push away and snap back to a leaning-forward stance on both feet.

BUCKING BRONCO A series of quick bucks.

BUTTERFLY A type of slanting cartwheel aerial.

CARTWHEEL Handspring(s) to the side with arms and legs spread.

CARTWHEEL HANDSTAND A cartwheel that is completed with the performer standing on his hands with his toes pointed upward.

CHEST ROLL A backward roll along the stomach and thighs until the toes touch, executed off a roll down from a handstand.

CRADLE A trampolining maneuver that begins from a back drop that half twists the gymnast half forward, with the final stage positioning the gymnast on his back.

DEAD-LIFT JUMP A springing up from a crouch unaided by a previous movement's momentum.

DIVE A roll forward after a headfirst leap in which the feet are cleared before there is hand contact.

DIVING HANDSPRING A dive onto the hands finished off with a front or back spring onto the feet.

DOUBLE BACKWARD SOMERSAULT Two complete turns in the air.

FLANGE A body extension off a backward roll into a hand balance.

FORWARD ROLL A roll forward with the body in a tucked position that moves the gymnast 360 degrees into a finish on both feet.

FRONT BRIDGE The positioning of the body only on the head, the toes, and the balls of the feet, looking down at the mat.

FRONT HANDSPRING A running forward handspring from hands to feet.

FRONT SOMERSAULT Total forward aerial rotation from a takeoff from the feet to a landing on the feet.

FULL GAINER A leaping forward run into a backward somersault, with body motion continuing forward.

FULL TURN Total body rotation on the long axis.

FULL-TWISTING BACKWARD SOMERSAULT A backward somersault that incorporates a full twist, with the body landing in the position it was in at the takeoff.

GAINER A reverse somersault executed with the body moving forward.

HAND BALANCE A position in which the body is poised vertically, the back is arched, the toes are pointed upward, and the performer is balanced on his or her hands (HANDSTAND).

HANDSPRING A forward or backward spring from hands to feet.

HEADSPRING A springing movement from the head aided by leg swing that enables the performer to take off and land with both feet even.

HEADSTAND A handstand with additional body support provided by the top of the head (HEAD AND HAND BALANCE).

JACKKNIFE A position with toes pointed, knees straight, hips flexed, and hands close to or touching the ankles.

JUMP THROUGH A maneuver executed from a face-down, body-and-arms-extended stance that enables the performer to "jump through" the stretched-out arms to a seated position.

KICKOVER A forward somersault initiated by a strong upward and backward kick from one leg and the other leg's spring takeoff.

KIP A projection of the body from a prone-back position to a vertical landing on both feet; a powerful hip snap and leg swing powers the move.

LAYOUT A body extension into an overall arch, legs straightened together, arms up and back.

LEAD-UP TRICK A basic move or trick that helps build skills for more difficult moves.

LEG DRIVE Extending the leg(s) to power the body up or forward.

LUNGE A quick and powerful forward-reaching movement.

MULE KICK A diving forward, into a hand balance, to a springing landing on the balls of the feet.

NECKSPRING A forward roll into a kip (NIP-UP).

NOVELTY A nonstandard maneuver.

ONE-HAND HANDSPRING A spring from a hand to either foot or both feet.

PIKE A position with the body fully bent forward at the waist, the legs straight, the toes pointed, and the hands either extended to the sides or grasping the ankles.

PIKE FULL A forward somersault aided by a leg swing from a pike into a layout.

PRESS A steady pull that enables a performer to move into a hand or head balance.

REVERSE BRIDGE A bridge accomplished with hips thrust up to arch the body with only the head and feet, or head, hands, and feet, touching the mat (WRESTLER'S BRIDGE).

ROLL A turning maneuver in a tucked position, head-over-heels.

ROUTINE A sequence of stunts generally performed in a straight line over a good part of the mat surface.

SHOULDER BALANCE A body position in which weight is placed only on the shoulders and there is a reversed hand placement; the legs are positioned upward.

SIT BACKWARD A fall backward to a seated position.

SNAPDOWN A pushing-off and at the same time downward kick from a hand balance to a balls-of-the-feet, springing landing.

SOMERSAULT A feet-to-feet complete turn in the air.

SPOT To help or guard a performer.

SPOTTER The performance of a move in a small area. Also, a takeoff and landing in almost the same spot.

SPRING A thrusting movement from feet to hands to feet.

SWINGTIME The flow of one stunt into another in such a professional manner that it is difficult to note when one ended and the other began.

THROW A bending forward or arching backward to start a handspring or somersault.

TIGNA A forward somersault after a tinsica landing.

TINSICA A half-twisting cartwheel move that enables the performer to finish by facing in the same position as he began.

TOE POINT Full feet extension.

TRICK A gymnastic maneuver.

TUCK A ball-like body position with knees bent, thighs drawn up tight against the chest, and hands clasping shins.

TWIST A body turn on the long axis.

WALKOVER A handspring with legs spread wide and positioned for a walking stride on takeoff and landing.

WHIP A forceful pullover to build momentum for a stunt.

WHIPBACK A backward handspring.

VOLLEYBALL

ABSORPTION A ''giving with'' the ball as it is hit by the passer.

ACCELERATION The application of forward momentum to the ball when passing.

ACE A serve that either lands untouched or is too difficult to return.

ATTACK Any procedure used to return the ball across the net.

BACK SET An overhand pass employed in sending the ball in a backward direction.

BACKWARD ROLL A tumbling-type fundamental that permits a player to dive laterally for the ball, land without injury, and quickly assume a defensive position.

BLOCK A defensive move by a player in which he or she jumps and reaches above the net to stop an offensive hit.

BUMP An inside-of-the-wrists-and-forearms pass from one player to another.

CATCHING (HOLDING) THE BALL A momentary coming to rest of the ball in the hands or arms of a player—a violation.

CHANGE OF PACE A spike that is softly hit to deceive the opposition.

COURT COVERAGE Offensive and defensive court assignments of a player while the ball is in play.

CUT To come in between another player and the ball.

CUT SHOT An offensive hit that results in a player slicing the ball barely over and parallel to the net, instead of hitting it with power.

DIG A defensive play to bring a spiked ball up into play.

DINK A soft hit that just goes over the net or beyond a blocker's hands.

DIVE AND SLIDE An advanced defensive technique enabling a player to spring forward to play a ball that is apparently out of reach.

DOUBLE ATTACK The ability to leap in the air and hit the ball with either hand.

DOUBLE FOUL Simultaneous fouls committed by players on opposing teams; the play is done over, with the same team that was serving given a chance to serve again.

DOUBLE HIT The hitting of a ball twice in succession by a player.

DRAW The position given in the bracketing of teams for competition that determines which teams a team will be matched against.

DRIBBLING The touching of the ball more than once by a player.

FAKE A feigned spike-swing at a ball by a player to keep the defense back.

FLOATER A spinless serve that performs like a baseball knuckleball.

FOOT FOUL A serving foul that takes place when a player steps on or over the backline.

FOUR-TWO OFFENSE A line-up in which there are four spikers and two setters.

FREE BALL A ball that is easy to handle given by one team to another just to keep the ball in play.

FRONTCOURT The area between the net and the attacking line.

FRONT LINE The front-row players lined up for a serve.

HALF-MOON DEFENSE A semicircular formation, as opposed to regular blocking.

INSIDE Closest to the center of the net.

JAPANESE SET A ball gotten just high enough to clear the net.

JUMP SET A play in which the setter jumps for a pass very close to the net.

KILL An unreturnable spike that scores a point for the offense.

LOW BALL A ball that comes in below the waist.

MYSTERY BALL A ball that curves, floats, drops, zigs, zags.

NET A foul called when any player touches the net while play is in progress.

NET ANTENNA Vertical projections on both ends of the net that aid officials in judging whether the net has been touched during the playing of a game.

NET BALL The hitting of the net by a ball.

OFF-HAND SPIKE A spike executed with the hand away from the setter.

OVERSET A set that goes over the net to the side of the defensive team.

QUICK SERVE A serve made before the opposing team is set.

ROTATION The shifting of positions by players.

ROUNDHOUSE An overhand serve hit with topspin that makes the ball drop.

SCREENING The blocking of the view of a server from the opposing team members.

SERVE To put the ball in play with a hand or arm strike.

SERVING ORDER The order in which team members play their positions and then serve.

SET Placement of the ball near the net to facilitate spiking.

SET-UP A method of setting the ball to another player on the team, which is positioned for such a play.

SHOOT A two-handed set made usually as a dink over the net.

SIDEOUT Failure of the serving team to score; the ball goes to the opposition.

SPIKE A forceful method of driving the ball into the opponent's court via a downward hit at the ball from a position above and close to the net.

SPIKER A player positioned close to the net who is looking for hard, downward hits of the ball.

STRIDE AND FLEX A passing technique in which the upper body is moved into a position in front of the descending ball, even though the lower body does not reach this position.

SWITCH An after-the-serve strategy that has two players exchange positions, enabling a setter to move from the back line to the front line to get the pass and to set the ball for the spiker; a frontcourt-to-backcourt move, or vice-versa, by a player.

TAPE SHOT A ball spiked or hit into the tape at the top of the net that continues on and over the net.

TECHNIQUE MAN A player skilled in spiking, setting, serving, and blocking.

THROW A mishandling foul when the ball is not set or hit cleanly.

WIPE-OFF SHOT A spike deliberately deflected off the blocker's hands.

WEIGHTLIFTING

BARBELL A steel bar approximately six feet long to which circular weights are affixed at each end.

BENCH PRESS The act of a weightlifter lying on a bench on his back and pushing a barbell out from his chest with arms extended, and then returning it to the chest position.

CLEAN To get a weight up to shoulder level by lifting it off the floor in one, nonstop motion.

CLEAN AND JERK The act of getting a weight to shoulder level, stopping, and then jerking the weight up over the head by shooting the arms straight up.

DEAD LIFT The lifting of a weight to hip level and then lowering it to the ground.

DUMBBELL A short, barlike device that can be lifted with one hand and that has balls or discs attached at either end.

INCLINE BENCH A 45-degree-angled bench used for pressing weights or for resting.

JERK The thrusting of a weight over the head from a starting position at shoulder level.

LIFTER Another name for a weightlifter.

OLYMPIC LIFTING International competition that involves only the snatch and the clean and jerk.

POWER LIFTING International competition that involves the
   bench press, the dead lift, and the squat.

PRESS A movement in which only the arms and the back are used
   to push a weight up from shoulder level to above the lifter's
   head (MILITARY PRESS).

SNATCH A lifting procedure performed in one continuous motion
   from the time the barbell leaves the floor until the arms are
   extended overhead; the lifter gets power into the move by
   squatting and then lunging upward with the barbell.

SQUAT A lifting procedure that involves moving from a squatting
   position to a standing position and placing the barbell behind
   the shoulder blades.

STANDARDS Barbell-supporting posts.

SUPER SET Exercises for one group of muscles that are done just
   before a set of exercises for an opposing group of muscles.

WEIGHT A disc that is attached to either a dumbbell or a barbell.

WRESTLING

ANCHOR Firmly holding an opponent to prevent or restrict movement.

ARMLOCK Holding an opponent's arm so that it cannot be moved.

BACKHEEL A backward pull of an opponent onto the mat, accomplished by a wrestler getting behind his man, locking his hands around the waist, and positioning his feet against the heels of the opponent.

BAR ARM The gripping of an opponent's upper arm in the bend of a wrestler's elbow (ARM BAR).

BODY PRESS The positioning of all of a wrestler's weight on top of an opponent who is lying on the mat under him.

BREAK DOWN To strip away arm or leg support from an opponent on the mat and get him onto his side or stomach in preparation for pinning.

BULLFIGHTER A technique used from a neutral standing position that incorporates movements similar to those of a matador avoiding a charging bull.

COUNTER To react to the moves of an opponent with the result that a wrestler is able to secure a hold.

CRAB RIDE A hold that simulates the position of a crab: the wrestler is behind his opponent and has his toes locked behind the knees and his arms around the waist of the opponent.

CRADLE A hold in which the opponent is held in a doubled-up position as a result of his head and one leg being caught between the interlocked hands of the other wrestler.

CRAM A quick shove or jolt without follow-through, as distinguished from a push.

CROSSANKLE PICKUP A takedown method in which the wrestler uses one hand to snatch his opponent's ankle and pushes with his body to move the opponent backward.

CROSSBODY RIDE While positioned generally to the back or behind an opponent, a wrestler locks one of the opponent's arms and scissors the other or opposite leg.

CROSSOVER A takedown method in which a wrestler positioned to the rear of his opponent with arms locked about the opponent's waist, crosses one leg over another and, by dropping to the opposite knee, is able to pull the opponent down and over the outstretched leg.

DECISION In the absence of a fall, a wrestler wins a match on the basis of the most points.

DEFENSIVE POSITION A stance assumed by a wrestler on his hands and knees; a coin flip by the referee determines which position—"offensive" or "defensive"—a wrestler assumes at the start of the second period, if no fall took place in the first period. Reversal of positions takes place in the third period if there was no fall in the second period.

DRAG A takedown method that consists of the grabbing of the upper arm of an opponent and pulling him down.

DRILL Dashing an opponent to the mat with much power.

ESCAPE To recapture a neutral position.

EVIDENT SUPERIORITY The scoring of at least eight points by a wrestler over an opponent, which is victory in a match.

FALL A match-ending situation in which a wrestler pins the shoulders of his opponent to the mat for one second in collegiate competition, or for two seconds in high-school matches.

FAR The side of the body farthest from the opponent.

FIGURE-4 SCISSORS A wrestler's encircling leg's foot locks behind the opposite leg's knee in this hold.

FIREMAN'S CARRY The gripping and placement of an opponent's arm over one's shoulder while positioning one's other arm through the crotch region of the opponent, so as to bring the opponent up onto one's shoulders in anticipation of a takedown.

FLATBACKING A stance in which a wrestler leans forward with his back parallel to the mat surface.

FLYING MARE Facing an opponent, a wrestler grips the wrist of the opponent, pivots, falls to one knee, and forces the opponent over his back and onto the mat.

FREESTYLE A mode of wrestling in which a wrestler may use his legs as scissors for gripping an opponent's arm or leg, but it is not legal to close the scissors around the head or body. Tripping and tackling is also permitted, but the rules ban injurious holds or ones that could cause an opponent much pain (CATCH-AS-CATCH-CAN).

GO-BEHIND To move around and behind an opponent.

GRANBY ROLL An escape technique that resembles a cartwheel performed from a seated position.

GRAPEVINE An intertwining leg hold.

GRAPPLING The jockeying about on the part of wrestlers as they attempt to get holds on each other while on the mat.

GRECO-ROMAN A style of wrestling that bans holds below the waist and the gripping of the legs of an opponent. Hooking, tripping, or lifting an opponent with the legs is also illegal. A wrestler's legs may only be used for support.

GROUND WRESTLING Wrestling on the mat (SAMBO).

GUILLOTINE A crossbody-ride fall that winds up with a wrestler gripping the shoulders of the opponent to the mat and applying pressure to the far leg of the opponent.

HAMMERLOCK The bending of an opponent's arm behind his back.

HEADGEAR Protective ear covering.

HIPLOCK A combination of a headlock and a throw that pulls the opponent over the wrestler's hip.

HOLD The gripping of an opponent.

HOLD-DOWN The art of pinning an opponent on his back to the mat.

LOCK A grip that completely immobilizes the part of an opponent's body that is being held.

MANEUVER A planned movement.

MAT The sport of wrestling.

MATCH The actual wrestling contest: high-school matches in the United States consist of 3 two-minute periods; college matches begin with a two-minute period followed by 2 three-minute periods.

MATMAN A wrestler.

MEPHAM A gripping hold of the opponent's far arm when a wrestler stationed alongside and behind the opponent reaches with both hands around the opponent from either side.

NAVY RIDE A locking of an opponent's waist with one arm and his far leg with the other.

NEAR The side of the body nearest to the opponent.

NEAR FALL A maneuver worth three points in collegiate wrestling, the conditions of which come close to an actual fall but do not meet the full criteria—holding an opponent's shoulders to the mat for one full second.

NELSON, HALF The positioning of a wrestler's arm under the like arm of an opponent while pushing up against the back of the opponent's head at the same time, and thus creating leverage in two directions. Variations of the "nelson" include FULL NELSON; QUARTER NELSON; THREE-QUARTER NELSON.

OFFENSIVE POSITION A stance assumed by a wrestler at an opponent's side, one arm placed around the waist of the opponent and a hand on his elbow. This position is given to a wrestler who has an advantage in a match. It is also determined by a referee coin toss.

OVER-ARM DRAG A swinging body movement from the mat that enables a wrestler to get his body around to the rear of an opponent.

PANCAKE A twisting, off-balancing throw of an opponent.

PENALTY Loss of a point by a wrestler for illegal procedures or unnecessary roughness; two points are lost when these violations take place for the third time.

PILE DRIVER A professional technique in which a wrestler lifts his opponent and slams his head to the ground.

PIN A method of winning a match by holding an opponent's shoulder blades to the mat for a full second in collegiate competition, or two seconds in high-school matches (FALL).

POINTS Ratings assigned wrestlers in evaluating their match performances: near fall (3), takedown (2), reversal (2), predicament (2), time advantage of two minutes or more (2), time advantage of one minute (1), escape (1).

POST To firmly fix an arm to the mat surface for use as a support in the execution of a technique.

PREDICAMENT Outmoded term for NEAR FALL.

PRINCETON LOCK A three-quarter nelson and leg lock combined.

REFEREE'S POSITION Stances that begin the second and third periods of a match. The top wrestler is on offense while the other wrestler, on the bottom, is on defense. The ability to use an advantage or to escape from a bad position can then be evaluated.

REVERSAL The moving from a handicapped position to one of superiority over an opponent, for which two points are awarded a wrestler (REVERSE).

RIDE Like a "reversal," one of several ways a wrestler gains points via control of an opponent's moves. Basically, a ride implies control of an opponent while in an offensive position—for example, gripping the ankle of an opponent to limit his ability to move about.

SCISSORS A locking of the legs about an opponent's body or head.

SET-UP Originating a move that causes an opponent to react in an expected manner that helps the originator.

SIT-OUT A defensive move used many times by the bottom wrestler in the referee's position. The wrestler moves into the sitting position to attempt to escape holds or to get into an offensive position.

SNAPDOWN A pushing movement used as an opponent jumps at a wrestler's feet, which results in the wrestler winding up behind the opponent for the application of a hold.

STALEMATE A condition in which neither wrestler can maneuver himself into an advantage position.

STAND-UP A method of escape that involves a crouched wrestler flexing his legs to assume a position above an opponent.

STEPOVER A method of escape that involves a wrestler using weight shifted to a leg placed over an opponent to his advantage.

SUGAR SIDE The side of the wrestler that is exposed in his stance.

SWITCH A change from defense to offense through arm leverage.

TAKEDOWN The forcing of an opponent down to the mat.

TIE-UP The coming to grips of two wrestlers while in a standing position.

TIME ADVANTAGE The time one wrestler was in an advantage position over an opponent during the course of a match; 60 seconds or more entitles a wrestler to one point.

TOTAL VICTORY A wrestler being awarded a win for application of a powerful submission hold or flawless throw.

UNDERHOOK A countering move that results in a wrestler hooking his arm beneath the arm or leg of an opponent.

UNLIMITED A weight class above 191 pounds.

WEIGHT CLASS Categories of maximum allowable weights into which wrestlers are grouped.

WRESTLING: THE WEIGHT CLASSES

Maximum Allowable Weights in Pounds

International	College	High School
105.5 (48 kgs.)	118	98
114.5 (52 ")	126	105
125.5 (57 ")	134	112
136.5 (62 ")	142	119
149.5 (68 ")	150	126
163.1 (74 ")	158	132
180.5 (82 ")	167	138
198 (90 ")	177	145
220 (100 ")	190	155
over 100 kgs.	unlimited	167
		185
		unlimited (minimum 75 lbs.)

WHIZZER A type of arm lock.

WRISTLOCK The gripping of an opponent's wrist to create a hold.

INDEX

Harvey Frommer is a true sports generalist. The author of A Baseball Century: The First Hundred Years of the National League, A Sailing Primer, The Martial Arts: Judo and Karate, *he is currently at work on a book on soccer. His* Sports Roots—*a work dealing with nicknames, namesakes, expressions, and trophies—will be published by Atheneum later this year.*

Dr. Frommer, a former United Press sports writer, has a Ph.D. in media ecology and communications and is a professor at The City University of New York.